1988

The Hitch-Hiker's Guide
to Artificial Intelligence

APPLESOFT BASIC VERSION

This book
is dedicated to the
first non-human being
capable of understanding it

The Hitch-Hiker's Guide
to Artificial Intelligence

APPLESOFT BASIC VERSION

RICHARD FORSYTH
and
CHRIS NAYLOR

LONDON
Chapman and Hall/Methuen
NEW YORK

First published in 1985 by
Chapman and Hall Ltd/Methuen London Ltd
11 New Fetter Lane, London EC4P 4EE
29 West 35th Street, New York NY 10001

© 1985 Richard Forsyth and Chris Naylor

Filmset by Northumberland Press Ltd,
Gateshead, Tyne and Wear
Printed in Great Britain
at the University Press, Cambridge

ISBN 0 412 27090 0

British library Cataloguing in Publication Data

Forsyth, Richard
    The hitch-hiker's guide to artificial intelligence.
    ——APPLESOFT BASIC version.
    1. Artificial intelligence——Data processing
    2. Microcomputers——Programming   3. Basic
    (Computer program language)
    I. Title   II. Naylor, Chris
    001.53'5'0285424   Q336

ISBN 0–412–27090–0

Library of Congress Cataloguing in Publication Data

Forsyth, Richard.
    The hitch-hiker's guide to artificial intelligence.
    Applesoft Basic version.

    Bibliography: p.
    Includes index.
    1. Artificial intelligence——Data processing.
    2. Apple computer——Programming.   3. Basic
    (Computer program language) I. Naylor, Chris, 1947–
    II. Title.
    Q336.F67 1985   001.53'5   85–7730
ISBN 0–412–27090–0 (pbk.)

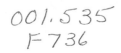

Contents

Preface

Now that you have spent a tidy sum of money on a home computer, why not do something clever with it? Artificial Intelligence (AI for short) has always been the 'department of clever tricks' within computer science. It is concerned with leading-edge problems which are hard for computers even if – like vision – they are easy for people. (Some AI problems, like playing chess well, are difficult both for people and computers.)

Our belief is that the home computer user can learn and profit from AI techniques. Today's microcomputers are as powerful as the mainframes that AI researchers were using fifteen years ago. Moreover, AI techniques tend to filter out into general computing practice if they prove successful. Expert systems are a case in point.

So this book is a practical do-it-yourself guide, the kind the authors would have liked to read when they first became interested in the field. No such book existed, so we had to write it ourselves.

All the programs in this book are in BASIC. There is a widespread myth that AI programs can only be written in LISP or PROLOG, and indeed most academic AI research is conducted in these two languages. But most readers simply do not have access to those languages, and in any case, once you understand the concepts, you can express them in the language that is convenient to you. The most important thing to realize is that AI is exciting, and that you can join in the excitement.

The version of BASIC used for the examples is Applesoft Basic but few machine-specific features have been used, and you should find that conversion to other BASIC dialects presents only minor problems.

January 1985

RICHARD FORSYTH
CHRIS NAYLOR

1
Introduction

Artificial Intelligence (AI) is a Jekyll-and-Hyde subject.

On the one hand, it represents the 'lunatic fringe' of computer science – peopled by researchers with long hair and hollow cheeks owing their inspiration more to Dr Frankenstein than Dr Feigenbaum. In this guise AI can be viewed as applied science fiction, dedicated to bringing the hyperintelligent robots of fantasy off the screen and into the home.

On the other hand, AI is big business. After a lean period in the academic wilderness, it has suddenly become respectable. Head-hunters in expensively tailored suits prowl the corridors of prestigious US universities with tempting offers designed to entice its leading practitioners into industry. AI has replaced biotechnology as the venture capitalists' flavour of the moment. This aspect of AI is simply an attempt to make computer software a little less dumb. (And not before time!)

So what exactly is AI?

The key notion is intelligent problem solving. And the key to intelligent problem solving, as opposed to a brute-force approach, is to apply the same kind of techniques that humans use.

One way to make this idea clearer is to take a step back and look at what AI workers have actually done in the thirty-odd years since the electronic computer brought AI out of the sorcerer's den and into the laboratory. We have divided our condensed history of AI into four decade-sized chunks, each characterized by the dominant theme of the time. It oversimplifies considerably; but it does bring out the main points.

Decade	Theme
1950s	Neural nets
1960s	Heuristic search
1970s	Expert systems
1980s	Machine learning

1.1 1950s: It takes a lot of nerve

In 1943 Warren McCulloch and Walter Pitts proposed a model of the neuron in the human and animal brain. These abstract nerve cells provided the basis for a formal calculus of brain activity. Other workers, notably Norbert Wiener, elaborated these and similar ideas into the field that became known as cybernetics; and it was from cybernetics that AI emerged as a scientific discipline in the 1950s.

Not surprisingly, early AI researchers took McCulloch's formalized neuron as their building block. Equally unsurprisingly, they failed to come up with intelligent systems as a result.

In effect, they were saying: 'the brain is an intelligent problem-solving system, so let's simulate the brain'. There was a feeling about that a richly interconnected network of artificial neurons could start out knowing next to nothing about its task, be subjected to a regime of reward and punishment and end up doing what its inventor wanted.

But the early hardware, to say nothing of the software, was not up to the job. The human brain contains 10 billion neurons. Even now, something apparently simple like a frog's nervous system would be beyond our capacity to simulate at the level of individual neurons.

One of the more successful systems of the time was Rosenblatt's Perceptron. It was an elementary visual system which could be taught to recognize a limited class of patterns. We will meet a version of the Perceptron algorithm again in Chapter 4.

A diagram of a Perceptron is shown in Fig. 1.1. It consists of a finite grid of light-sensitive cells. This constitutes a miniature retina. In addition

Fig. 1.1 A Perceptron

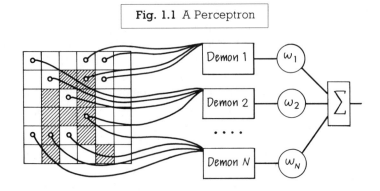

'Demons' respond to particular configurations in the subset of cells they monitor. Output from each demon is multiplied by a weighting (w_1 ..., w_n) and all outputs are added up. The final decision is reached by comparing the sum of weighted outputs to a threshold. (Quiz: Is it an 'A' or an 'R'?)

there are a number of feature-detecting elements – picturesquely called 'demons' – which monitor the state of groups of cells in the grid. They respond when characteristic subpatterns are present by sending a signal to a higher-level decision-maker. The decision-maker multiplies each signal from a local demon by a positive or negative weighting factor and the resulting numbers are added. If the total exceeds a set threshold the Perceptron says 'Yes'; otherwise it says 'No'. Thus one Perceptron can discriminate two classes of images. To recognize more patterns requires more Perceptrons – 26, say, for the letters of the alphabet.

By adjusting the weightings attached to each demon, the Perceptron can be made to learn (in a sense). Recently Professor Igor Aleksander at Imperial College has extended the Perceptron concept and built special hardware to exploit its flexibility. His system can be taught to make rather subtle distinctions such as that between a smiling and a frowning human face.

1.2 1960s: In search of intelligence

The next major step forward was the idea of heuristic search. AI workers abandoned the attempt to build artificial brains from the ground up. Instead they looked on human thinking as a complex coordination of essentially simple symbol-manipulating tasks. Here they were on firmer ground since computers can do things like searching, comparing symbols and so on, which they identified as the foundations of intelligent problem solving.

The hard part was putting these simple activities together.

The most influential workers at this time were Allen Newell and Herbert Simon of Carnegie–Mellon University, who worked on theorem-proving and computer chess, among other things. Their masterwork was a program called GPS, the General Problem Solver.

GPS was general in so far as the user defined a 'task environment' in terms of the objects of a particular domain and the operators which could be applied to those objects. However, its generality was restricted to puzzles with a relatively small set of states and well-defined rules. It could work on the Towers of Hanoi, cryptarithmetic and other problems of a similar nature (Fig. 1.2). It functioned in formalized micro-worlds. What it could not do was solve what people would regard as real-life problems – e.g. Has this patient got cancer? Should I sell my shares now?

Real problems are characterized by a lack of precise rules; but GPS and contemporary systems could only work in a very clearly defined environment.

Another criticism of GPS was its reliance on what is now known as depth-

Fig. 1.2 A cryptarithmetic puzzle

$$
\begin{array}{r}
\mathsf{H\,I\,T\,C\,H} \\
+\ \mathsf{H\,I\,K\,E\,R} \\
\hline
\mathsf{G\,U\,I\,D\,E}
\end{array}
$$

The object is to assign digits to letters so that the addition sum makes sense and the letter assignment is consistent. Thus if I stands for 7 in one column it must stand for 7 in all the columns where it occurs.

GPS attacked such problems by noting constraints (e.g. H < 5) and then solving subproblems. For instance, assume H = 4 and solve for the other digits. Then, within that, assume I = 5, for example, and solve for the remaining digits, – and so on.

first search, which involves splitting larger problems into progressively smaller subproblems until one trivial enough to be solved directly is reached. It is an elegant idea, but it is not an optimal search strategy, since it can involve an unnecessarily thorough examination of unsuccessful pathways, requiring a lot of backtracking.

Nevertheless, the trail-blazing work of GPS could not be said to be wasted, as we shall see in Chapter 7.

The central idea behind GPS was that problem solving was a search through a space of potential solutions. To make the search efficient, it had to be guided by heuristic rules that directed it towards the desired destination. Thus, an automaton wandering around a maze would have to use an exhaustive search technique if it knew nothing about the structure of that maze; but if it had some way of telling when it was getting 'warm' it could normally reach its goal state sooner. (Not always, since heuristics are not guaranteed to work, and occasionally may lead it down a blind alley.)

During this period, AI workers devised several heuristically guided search strategies, such as the A* algorithm, which are still valid. (See Chapter 7 for details.) In addition, concepts such as list-processing were introduced into general computer practice.

List-processing was once a specialist AI topic, motivated by the desire of AI programmers to handle diverse and flexible data structures, i.e. to 'represent knowledge'. Now it is standard computing practice. This tendency for AI to 'export its successes' is remarkable, and continues to the present day. AI has always been a fertile breeding ground for new ideas, and if they are good ideas they soon cease to be regarded as belonging to AI.

One of the best ideas that has spread outwards in this way is the notion of the expert system.

1.3 1970s: Knowledge is power

GPS, as we have said, was not much good at real-life problems. In the 1970s a team led by Edward Feigenbaum at Stanford University began to remedy that defect.

Rather than trying to computerize general intelligence, they focused on very narrow areas of expertise. Thus was the expert system born.

The first expert system was DENDRAL, a mass-spectrogram interpreter built as early as 1967; though the most influential has proved to be MYCIN, which dates from 1974.

The problem addressed by DENDRAL is to take data about the fragmentation of an organic molecule provided by the mass-spectrogram and use it to infer the structure of that molecule. The knowledge used to guide the interpretation is of two kinds – knowledge about the chemical composition of the molecule, and knowledge about the way the chemical bonds break up within the instrument. Without the second kind of knowledge there could be literally millions of ways that the molecule might have been put together.

MYCIN diagnoses bacterial infections of the blood, and prescribes drug therapy. (See also Chapter 2.) It has spawned a whole family of medical diagnostic 'clones', some of which are in routine clinical use. For instance, PUFF, a lung-function diagnostic tool based on the MYCIN plan, is routinely employed at the Pacific Medical Center near San Francisco.

MYCIN's importance lay in the introduction of various new features which have become the hallmarks of the expert system. Firstly, its 'knowledge' consists of hundreds of rules such as the following.

Rule No. 50:
IF   (1) the infection is primary bacteremia, and
        (2) the site of the culture is a sterile site, and
        (3) the suspected portal of entry of the organism is the
        gastro-intestinal tract
THEN   there is suggestive evidence (0.7) that the identity of the
        organism is bacteroides.

Secondly, these rules are probabilistic. Shortliffe, the inventor of MYCIN who was also a doctor, devised a scheme based on certainty factors to allow the system to reach plausible conclusions from uncertain evidence. Thus the number 0.7 is not strictly speaking a probability: really it is just a fudge factor. The significant point, however, is that MYCIN and systems like it can arrive at correct conclusions even with incomplete and partly incorrect information. They have some method of approximate reasoning – whether based on probabilities, Fuzzy Logic, certainty factors or some other likelihood calculus – for deriving a good estimate of the truth even from imperfect data.

Thirdly, MYCIN can explain its own reasoning process. The physician using it can interrogate it in various ways, either to ask how it reached a particular conclusion or why it is requesting a certain item of information. The system answers by retracing and describing the deductive process that led to the current state. This degree of user-friendliness was essentially a by-product of the rule-based style of programming. Today hardly anyone doubts that the more important the task a computer system performs, the more necessary that it can explain and justify its own behaviour to the users.

Fourthly, and crucially, MYCIN works. It does what requires a human years of training. In fact, MYCIN is more used in teaching than diagnosis, but the point is that large corporations, governments and the media are all growing interested.

One of MYCIN's successors, the PROSPECTOR geological exploration system, has been widely quoted as helping to discover a vast unknown molybdenum deposit in Washington state. It is early days yet but corporate America has scented the sweet smell of profits. AI has lost its innocence.

1.4 1980s: The state of the art

This brings us up to the 1980s. Expert systems are in fashion, and the magic ingredient is knowledge. For it is the scope and quality of its knowledge base that determines the success of an expert system.

But knowledge is not something you can squeeze into a computer program like toothpaste from a tube. In fact it is often harder to quarry out of the unyielding rockface of ignorance than that famous molybdenum deposit! Codifying a human expert's skill can be a long and labour-intensive process.

So while the world is marvelling over expert systems, AI has moved on to concentrate on the problem of machine learning – which is one way of synthesizing knowledge automatically. AI always has been a moving target, and at the centre of that target right now is a program called EURISKO.

EURISKO is a discovery program which extends and improves its own body of heuristic rules automatically, by induction. Apart from winning the 'Trillion Credit Squadron' naval wargame three years in succession (despite rule changes intended to prevent it) EURISKO has also been applied to practical problems. One result was the invention of a novel three-dimensional AND/OR gate in the field of integrated-circuit design. Indeed, EURISKO is thought to be the first computer program holding a patent, though most of the credit rightly belongs to its author, Doug Lenat.

There can be little doubt that systems like EURISKO represent the leading edge of AI research. And since AI is itself the leading edge of computer science, this is the place to look for a peek at the future of computing.

Ironically enough, by concentrating once again on learning AI has returned to its roots, because learning was seen as the key problem in the early cybernetic days. A lot of silicon has flowed under the bridge since then, however, and the present attempts to build systems that can improve their problem-solving abilities have a far higher chance of success.

1.5 AI on small computers

The well-equipped AI investigator will have a roomful of dedicated LISP-machines, or at the very least a VAX. All you have is a home computer. How can you write AI programs on a small computer in a language like BASIC?

Well, in the first place, your microcomputer is just about as powerful as the mainframes that AI workers had to use 15 years ago. So provided that you only want to be at the leading edge (and not the leading edge of the leading edge!) you can go quite a long way with what you have.

Secondly, it is always easier to come second. You will be adapting, and perhaps improving, AI techniques that have already been proven in the field.

Thirdly, while BASIC is not the ideal AI language, it is at least commonly available. You do not have to wait for the promised 'fifth generation' inference machines to explore AI concepts. You can get started right away. Once you understand the concepts, you can express them in any language. Even in BASIC some pretty impressive feats can be accomplished. Nor should you succumb to the popular misconception that just because you write in LISP or PROLOG you are thereby writing AI programs: this is a fallacy.

And, finally, AI is too important to be left to the 'Artificial Intelligentsia'. As computers become more commonplace and more powerful, the range of tasks they perform widens. Inevitably they become used for tasks that would require intelligence if done by a person – finding routes through traffic, comprehending spoken instructions, planning a factory's production, playing games of skill. So intelligent problem solving will become the norm.

If you know some of the tricks of that particular trade, not only will you be better prepared for the future, but so will your software.

2
Expert systems

The study of expert systems has two distinct attractions. In the first place, most people can see the potential usefulness of an expert system; and, in the second place, many people have come to believe that expert systems are not just a nice theoretical idea but are something which could actually be implemented and made to do something useful now, rather than in the distant future.

After all, an expert system is, simply, a computer program which replaces a human expert. Human experts have many disadvantages – they are scarce, they are unreliable (sometimes, anyway), they want payment for their expertise, they fall sick and, eventually, they die, taking their expertise with them. Now, if their expertise could be encoded into a computer program this program would be every bit as good as the human expert, it would always be completely reliable, it would never want payment, fall sick or die. The expertise would always be instantly and cheaply available at the flick of a disc to anyone who wanted it.

All of which constitutes a powerful set of arguments in favour of pursuing the goal of expert systems.

And, broadly speaking, this goal is attainable even on quite a modest microcomputer. Some of the techniques used are not particularly hard to learn or to implement and do not necessarily involve you in anything more complex than, say, a knowledge of BASIC and a little common sense. So expert systems are something which you could quite reasonably have a go at yourself. All that is needed is a computer, a bit of imagination and, possibly, some background ideas to get you going – and, as with other chapters in this book, the purpose of this chapter is to give you some of those background ideas to see if they help. If they do not, if you can think of better ways of doing things, then that is fine – because there is no reason why you should not dream up another method of your own which works just as well (if not better) than any currently existing methods. After all, many people are carrying out research into expert systems and if you feel like carrying out your own research then more strength to your elbow (or, more accurately, more strength to your brain cells).

2.1 The human expert

If you plan to produce an expert system which, by its nature, is intended to replace a human expert then it makes sense to start at square one and ask: How do human experts work? For if you knew the answer to that one you could readily code up the methods which human experts use and there you would have it – your very own, absolutely true to life, expert system.

The snag with this approach is that nobody really knows just how a human expert does work. Or, to be more precise, nobody knows well enough to enable you to write a computer program on the basis of it. Intuitively, we all know how human experts work. They study their subject, often over a period of years, then gradually they begin to practice that subject gaining expertise as they go along. Eventually, and to an ever-increasing degree, they arrive at a situation in which most people acknowledge their expertise – they are experts. When faced with a problem in their field they can usually solve it. They can often say how they solved it, giving some justification for their actions. Also, the way they proceed to a solution is often very economical – they do not need to be told everything concerning a given situation nor do they ask for all the information – they just seem able to home in quite nicely on a solution in an intuitive, common-sensical way.

Which would be fine if you could write programs in an intuitive, common-sensical way. Unhappily, computers require explicit instructions of one kind or another so we have to dig up something a little more precise – and it is here that the human expert lets us down. For the reality is that many human experts do not really know how they themselves work. At a low level of expertise the human expert may well be able to give a good account of how he or she works – take the example of a student in some subject being drilled with the basics in his field. This drilling will, for a time, enable the student (hopefully!) to give a good account of what he or she is doing and why – and that might be computerized. But as soon as the level of expertise starts to rise the ability of its practitioners to explain exactly how they are working seems to diminish. Possibly, it is just that they less frequently have the need to exactly formulate the steps they go through and so their methodology remains largely unconscious – but, even if this is the case, it does not help the computer programmer much. What is needed is an exact specification on how human experts work and, sadly, this is not in general forthcoming.

2.2 The domain of inquiry

In some measure a reason for this difficulty lies in the concept of the domain of inquiry of the expert system – that is, the area of expertise which is being considered. Human experts exist in such a wide diversity of fields that it would be unrealistic to suppose that every expert in every single field used exactly the same kind of general method as every other expert in different fields. After all, why should an expert in medical diagnosis use the same methods when exercising his expertise as an expert in, say, personnel administration? The former has to know how the human body works and the latter has to know how personnel procedures work and it takes some stretch of the imagination to suppose that techniques applied to the one are readily applied to the other.

And yet, if we take this argument to its final conclusion, we might finish up by saying that every expert system would have to be different in design to every other expert system which worked in some different domain. The implications of this being that every time you wanted to produce an expert system you had to start off from scratch using methods applicable only to the new situation and ignoring any methods which might have been used in other situations. Clearly, this would be a wasteful approach and – just as much to the point – if this were the case, then the justification for having a subject labelled 'expert systems' would be very slight indeed. If there is no commonality between different expert systems then there is hardly anything to tie the subject together as a whole.

The answer to this problem (to the extent that there is an answer) lies in the fact that some areas of expertise do have *certain* aspects in common – which enables you to use common techniques. But not all areas of expertise have *everything* in common – which means that you can not just pick one standard set of methods and expect to solve every expert-system problem with just this one set. You have to think about the nature of the problem and choose methods which apply to that situation. Hopefully, some of the 'standard' methods will enable you to make some substantial progress – but that does not preclude the possibility that you might have to dream up methods of your own for particular domains of inquiry.

2.3 The knowledge base and the inference engine

Of all concepts used in expert-systems work the most rock-bottom, standard concept is the distinction between the knowledge base and the inference engine.

The idea, in theory, is that every expert has the capacity to reason and, given the diversity of domains over which the human expert can reason, it makes sense to suppose that people have a general-purpose reasoning mechanism of some sort. All that varies between an expert in one field and an expert in another field is the knowledge which each expert has. A medical diagnostician has the same basic reasoning power as an analytical chemist, we might suppose, but the former has knowledge concerning human disease and the latter has knowledge concerning the structure of chemical compounds. So, why not design a general-purpose reasoning program which can apply itself to any particular domain? That way, all you have to do is to alter the knowledge you give it and the program becomes expert in whatever field you like.

In many respects this approach works (you will be relieved to hear). It is possible to design general-purpose reasoning programs which become expert in different fields depending on the knowledge you give them. In expert-systems terminology, the reasoning program is the inference engine and the knowledge you give the program is the knowledge base. By writing a generally applicable inference engine it is possible to unplug one knowledge base and plug in another with the effect that the expert system then becomes expert in some different domain, as shown in Fig. 2.1.

Fig. 2.1. Inference engines and knowledge bases

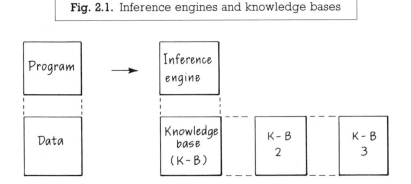

In expert-systems work the concept of a program and data has been largely replaced by the concepts of inference engines and knowledge bases. The idea is that an inference engine is a general-purpose reasoning program and the knowledge base simply provides this program with concrete knowledge about which the program shall reason. By producing a standard inference engine and knowledge bases in a standardized format it becomes possible to 'unplug' one knowledge base and plug in other knowledge bases to the same inference engine, but in different domains of expertise. The result is an expert system which can be expert in a wide variety of fields with a minimum of programming effort.

Obviously, the practical advantages of doing this are enormous – for one inference engine can be used over and over again without modification in order to construct expert systems in a wide range of fields. All that needs altering is the knowledge base.

But this seems almost to contradict the comments made when we mentioned the problems involved in different domains of inquiry. There, we said that each domain had methods which tended to be very different from any other domain; and, here, we are saying that one inference engine can be made to cover problems in any domain.

Fig. 2.2. Domains and inference engines

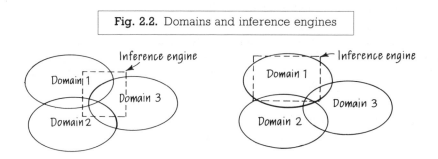

Different areas of expertise can be represented as existing in different domains which may or may not have some common areas of overlap. The problem then is to construct an inference engine which is able to operate in these domains. Ideally, the inference engine should be as general purpose as possible, being able to operate in a large number of domains – however, to do this may result in an engine which is only partially able to satisfy the requirements of each individual domain (as on the left). On the other hand, an inference engine which was able to satisfy the requirements of one particular domain almost completely might prove to be of very little use in any other domain (as on the right). The answer is, in general, a compromise and is greatly helped if a large number of domains can be found which have a very large common area of overlap at which the inference engine can be targeted.

The solution to this apparent contradiction is, in fact, a kind of balancing act. For, when you get down to it, you will find that one inference engine cannot be made to cover all possible domains of inquiry (which is in line with what we said earlier). But, and here is the hopeful news, one inference engine might be designed which covers a largish number of similar domains – even though it will not do everything (Fig. 2.2). The balancing act consists of trying to design an inference engine which does have some fairly broad area of application – an engine which is good for more than just one area of expertise. And it is here that the balancing act becomes particularly acute. For the fact is that the more general purpose the inference engine is made (i.e. the more different domains to which it can be applied) then the less effective it is liable to become in any of these domains.

In a way, it is almost true to say that if you want to design an expert system which is absolutely wonderful in some particular domain then you will be likely to find that the inference engine it uses is virtually useless in any other domain whatsoever. In making the system good in some particular field you will have to build in so many special cases and techniques that to move it to another domain is likely to involve a complete re-write.

On the other hand, if you design an inference engine which has a very wide area of application you will be likely to find that it lacks all of the special cases and techniques which would make it really good in any particular field. So the choices involved are a balancing act between designing a system which is perfect (but only for one particular domain); and designing a system which can be applied to any domain you care to think of (but is not much good in any of them).

The greatest light that can be shed on this problem almost certainly comes from considering the knowledge base – the information which is domain specific that the inference engine uses when exercising its expertise.

To get this picture in context, think back to the days before expert systems became so well known. In those days people talked not about inference engines and knowledge bases but about programs and data. Clearly, the inference engine corresponds (roughly) to the 'program' and the knowledge base corresponds (roughly) to the 'data'.

What expert-systems workers have tried to do is to make the program as general purpose as possible, so that it can handle as wide a range of data as possible. Unlike, say, the payroll program which could handle a lot of different data, as long as they were data concerning payments to employees, the inference engine is able to handle lots of different data which might not necessarily concern payments to employees. An expert system which could do the payroll might also be able to do something else as well – such as telling you how to bake bread – simply by giving it a different set of data to work from (i.e. a different knowledge base).

It sounds fine to suggest that one program might alternatively be able to work out the payroll, acting as an expert on the subject of pay regulations, and then be able to tell you how to bake bread, acting as an expert baker – and, in fact, this is what expert-systems theory is aiming for.

But, in practice, you will realize that you can not take an existing payroll program, give it fresh data, and expect, say, fresh bread as output. The reason for this is the plain fact that the data formats are different for the two subjects – even if an inference engine could be devised which could, in some way, handle both cases. And that, roughly, is the problem when it comes to designing a truly general-purpose inference engine – that the engine has to operate on a knowledge base and the knowledge base has to be in some particular format. True, with expert systems you try to relax the format as much as possible in order to increase the generality of the program. But equally true is the fact that, just like ordinary data, you can not relax it so much that the program will not accept it – there has to be some kind of format to the knowledge base just as there had to be a format to the data in more conventional programs.

These considerations tend to help in formulating the balancing act between a totally general-purpose expert system and a highly specific one. For, when designing an expert system, if you look at the likely format of the knowledge base then you can see to what extent this format might be extended to other domains than the one which you originally had in mind when you started first to think about expert systems.

For instance, one of the main fields in expert-systems work is that of structured selection (or, 'classification') – choosing which of a number of possibilities might be the right one in a given set of circumstances. So common is this problem that an inference engine which worked in this area in one domain would have a very good chance of being applicable to another domain if it was supplied with a different knowledge base. Conversely, an inference engine which was able to work out the structure of chemical compounds would have very little chance of being useful in another domain – and the fact can be spotted simply by considering the format of the knowledge base which each expert system might require. Clearly, the structured selection problem requires basic information concerning the hypotheses to be considered and the evidence available to support or contradict these hypotheses – and that is something which might apply over a very wide variety of domains. But the chemical-analysis program will require in its knowledge base information on the chemical structure of various compounds along with a lot of very detailed chemical knowledge. The language of chemistry is so specialized that it is hard to see how an inference engine capable of driving this particular knowledge base could be fed with information concerning anything else and still work.

2.4 Structured selection

Although expert systems have been produced which work in a variety of different problem areas the most common area by far is that of structured selection (or 'classification') – and the reasons for this are not at all hard to see (Fig. 2.3). It is the area which currently seems to have the greatest amount of generality to it, inasmuch as the techniques used in structured selection tend to be broadly similar from one domain to another. This means that, within the area of structured selection, it seems most possible to design an inference engine which will be genuinely multi-purpose and to produce knowledge bases which can be plugged in and unplugged at will in order to change the area of expertise of the expert system readily. In short, this is the area in which the theory of expert systems seems to be most nearly capable of being realized in practice.

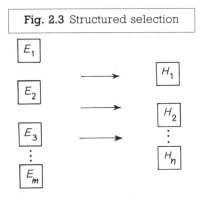

Fig. 2.3 Structured selection

The most common area of application for expert systems is in the field of structured selection (or 'classification'). This essentially consists of acknowledging that any given problem has a finite number of hypotheses associated with it, H_1 to H_n, and the task of the expert is to select which of these hypotheses are the most likely given certain items of evidence, E_1 to E_m.

The most commonly known area of structured selection is the field of diagnosis. In medical diagnosis one out of a number of possible diseases may be suggested by the evidence. In fault diagnosis one out of a number of distinct faults may be suggested by the evidence.

The general form of the problem can often be applied to other fields as well, such as weather prediction, in which the hypotheses might be reduced to the question, say, of whether or not it will rain tomorrow.

But what, exactly, is 'structured selection'?

We have already mentioned that it is a system which contains various hypotheses and various items of evidence which might help the system to judge which of the hypotheses are correct and which incorrect – but that might sound a little abstract.

For many people, structured selection simply means 'diagnosis'. Medical diagnosis is the classic example of this and, possibly, the classic example of expert systems altogether. A doctor is obviously an expert in the field of medicine. He, or she, has had a long training supplemented by years of experience. Their services can be expensive and can be in short supply. Eventually they grow old and die and a whole new generation of doctors needs to be trained, laboriously, to take their place. On the face of it, medical diagnosis is a prime candidate for expert-systems applications.

But, sticking with that word 'diagnosis', there are obviously lots of non-medical fields in which diagnosis is carried out. Next time your computer goes wrong, you are carrying out a diagnosis as you try to work out what has gone wrong with it – and that is an example of fault diagnosis in general.

However, there is something about the word 'diagnosis' which always brings faults (whether in human or machine) to mind. And yet the techniques used in diagnosis are generally applicable to a wider field than simple fault finding. Suppose that you are planning a holiday and can not quite decide where to go. Or planning on buying a new computer (or washing machine). Suppose that you would like to know what tomorrow's weather is going to be like.

All of these problems can be reduced to the one problem of structured selection – the expert is faced with a number of hypotheses and, on the basis of the available evidence, he has to come to a decision regarding these hypotheses. The hypotheses might concern possible illnesses, possible holiday destinations, possible consumer purchases or possible forthcoming weather. And the evidence available might range from the patient's temperature to the computer's price.

But, to a very large degree, the structure of the problems is the same – which means that one inference engine might be able to deal with all of them and the knowledge bases might be formatted in a very similar way.

For this reason, we will concentrate on structured selection to see in some detail the techniques that might be used.

2.5 The inference engine

2.5.1 The inference

When designing an inference engine for use in structured selection the first point to consider is the exact form that each individual inference is to take. To get this clearer, consider a human expert who is working on some problem. Either this expert requests some information or some information is presented to the expert. Either way the expert has to do something with that information. It may tend to support some particular hypotheses and discount some other hypotheses. It may lead the expert to decide that some particular course of action needs pursuing or that some other item of evidence needs gathering. But all this amounts to is that, given some item of evidence, the expert has to be able to make some inference from it and, by the same reasoning, the expert system has to have some means of making inferences from the evidence it receives.

The problem is, of course, that there are a wide range of inferences which can be made – not wide solely with respect to the number of hypotheses to which they might apply, but wide in the range of inferencing techniques that might be applied.

Broadly speaking, there are two main types of inference which can be made – probabilistic and deterministic inferences.

Deterministic inferences are quite certain items. You switch your computer on and find that absolutely nothing happens – no lights go on, nothing moves, no sound comes out – so you can be sure that you have had a power failure. Or you decide, maybe, to buy a new computer and you want one with an exact 31K of main memory – only Bytesnatcher Inc. produce such a machine so you can be sure that this is the machine you want. These inferences are quite exact and can be expressed in terms of ordinary Boolean operations within your program – it hardly needs an expert system to do the work for you.

Probabilistic inferences are a different matter. The doctor observes that you have a fever and thinks it might be influenza. You switch your computer on and get intermittent errors so you think it might be a faulty RAM chip. You decide to buy a new computer and want a fairly ordinary 48K machine so, maybe, there are a dozen or so models you might consider. All of these are probabilistic inferences in which the evidence, as it comes in, tends to support or deny certain hypotheses but not with any absolute degree of certainty.

To make matters worse, most experts of the human variety (and hence most ideal expert systems) use both deterministic and probabilistic methods in something that resembles a witch's brew more than anything else.

When the doctor says that you have got a fever and spots on your face so it may be measles but, on the other hand, it might just be a dose of flu plus acne then he is using precisely that witch's brew in his own internal inference engine. The problem is: How to convert this brew into a machine form?

There are several approaches which might be tried, but one of the theoretically soundest involves Bayesian inferencing. This relies on the supposition that every hypotheses has some probability of being true prior to any information coming in at all – this is called the 'prior probability'. After an item of evidence has come in this probability can be updated to incorporate the new evidence to give a 'posterior probability' for that hypothesis – and this posterior probability can then be used as the prior probability of that hypothesis as some new item of evidence comes in. So the whole process can be made to go cycling around as each new item of evidence comes in – a process which is computationally very elegant.

Consider, by way of example, some hypothesis H and some item of evidence E. The prior probability of H we call $P(H)$ and it is the probability of H given no knowledge of E. What we want to know is the posterior probability of H given evidence E, which we call $P(H:E)$.

Bayes's equation gives a very convenient method of calculating this. It relies on the definition of $P(H:E)$ as

$$P(H:E) = \frac{P(H\&E)}{P(E)}$$

i.e. the probability of H given E is the probability of both H and E (the joint probability of H and E) divided by the probability of E.

Because of the symmetry in the equation, it follows that

$$P(E:H) = \frac{P(E\&H)}{P(H)}$$

and, as $P(E\&H) = P(H\&E)$ then $P(H\&E) = P(E:H)P(H)$ giving

$$P(H:E) = \frac{P(E:H)P(H)}{P(E)}$$

So, in order to find the posterior probability of H all we need to know is the prior probability of H and those other two terms – $P(E:H)$ and $P(E)$ – which are, respectively, the probability of observing the evidence given that H is true and the probability of observing the evidence in isolation.

So, if you wanted to know whether you should buy Model X as your new computer all you need to do is have a prior probability for buying Model X (which might be very low initially and the same as the probability of buying any other model of computer); the probability of your wanting to buy a 48K machine given that you are going to buy Model X; and the probability of your wanting to buy a 48K machine at all. Put these into the equation and the result is that you can work out the probability that you should buy Model X given that you want a 48K machine.

This may seem like rather a roundabout way of going about the matter and, for some applications, it may be. It all depends on which is the easier probability to provide in the knowledge base – $P(H:E)$ or $P(E:H)$. If you knew $P(H:E)$ then there would be no need to go through this equation because the knowledge base could contain it quite adequately. But the fact is that you might know $P(H:E)$ if only one item of evidence were being considered throughout the whole system, but you would probably not know it if there were several items of evidence to consider. It is rather as if $P(H:E)$ is the final 'score' for the hypothesis in question and, where there are a large number of items of evidence to be considered, you would not know the final score until all, or most, of the evidence had been gathered in.

But, even if you did not know $P(H:E)$ you might very well know $P(E:H)$, the probability of observing some evidence given the hypothesis is true, because this would be less likely to change.

This point might become clearer if we resort to the medical diagnosis example again. The doctor observes that the patient has a fever and wants to know whether or not he should consider influenza. Well, it would be hard to say just what the probability of influenza, given the patient has a fever, was because so many other items could have a bearing on the matter. But it would be very easy to say what the probability of observing a fever, given the patient has influenza, was and it would also be fairly easy to say what the probability of fevers were in general.

It is simply that the information $P(E:H)$ and $P(E)$ is much less liable to change and much more liable to be known in advance that makes this method attractive. And, as other items of evidence come in, these can be incorporated into the equation in exactly the same way.

The main basic disadvantage with constructing a Bayesian inference engine in this way is that it assumes that each item of evidence is independent of each other item of evidence. To the extent that the items are not independent the final posterior probabilities obtained will be wrong. This situation occurs at its strongest when probabilistic methods are mixed in with deterministic methods.

For suppose that you wanted to include in the system a statement along the lines of 'You should probably buy Model X computer if you wanted something with 48K and disc drives.' The point about this example is that you might consider buying a machine without disc drives if it had much more than 48K on it (because the disc drives might be unnecessary if there was enough RAM to hold everything in memory without them). So, clearly, the two items of evidence are not independent of each other and yet the way they depend on each other is fairly explicit – they are joined by the logical connective 'and'. So what you need is some way of handling both probabilistic inferencing and logical connectives.

One way of dealing with this is to consider two items of evidence, E_1 and E_2, and allow for the logical connective AND and OR by saying that

$$P(H:E_1 \text{ AND } E_2) = \min[P(H:E_1), P(H:E_2)]$$
$$P(H:E_1 \text{ OR } E_2) \;\;= \max[P(H:E_1), P(H:E_2)]$$

In other words you use the same Bayesian equations as before but if two items of evidence are joined by the logical connective AND then you take the minimum of the posterior probabilities of the two because the AND relationship is rather a tight constraint on the situation and if two items of evidence are joined together by the logical connective OR then you take the maximum of the posterior probabilities of the two because OR is a less tight constraint on the situation.

The end result of this is that it enables you to construct a knowledge base which contains statements of the general form:

'If the patient has influenza then the probability that he has fever is 0.9.'

'The probability of a patient having fever is 0.1.'

'If the patient has measles then the probability that he has a fever is 0.99 and the probability that he has spots is 0.5.'

'The probability that the patient has spots is 0.2.'

At which point one of the potential advantages of this approach to expert systems should be fairly apparent, namely that the knowledge base makes sense, not just to the computer but also to the moderately casual user. A human being could, in theory, read this knowledge base and say fairly rapidly whether or not he agreed with it – which makes a very good check on the basic reasonableness of the expert system as a whole. And, as the methods are available to write an inference engine to work off this knowledge base, no sooner has it been written and checked than it can then be run to see whether the results it gives are the sort of results which a human expert would be happy with.

2.5.2 The engine

It might not at first seem obvious that there is anything more to an inference engine than the making of inferences – as long as the engine can do that then, surely, it is doing everything we might want of it?

In a very simple system this is probably true – but as the systems become more complex, or as we go for something a little more subtle, we find that the framework within which these inferences are made becomes increasingly important – and it is this framework which we call the 'engine' part of the inference engine.

With just one hypothesis to consider and a small number of items of evidence then the precise nature of the framework scarcely matters – but, even in this situation, consider the following problem.

There is only one hypothesis in the expert system and there are a small number of items of evidence which the expert system can use in order to form an opinion. Which item of evidence should the system consider first?

Obviously, if all the items of evidence have to be considered before the expert can express any opinion at all then the order in which they happen to be considered is immaterial. But suppose there was one item of evidence which was more important than any other, so important that knowledge of that item could enable the expert to form a final opinion without reference to any other material, then obviously we would like our expert system to consider that item first. One example of this might be our hypothetical expert system to help you decide which computer to buy next – if Model X is being considered and Model X is the only one with 31K of main memory then the question as to whether or not you want exactly 31K of memory will obviously settle the matter.

Now consider the situation when there are several hypotheses within the expert system. Obviously some hypotheses are more likely than others right from the start – so it would make sense to have the system concentrate on those hypotheses more than on some very rare, special case, hypotheses.

It is this that constitutes the 'engine' – the procedures the system uses to decide which items of evidence it will look at next and which hypotheses it will consider next.

In general, there are three main types of structure used in expert systems. These three main types, forward chaining, backward chaining and the rule-value approach, are shown in Fig. 2.4.

Foward chaining, sometimes called a data-driven strategy, consists of giving the system some information and letting it make what inferences it can from that information. After which you give it some more information, and so on until it reaches a conclusion. Maybe you, the user, do not personally decide exactly which bits of information to give the system – it may be that the system decides that for you – but essentially, it is as if there were a list of items of evidence and either you or the machine simply worked systematically through that list, rather like filling in a form.

Backward chaining, sometimes called a goal-driven strategy, consists of the system thinking of a hypothesis and trying to set about deciding whether or not this hypothesis might be true. To do so it chains backwards to see what items of evidence are relevant to this hypothesis and interrogates the user on these items. Once it's made up its mind about a particular hypothesis it then moves on to consider another hypothesis. Essentially, if forward chaining is like working through a list of items of evidence, then backward chaining is just the same except that it is working through a list of hypotheses.

The rule-value approach, which is sometimes called sideways chaining, does neither of these things, its approach is to ask the user those questions that seem like interesting questions to ask at the time, given the current state of the various hypotheses within the system and the items of evidence which are still outstanding. The way it decides which items are interesting

Fig. 2.4 Engine strategies

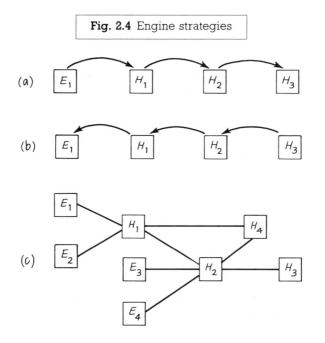

(a) The most common strategy used by inferencing engines is forward chaining. In this the system starts at the beginning and establishes evidence E_1 from which it can establish H_1 and so on forwards through the chain until it comes to its final conclusion.

(b) An alternative strategy is backward chaining in which the system first considers a final hypothesis H_3 and then finds that, to establish the worth of H_3, it needs to know about H_2 and to establish that, needs to know about H_1, and so on until it has come to the back of the chain – at which point it inquires about evidence E_1.

(c) The difference between these two strategies may not seem so obvious on a simple system. But where there are a large number of items of evidence and hypotheses and these are interlinked in a complex fashion it can make considerable difference to the running of the system which strategy is chosen.

An alternative approach to either forward or backward chaining is the Rule-Value approach. This always concentrates on that item of evidence which is able to produce the greatest change in subsequent hypotheses further down the reasoning chain, thereby reducing the uncertainty in the system by the greatest amount every time it asks for information.

is by looking to see how much total change each item of evidence could bring about in the hypotheses under consideration. That item which can bring about the most change is obviously the most interesting because, once information is available on that item, the greatest amount of uncertainty will have been removed from the system.

Of the three approaches forward chaining is by far the easiest to program – so easy that it hardly requires any conscious thought to do it. After all, the expert has to interrogate the user somehow and the easiest way is just to work through a list of all the items about which the user might be interrogated in the order they appear.

The snag with forward chaining is that, as mentioned earlier, it might not always ask the best questions first – but for some applications this may not matter.

Backward chaining is easy to implement as long as there is not a long reasoning chain involved. On a short reasoning chain involving only a single step from evidence to hypotheses it, again, amounts to little more than working through a list.

However, on a long reasoning chain involving several intermediate conclusions in which evidence leads to a hypothesis which is in turn the evidence which leads to other hypotheses, backward chaining can give rise to programming problems (not insurmountable ones) as the program examines each hypothesis in turn and tries to establish exactly which items of evidence relate to this hypothesis.

In its favour is the fact that backward chaining can appear to the user to be very purposeful – it always has a particular hypothesis in mind and is able to justify any question it asks by telling the user that it is asking that question because of its relevance to a particular hypothesis.

Both forward and backward chaining suffer from the basic criticism that, in the end, they are both simply working through lists. The one works through a list of evidence and the other works through a list of hypotheses, but if these lists are not ordered in any particularly optimal way then the user will not get asked questions in any particularly optimal way either.

The rule-value approach attempts to ask questions in an optimal order and is fairly easy to implement. If you think in terms of Bayesian inferencing you will realize that each hypothesis can have two extreme outcomes with respect to a particular item of evidence – the outcome when the evidence exists and the outcome when it does not. In terms of our earlier formula this is the absolute difference of

$|P(H:E) - P(H:\text{not } E)|$

If, for each item of evidence, we add up these terms (the maximum probability shifts) for each hypothesis for which the evidence applies the system can then ask that question with the highest rule value, where the rule value is the sum of these shifts. This method is fairly easy to program and can deal with moderately long reasoning chains without too much difficulty – it only has to search forward through the reasoning chain for each item of evidence totting up the rule value as it goes along. Its main disadvantage is that it can prove a little slow at run time because of the amount of calculation needed – after each item of evidence has come in the rule values need to be re-calculated, sometimes in their entirety, because the possible values for $P(H:E) - P(H:\text{not } E)$ will have changed due to the addition of the last item of evidence.

2.6 How and why?

If our expert system is to be a perfect (well, nearly perfect) replica of a human expert it needs to be able to do more than simply take in evidence and spew out conclusions. It would be nice if we could ask it *how* it came to these conclusions; and, when it asks a question, it would be nice if we could get it to say *why* it was asking that question.

Neither of these two facilities (Fig. 2.5) have anything particularly complex about them – but they can help to make the user of the system feel much more at home with the computerized expert than they might well have done otherwise. It makes it all seem so much more human and the fact that the system can explain itself, even on a simple level, does help to inspire confidence in its abilities. It also helps when the system is being developed – after all, everyone has problems debugging their programs occasionally and if you were able to ask the system to explain itself when you felt it had made a mistake then this might well help in the debugging process.

Fig. 2.5 How? and Why?

Expert systems become increasingly useful if they are able to explain their workings to the user. This is commonly achieved by means of the How? and Why? facilities.

How? is a question the user may ask of the system in an attempt to discover why the system came to some particular conclusion. In effect, it is: How did you come to that conclusion?

Why? is a question the user may ask of the system in an attempt to discover why the system is asking for a particular item of evidence. In effect, it is: Why are you asking me this question?

130,201

Essentially, as *How?* is simply an explanation of the conclusions which the system has reached all that is necessary is to have the system recite the reasoning steps it has gone through to date in order to arrive at its conclusions – rather like giving a trace of what has happened so far, but dressed up so that it looks nice. Obviously, if the system is explaining how it came to some conclusion regarding a particular hypothesis then only those items relating to that hypothesis need to be mentioned by the system and this can be done in one of two ways. In the first, if the system is backward chaining, then the currently existing method of backward chaining can be used on the hypothesis the system is explaining in order to show the reasoning chain to date. Otherwise, if backward chaining has not been used, then the trick is to more or less present everything that has occurred so far but to mask out those items which appear to have no relevance to the hypothesis being explained.

The *Why?* facility proceeds in much the same way inasmuch as it can be used to give the current state of reasoning of the system – but the main point about *Why?* is that it should be able to say which hypotheses are influenced by the current question. In a backward-chaining system there will only ever be one hypothesis under consideration and *Why?* can consist simply of naming that hypothesis – although, in a long reasoning chain, it is possible that this hypothesis is only a subgoal in which case the system may also look forward and state which further hypotheses are influenced by the current question. In forward-chaining and rule-value methods the system has to be able to look forward to see which hypotheses are going to be influenced by the question but this usually presents no special difficulties because, when the question eventually gets answered, the system is going to have to find these hypotheses anyway – the only alteration to the program design is that, to answer *Why?*, it helps to have these hypotheses identified in advance. The pros and cons of different engine strategies are summarized in Fig. 2.6.

2.7 Expert systems shells

If all, or most, of the aims of an expert system are realized then the result would be an inference engine which worked well in a variety of different domains of similar type, and a knowledge base which could be varied in order to vary the domain of expertise. Because we attempt to make the knowledge base represent human knowledge in some fairly close way it should be fairly easy to produce and to modify, often consisting of a number of fairly intelligible rules on which the inference engine can act (which, incidentally, is why such systems are often called 'rule-based systems').

At which point it should be clear that an expert system without its knowledge base, but with a well-known structure for the knowledge base, is little more than a shell into which new knowledge could be placed. These are expert systems shells – 'empty' expert systems just sitting there waiting to be turned into a fully fledged expert. Typically, they have to them rather more than a simple expert system because, if new knowledge bases are going to be added or altered frequently, then some relatively easy way of building up a knowledge base would be useful. There are three main methods of building up a knowledge base easily should you want to extend your activities into the area of expert systems shells.

The first, and most common, is to define the format of the knowledge base very exactly and to allow within it for a slightly wider range of options than might be encountered in any one expert system built for some specific purpose. This is roughly equivalent to defining a computer

Fig. 2.6 Pros and cons of engines

Each different strategy has its own particular advantages and disadvantages. In summary, these are some of the main factors to be considered:

Forward chaining
Pro: Easy to program.
Con: It may just work through a list of questions in an apparently purposeless fashion. How? and Why? can be answered but only in a very simple fashion.

Backward chaining
Pro: Purposeful, the system is always considering a particular hypothesis. How? and Why? can be readily answered by backward chaining through the evidence on a particular hypothesis to give an account of the reasoning chain involved.
Con: Can be hard to program as it involves the use of recursive techniques which are not always available in all languages. Will always consider hypotheses in some rigid order which may not be optimal.

Rule values
Pro: Relatively easy to program especially for short reasoning chains. Always asks that question which seems the most 'interesting' to the system at the time, as it attempts to reduce uncertainty about the whole spectrum of hypotheses.
Con: How? and Why? can be difficult to program except for simple systems unless recursive techniques are used.

language and it means that users of the shell can write a new knowledge base in this language and, having done so, submit their efforts to the inference engine which will then act upon that knowledge base. The similarity to a computer language is often quite marked with this approach – even down to having a specific compiler for the knowledge-base language which checks the statements in it for correctness before allowing them near the inference engine.

The second approach is more along the lines of the method used by current program generators and is generally more suitable for inference engines which have rather more limited facilities. In these the knowledge base is built up via a question-and-answer session on the screen and by filling in the blanks in screen templates – rather like designing a database system using a program generator. This method is easy to use and is suitable for simpler systems.

The third approach is to use a learn-by-example system for building up the knowledge base in which the system is given examples of what it has to know and, from these examples, it works out the appropriate rules for its knowledge base. This approach has the advantage that the user who is establishing an expert system does not need to know much about the problem domain himself – all of the previous methods assume that the person constructing the system either knows, or can find out, just what the system should know in order to become an expert. Learn-by-example systems do not make this requirement which means that they can rapidly become more expert in some domain than the person that taught them. However, a full discussion of such systems really belongs under the heading of Machine Learning.

2.8 Expert systems

It should be apparent by now that there are some strong things going for expert systems – and also some strong things going against them.

In several cases they have been found to perform as well as human experts or even to outperform them and there are probably two reasons for this.

The first is that expert systems, once produced, are always consistent – the computer never forgets or has an off day. This, over a large number of cases, often gives the expert system a decided advantage over its human counterpart. The consistency of the system should tend to give it a better track record simply because, whilst it may not be perfect, it will always avoid making any really horrendous mistakes due to, say, forgetfulness.

The second is that designing and producing an expert system requires a great deal of careful thought – and, in many areas of human expertise, the human experts may have spent years with their subject but never really sat down and analysed what it is that they do. To produce an expert system requires someone to sit down and analyse the problem and it could be that this is a useful exercise in its own right. Maybe, even if the system was never used, the exercise of having produced it would lead to greater human expertise in the domain which was analysed.

Working against expert systems are two main items.

The first is simply that computers have a screen and keyboard as their sole means of communication (leaving aside speech and vision for the moment – these being non-standard and barely available anyway). It would, therefore, be quite possible for you to crawl up to a medical expert system with a broken leg and, unless you specifically told the system about your misfortune, it would never spot the fracture. Or you could go to your expert system which was to advise you on your choice of a new computer. With a tattered jacket about your shoulders and an over-due telephone bill tucked under the keyboard you could swear blind that you had a budget of millions and the expert would have no way of saying otherwise. The basic limitation of expert systems is that, at best, they can only offer expertise of the sort which might be offered by a human expert who had never met you and who chose to advise you via telex messages back and forth between yourself and himself.

The second disadvantage which currently affects expert systems relates to the points made earlier about different domains of inquiry. Different domains require different methods of working within them – different inference engines. Which is fine as long as the problem on which expertise is required falls relatively neatly into some particular type of domain. If it does not then there are problems because the big advantage of the human expert is that he, or she, is adaptable. If you go to your doctor to complain of weight loss then your doctor can do what many expert systems might be able to do – check you out on various wasting diseases. But if the real problem was that you had not been eating recently then a human doctor might come to this conclusion and start to make some tentative inquiries as to your financial standing. In other words, the doctor expert would be able to switch immediately into a social-worker expert with a new knowledge base and a different inference engine. Now, there is no reason why you should not write a series of expert systems each of which could call the others as necessary. But you would be hard pressed to write expert systems to cover absolutely everything which might turn up under every conceivable circumstance. You could try, of course, and it might be quite interesting to do so.

But, in general, expert systems currently work best on problems which are well defined and in a tightly restricted domain. To do more than this requires only one thing though – that you should dream up a method of doing it yourself. Nobody else has.

Listing 2.1 Simple, deterministic, forward-chaining expert system

Probably the best overall word to use to describe this particular expert system is 'simple'. In its present form it is designed to enable you to use the system to decide which computer you should buy next. It involves no long reasoning chain and is non-probabilistic (i.e. it is deterministic). It is, however, divided into an inference engine (in lines to 580) and a knowledge base (in lines 1000 forwards). So, you could modify the knowledge base to include details of real models of computers which you know about. You could even modify it to cover some other field in the general area of structured selection – as long as it was possible to fit the new knowledge into the same format in the knowledge base.

Although it is forward chaining in the strict sense, because it only proceeds from a single set of questions to a single set of conclusions this really amounts to nothing more than working through a list of questions in a fixed order.

It will recommend that hypothesis which exactly suits your answers to the questions it asks. So, if you say that you are willing to pay, say, £200 for your computer, it will only consider those computers which cost exactly £200 and discount all others. It will not make allowance for the fact that you might be happy to pay less! Nor, if you state that you would be happy with black and white (i.e. *no colour*) will it suggest a suitably priced colour model even if it falls within your price tag.

So, you should definitely regard this program as a starting point for your own work (a comment which will be true of many of the programs in this book) rather than as a complete finished program in its own right.

Run the program as it is and then try adding a few more models in order to see that you understand the structure of the knowledge base correctly. Then try adding a few more variables for each computer (you will need to increase the value of V in line 90 from its current value of 3 in order to do this). Once you have got the hang of that, try asking yourself how you would modify the program so that it could take account of the fact that when you state that you are willing to pay a given price you might only be giving an approximate answer, or an upper limit. Or, how you would modify it in a similar way to allow for the fact that a willingness to put up with black and white would not necessarily exclude a willingness to accept a colour model. Or, that a willingness to have only 16K of RAM would not prejudice you against a model with more.

Once you have thought along these lines, try changing the knowledge base to cover some other field – maybe some other purchasing decision – and see if your modified inference engine will still deal with the new problem. As likely as not, you will find that the better it gets at advising you on which computer to buy the worse it gets at other problems which you might give it – but every time you improve the knowledge base for some particular field without losing its general usefulness you have made a substantial step forward.

Note that the 'How?' facility (in line 520) gives a strictly deterministic summary of how the system came to its final conclusion. The 'Why?' facility (in line 460) is not 'Why' in strict relation to the usual 'Why did you ask that question?' (in this system the only answer would be that it needed to know the answer in order to solve the problem). Instead, it gives an answer to the question 'Why did you reject that particular hypothesis?'

Incidentally, as a clue, if you want to modify the system so that it will act a little more intelligently, possibly being able to allow for the fact that when you say you are willing to pay £200 that is only an upper figure, you will find that you have to alter the knowledge base as well as the inference engine. If, for instance, you were only to alter the inference engine so that the first variable was to be taken as an upper limit this would then mean that, with any other knowledge base, the first variable would also be taken to be an upper limit – which might not be appropriate with a different knowledge base. So, the *price* field would need to contain additional information to indicate that this model had a particular price but that it might still be of interest to someone willing to pay more. The introduction of a 'greater than' or 'less than' sign at a suitable point in the field could be interpreted by a modified inference engine to deal with this problem.

```
10   REM   *****************************
20   REM   ** LISTING 2.1             **
30   REM   ** SIMPLE,DETERMINISTIC    **
40   REM   ** FORWARD-CHAINING        **
50   REM   ** EXPERT SYSTEM           **
60   REM   *****************************
70   REM   INFERENCE ENGINE
80   HOME : PRINT ,"EXPERT": PRINT ,"------"
90   X = 100:V = 3: REM    X IS THE NUMBER OF DIFFERENT MODELS THE
           PROGRAM CAN CONSIDER AND V IS THE NUMBER OF DIFFERENT VARIAB
           LES ON EACH MODEL
100  REM   S%(X) IS FLAG ARRAY = 1 IF HYPOTHESIS IS STILL TO BE CO
           NSIDERED
110  REM   A$(X,V) IS ANSWER SUBMITTED BY USER
120  REM   Q$(X,V) IS NAME OF QUESTION VARIABLE
130  REM   R$(X,V) IS CORRECT ANSWER
140  REM   N$(X) IS NAME OF HYPOTHESIS
150  DIM S%(X),A$(X,V),Q$(X,V),R$(X,V),N$(X)
160  REM   READ IN KNOWLEDGE BASE INTO THESE ARRAYS
170  RESTORE
180  READ A$: IF A$ = "999" THEN 250
190  C = C + 1:S%(C) = 1:N$(C) = A$
200  FOR I = 1 TO V: READ A$
210  FOR J = 1 TO  LEN (A$)
220  IF  MID$ (A$,J,1) = " " THEN :L = J:J =  LEN (A$):Q$(C,I) =
         LEFT$ (A$,L):R$(C,I) =  RIGHT$ (A$, LEN (A$) - L)
230  NEXT J
240  NEXT I: GOTO 180
250  X = C
260  REM   START QUESTIONING THE USER
270  FOR C = 1 TO X
280  IF S%(C) = 0 THEN 540
290  FOR I = 1 TO V: IF A$(C,I) <  > "" THEN 500
```

```
300   PRINT : PRINT "WHAT IS ";Q$(C,I);" ?"
310   PRINT "(YOU COULD REPLY :"
320   FOR Q = 1 TO X: IF S%(Q) = 1 THEN : PRINT  SPC( 20);R$(Q,I)
330   NEXT
340   PRINT "TO MATCH THE CURRENT POSSIBILITIES )"
350   INPUT A$(C,I)
360   REM  LOOK FOR ANY OTHER QUESTIONS THIS ANSWER MIGHT ALSO APP
      LY TO
370   FOR Q = C + 1 TO X
380   FOR P = 1 TO V
390   IF Q$(Q,P) = Q$(C,I) THEN :A$(Q,P) = A$(C,I)
400   NEXT P: NEXT Q
410   REM  LOOK FOR ANY THEORIES WHICH CAN BE DISCOUNTED DUE TO TH
      IS ANSWER
420   FOR Q = 1 TO X
430   FOR P = 1 TO V
440   IF (A$(C,I) = R$(Q,P) AND Q$(Q,P) = Q$(C,I)) OR Q$(Q,P) < >
      Q$(C,I) OR S%(Q) = 0 THEN 470
450 S%(Q) = 0
460   PRINT : PRINT N$(Q);" IS RULED OUT ": PRINT "WOULD YOU LIKE
      TO KNOW WHY (Y/N) ";: INPUT A$: IF A$ = "Y" THEN : PRINT "IT
       HAS ";Q$(Q,P);" OF ";R$(Q,P)
470   NEXT P: NEXT Q
480 P = 0: FOR Q = 1 TO X:P = P + S%(Q): NEXT : IF P = 0 THEN : PRINT
      : PRINT "NO THEORIES ARE SUITABLE FOR YOU":I = V:C = X: GOTO
      500
490   REM  NOW TRY THE NEXT QUESTION
500   NEXT I
510   REM  NOW DISPLAY ANY THEORIES WHICH SUIT THE USERS ANSWERS
520   IF S%(C) = 1 THEN : PRINT : PRINT N$(C);" IS POSSIBLE": PRINT
      "WOULD YOU LIKE TO KNOW HOW (Y/N)";: INPUT A$: IF A$ = "Y" THEN
      : PRINT : PRINT "IT HAS :": FOR Q = 1 TO V: PRINT Q$(C,Q);"
      OF ";R$(C,Q): NEXT Q
530   REM  NOW TRY ANOTHER THEORY
540   NEXT C
550   PRINT : PRINT "WOULD YOU LIKE ANOTHER RUN (Y/N)";: INPUT A$:
      IF A$ = "Y" THEN : FOR Q = 1 TO X: FOR P = 1 TO V:A$(Q,P) =
      "": NEXT P:S%(Q) = 1: NEXT Q: GOTO 260
560   END
1000  REM   KNOWLEDGE BASE
1010  REM   FORMAT OF K-B IS :
1020  REM   NAME OF HYPOTHESIS(,VARIABLE NAME(SPACE)VARIABLE VALUE
      )
1030  DATA  MODEL A,PRICE 200,COLOUR YES,RAM(K) 48
1040  DATA  MODEL B,PRICE 300,COLOUR YES,RAM(K) 64
1050  DATA  MODEL C,PRICE 100,COLOUR NO,RAM(K) 48
1060  DATA  MODEL D,PRICE 50,COLOUR NO,RAM(K) 16
1070  DATA  999
1080  REM   999 IS THE STOP CODE AND FOLLOWS THE FINAL ITEM

]RUN
```

```
              EXPERT
              ------

WHAT IS PRICE   ?
(YOU COULD REPLY :
                    200
                    300
                    100
                    50
TO MATCH THE CURRENT POSSIBILITIES )
?50


MODEL A IS RULED OUT
WOULD YOU LIKE TO KNOW WHY (Y/N) ?Y
IT HAS PRICE   OF 200

MODEL B IS RULED OUT
WOULD YOU LIKE TO KNOW WHY (Y/N) ?Y
IT HAS PRICE   OF 300

MODEL C IS RULED OUT
WOULD YOU LIKE TO KNOW WHY (Y/N) ?N

WHAT IS COLOUR   ?
(YOU COULD REPLY :
                    NO
TO MATCH THE CURRENT POSSIBILITIES )
?NO

WHAT IS RAM(K)   ?
(YOU COULD REPLY :
                    16
TO MATCH THE CURRENT POSSIBILITIES )
?16

MODEL D IS POSSIBLE
WOULD YOU LIKE TO KNOW HOW (Y/N)?Y

IT HAS :
PRICE   OF 50
COLOUR   OF NO
RAM(K)   OF 16

WOULD YOU LIKE ANOTHER RUN (Y/N)?Y

WHAT IS PRICE   ?
(YOU COULD REPLY :
                    200
                    300
                    100
                    50
TO MATCH THE CURRENT POSSIBILITIES )
?200
```

```
MODEL B IS RULED OUT
WOULD YOU LIKE TO KNOW WHY (Y/N) ?N

MODEL C IS RULED OUT
WOULD YOU LIKE TO KNOW WHY (Y/N) ?N

MODEL D IS RULED OUT
WOULD YOU LIKE TO KNOW WHY (Y/N) ?N

WHAT IS COLOUR  ?
(YOU COULD REPLY :
                      YES
TO MATCH THE CURRENT POSSIBILITIES )
?NO

MODEL A IS RULED OUT
WOULD YOU LIKE TO KNOW WHY (Y/N) ?Y
IT HAS COLOUR  OF YES

NO THEORIES ARE SUITABLE FOR YOU

WOULD YOU LIKE ANOTHER RUN (Y/N)?N

    ]
```

3
Natural language

From the very earliest times Man has been trying, without much success, to speak to, and receive intelligible replies from, non-human objects. These attempts at communication have taken various forms, one of the best-known early attempts being that of Saint Francis of Assisi who is said to have preached to the animals, presumably on the basis that his words would be understood.

More recent times have seen people supposedly communicating with animals for less exalted reasons. Psychologists have spoken to horses in order to demonstrate the horses' grasp of mathematics in an early psychological experiment which is not, nowadays, highly regarded. From time to time various people have appeared who claim to have learned the language of animals and, thereby, been able to communicate with them. Linguists have tried to demonstrate that dogs can talk by manipulating the dog's throat with their hands while the dog growled, thereby producing the semblance of words. And highly respectable modern psychologists have attempted, with fairly widely acknowledged success, to teach the English language (or, at least, American Sign Language) to chimpanzees. Whilst all over the world people fondly talk to their pet dogs and budgerigars and listen to the utterances of parrots.

With a background like this, it only seems natural that people would also try to hold sensible conversations with inanimate matter as well – and it could be that part of the interest in sound-reproduction systems, such as record players and television sets, is in some way a response to an apparently deep-rooted desire in people to talk to something other than mere people.

So, when the computer appeared on the scene one of the first things that researchers tried to do was to talk to it and get it to answer back. And it is very easy to see the attraction of this aim. After all, it *would* be interesting to be able to talk to a computer and listen to what it had to say in return. In traditional science fiction it goes without saying that this is possible with computers. Surely, it just needs a little concentrated thought to work out how to do it and in next to no time we will all be chatting away happily to our machines?

The only fly in the ointment seems to be the fact that, so far, we are not – and the reason we are not is essentially the problem of natural language.

Natural language is what you and I speak and understand. It is called 'natural' language because that is exactly what it is – natural. Nobody invented it, nobody ever defined it. It just grew over the years and, if it carries on growing, it can change in any way it likes and we will still be able to understand it and use it just as easily as we can now.

This is in sharp distinction to that other class of languages – formal languages. These are called formal languages because that is exactly what they are – formal. They have been invented and they have been defined and, talented people that we are, we can understand them almost as well as we can understand natural languages.

The traditional example of a formal language is a computer programming language – such as BASIC, COBOL, ALGOL, FORTRAN, ASSEMBLER or machine code. These languages have been rigorously defined so that when you use statements in these languages you know (if you study them a little) exactly what those statements mean.

But there is a deceptive trap waiting when you consider programming languages, and it goes like this. In the early days of computers, programming was carried out in machine code which, as often as not, meant keying in strings of binary digits. Then along came ASSEMBLER which, with its mnemonics, made the language more memorable and easier to use. Then, along came the high-level languages, such as BASIC, which were easier still to use. All the time, computer languages have been getting easier to use and more English-like in their appearance. Surely, if this trend continues, we will finish up with a computer language that is actually indistinguishable from natural language? That is the trap.

For, whatever developments are made, the very definition of a natural language against a formal language makes this impossible. Whilst computer languages are defined exactly and natural languages are not there is no bridge that will completely cross the gulf between the two.

But, if that is the case, why are people trying to talk to computers – what can they seriously hope to achieve and why, apart from the intrinsic fascination of the subject, are they trying at all?

3.1 Four types of problem

The answer will become a little clearer if we break the problem down into four distinct sections. For, whereas 'talking to computers' might seem like a single act there are several distinct categories within that act.

The first broad distinction to make depends on whether or not we are talking to the computer, or the computer is talking to us; and the second broad distinction to make depends on whether this talking is going to take place via the keyboard and screen or via some acoustic signals. If we use these two broad distinctions we can divide the subject into four distinct categories and state quite clearly where the problem areas lie. Roughly we get:

Communication	Who is doing the talking?	
via	The computer	The human
Keyboard and screen	Easy	Hard
Acoustic signals	Easy/hard	Extremely hard

From this we can see that if the computer is doing the talking via the screen this is easy to program. If the computer is doing the talking via an acoustic medium (i.e. through a loudspeaker, say) then this varies between being easy and being hard. If the human is doing the talking then this a hard problem even via the keyboard; and, if the human is doing the talking via an acoustic medium (i.e. a microphone, say) then this is an extremely hard problem.

There are good reasons why this should be the case as we will see if we examine each category more closely

3.1.1 Computer talks via the screen

In this, the simplest case, the computer has something it wants to say to the user. It is going to say it by displaying its message on the screen. Well, that is easy – that is what the BASIC PRINT statement is for. Also easy was that particular explanation for, surely, with such a difficult problem as that of natural language there must be more to it than that?

In fact, there is not much more to it than that – but the reasons for its simplicity are quite interesting.

The first point to make is that language, in any form, is an attempt to communicate something. When you speak to another person you are seldom making noises just for the fun of it – you have a purpose, an intention to communicate something to that other person. So, when you say 'Would you pass the sugar?' you can, for the moment, forget about the complexities of decoding that particular sentence and concentrate instead on the one basic fact – that the reason you said it was because you wished to communicate with someone that you wanted them to pass the sugar to you. If they pass the sugar then your attempt at communication has been successful and it does not matter too much what anyone thinks of the way you phrased your request. As long as your message was received correctly, then your attempt in natural language has succeeded. In fact, all language can be viewed as a communication chain like this:

message → encode → transmission → decode → message

where, in this case, the message was that you wanted the sugar passed to you; this you encoded as the set of words 'Would you pass the sugar?'; which you then transmitted acoustically (using your mouth) to the ears of your companion; which your companion then decoded until, finally, he got the message. And, just to round the picture off nicely, you know he got the message because he then passed you the sugar – a sort of 'answerback' or 'message received' signal of the sort that would keep most communication engineers quite happy.

But now suppose that you are sitting at the table taking tea with the same companion only, this time, you have decided that your waistline needs some attention and have therefore given up sugar in your diet.

Conversation now drags because you are no longer interested in the sugar – you have everything else that you need to hand and so you both sit there heads deep in your newspapers. In other words, you have nothing to communicate to your companion so you remain silent.

Well, that is O.K., you are not breaching any laws of natural language by remaining silent – but it does illustrate an important point. If you are going to speak you must have some reason for speaking. There must be something which you wish to communicate – and this is an extremely important point.

Superficially, you can argue that many people speak frequently and at length without having anything to communicate – you only have to think of your favourite bore to demonstrate that point – but, in fact, this just is not true. Your favourite bore does have something to communicate, it is just that what he wishes to communicate you do not wish to know. As far as people are concerned the message to be communicated may be important and packed with facts of a very obvious nature, but there are other messages that humans like to communicate using language. They may want to communicate the fact that they are bored, or that they are lonely or that they just do not like silence too much. But at the bottom of all language is something which the speaker wishes to communicate with the hearer. That is the purpose of language.

Now turn back to your computer which, in this simple case, is displaying a message on its screen. As the message is in a language it is an attempt to communicate with you. Like any natural human being, the computer has something which it wishes to communicate with you and it is using language in order to do so. But what on earth could a computer possibly want to communicate with you about?

Unlike you, it will not want the sugar passed to it, nor will it feel bored, or lonely, or object to long periods when nothing is happening on its screen. For the most part, a computer simply does not have anything it might want to communicate. It has nothing to talk about. Except, of course, for those very rare occasions when it, like you, feels a desire to communicate. When something is weighing on its mind and it simply has to talk. At which time it will communicate with you. It will say something like:

UNABLE TO READ DRIVE A

because that is the message it wanted to communicate. Now, on some machines, it may not make such a crystal-clear statement as this. It may say something like:

BDOS ERR ON A

and it is up to you to figure out what that means. But it is not very hard to make the computer's messages much more natural – to place them in natural language – simply because the actual messages that the computer will want to communicate are, essentially, so few and far between and so simple when they do arise that a bit of careful thought when writing a program can make its output almost as clear as you want to make it.

It is not that the problem of natural language is an easy problem – it is just that the things that a computer might want to say are so restricted.

The second point to make about the computer talking to you via the screen is that encoding a message is much easier than decoding it. You only have to think of the often-publicized efforts of intelligence agencies to break codes and compare that with the complete dearth of stories concerning the difficulties of encoding those messages in the first place to realize this. Coding a message is easy – breaking the code of that message to decode it is hard.

So, when the computer is talking to you, the computer has it easy. It displays a message on the screen and it is up to you to work out what that message means. By and large, most people have far greater processing power than any computer so the hard bit is being passed on to the most-powerful processor (yourself) whilst the easy, encoding, bit is handled by the least-powerful processor (the computer).

So, that is why producing natural language on a computer screen by the computer is relatively easy – because computers have very limited things which they might want to say and it is up to you to understand the message anyway.

Not that things could not be improved quite a bit. Paying attention to screen messages to make them seem more natural can improve the 'user-friendliness' of a program enormously, making it much easier to use and understand. But for the most part this simply consists of putting more thought into 'canned' messages within the program. For instance, if a stock-control program is to output a warning message when there is only a certain number of widgets left in stock then it makes things look a lot nicer if you program the computer to use the singular form 'widget' when the number in stock is equal to one. But changes such as these really border on the cosmetic and are not where the main thrust of research into natural language lies.

3.1.2 Computer talks acoustically

For the casual user this is where things start to get a little more interesting. The same comments apply here as for the previous section inasmuch as the computer has a limited number of things it might want to communicate and it is you who have to put in the real effort involved in decoding the computer's messages. But, because the computer is talking via a loud-speaker this time, what it is saying begins to sound much more like a human being speaking (in theory, that is) and the problem becomes that bit more interesting. It also becomes substantially harder.

To illustrate the point, suppose that we go back to that problem the computer had earlier – about its being unable to read drive A for some reason. The computer knows it can not read drive A because a bit has been set somewhere in the disc interface and it wants to communicate to you that this bit has been set. Because the meaning of that bit being set is that it is unable to read drive A it was perfectly adequate to produce a nicely worded message on the screen which said as much. This is because there was a one-to-one correspondence between that bit being set and the message to be displayed on the screen. Well, why could not there also be the same one-to-one correspondence between that bit being set and the same message being spoken by the computer via a loud-speaker? The answer is that this is perfectly feasible. All that is needed is to store the speech signal somewhere and get the computer to play it back again every time it gets a disc error, rather like a tape recording. In fact, if the message was recorded from a human speaker then it would be very much like a tape recording. The computer could then speak, what it said would express the message it wished to communicate, and everyone would be able to understand it.

The only real snags are practical ones.

Chief amongst these practical snags is the fact that the recording would take up rather a lot of room. To get an idea of what it might be like one of the authors carried out the following experiment. A sample of speech was recorded onto a normal domestic cassette recorder (a good one, but normal). The output from the cassette recorder was then input to a computer (an Apple II in this case) by means of an analogue-to-digital (A-D) converter (Fig. 3.1). The computer then took this input and re-converted it back into an analogue form using a digital-to-analogue (D-A) converter and this signal was fed back into the amplifier of a hi-fi set so that it was possible to hear what came out of the loudspeakers.

Fig. 3.1 Resolution and sampling rate

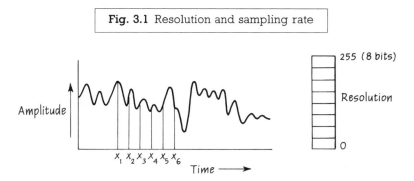

An acoustic, analogue, signal may be turned into a digital signal by sampling the waveform at regular intervals of time and converting the amplitude of the waveform into a digital representation (A-D conversion). The number of times each second at which the waveform is sampled is known as the sampling rate and the number of bits used to represent the waveform gives the resolution of the system. So a system which stored the signal in 1 byte would give 8-bit resolution. As 8 bits can hold the numbers 0–255 this gives a total of 256 different levels of amplitude which can be resolved. Sampling rates of the order of 6000 s^{-1} may be needed for good quality speech storage.

The result was that there was little perceptible degradation in the sound quality as long as the sampling rate was kept as high as some 6000 times per second.

For the more technically minded, the A-D and D-A converters were 8-bit jobs so this means there was a sampling rate of 6000 s^{-1} with 8-bit resolution – compare this with a compact disc in which music is encoded digitally and, typically, you will find that the compact disc encodes and decodes music at a sampling rate of 44 000 s^{-1} with around 16-bit resolution, depending on the player being used. So, in strict terms, the experiment carried out on the Apple was very low-fi indeed. But it worked for speech – which has a fairly restricted bandwidth.

But now do the arithmetic on this experiment and you will see that 6000 8-bit samples per second would fill up approximately 6 kbytes of memory every second it was running. The same author found he could not say 'Unable to read drive A' more than about once every $1\frac{1}{4}$ s – and that was hurrying things. A more leisurely speech gave some $2\frac{1}{2}$ s for the message.

So, to hold that simple piece of English in memory in an acoustic representation of this sort would use something like 12K of memory. Do that for every message that the computer might ever want to communicate and you quickly have no memory left.

So, obviously, this method is not going to work if you want to output a large and varied set of messages – as large and varied, say, as is possible using PRINT statements direct to the screen. Something more economical has to be dreamed up.

The first line of attack on the problem is, instead of storing an exact representation of the sound waves, to only store an approximate description of them – an acoustic description. The essence of this approach is that although the actual waveform of spoken language is continuously varying over time the *way* in which it varies changes much less rapidly. For instance, if you say 'Home' then the 'o' gives rise to a waveform which is continuously varying but, for the duration of that 'o', it is the same basic waveform. So, all you need to know is what it looks like and how long it lasts – a snapshot or average picture with a time associated with it.

Specifically, there are three main ways in which this is carried out.

Fig. 3.2 Vocoder representations

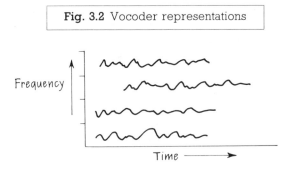

The acoustic signal may be conveniently compressed by separating the signal into a number of different frequency bands and merely recording the duration of the signal in each of these bands, possibly also with some indication of its amplitude. The above figure shows a signal separated into four such bands. Many vocoder representations use more frequency bands than this, often as many as 16.

The first is to treat the signal as if it were any acoustic signal, not necessarily speech, and to break it up into a number of different bandwidths, as shown in Fig. 3.2, and then record how much energy is in each band and roughly how long this burst of energy lasts. This is generally called a vocoder representation and does not rely on the fact that the incoming signal is speech – within the available bandwidths it can be used to compress and store information on any acoustic signal coming in and can be played back again afterwards.

After vocoder representations come two methods which rely on the fact that what is being input is speech.

The first of these is a formant representation which may need a little explanation.

In the early days of acoustic linguistics people started studying the waveforms that were associated with various speech sounds. Very much like modern vocoder representations, they studied the frequency bands which occurred in speech and the amount of energy present in each of these bands. After a while it became apparent to them that there were some distinctive patterns in all speech sounds – it seemed that whenever someone was speaking the bulk of the energy was concentrated in three main frequency bands and they called these the formants. Formant 1 had, typically, the lowest frequency and the greatest energy in it, Formant 2 had a slightly higher frequency and slightly less energy in it and Formant 3 had a still higher frequency and even less energy. These three formants are shown in Fig. 3.3.

The characteristic pattern that appeared was of speech being identifiable solely by reference to the relative position of these three formants. And, as the relative position of these three formants changed

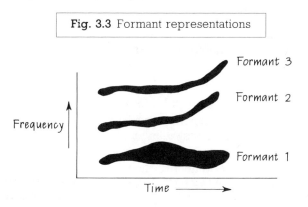

Fig. 3.3 Formant representations

Greater compression of speech signals may be obtained by using a formant representation. This derives from the observation that speech appears to fall into three distinct energy bands, known as Formants 1 to 3. Formant 1 is the lowest frequency and typically contains the most energy whilst Formant 3 is the highest frequency and typically contains the least energy. The speech can be encoded by simply recording the frequency, duration, and sometimes the energy, associated with each formant.

In this figure the energy associated with each formant is shown as variations in the 'area' occupied by that formant at each moment in time.

relatively slowly they became prime candidates for compressing the speech signal – all that would be necessary would be to store the information regarding the three formant positions and their duration and the speech would have been encoded.

In many ways, this approach is very much like a vocoder representation except that whereas a vocoder might be simultaneously recording information on as many as, say, 16 channels the formant encoder would only need to store information on the position of three formants – so the saving in storage space would be quite substantial. And the speech could be reconstructed simply by generating sound waves to correspond to the frequency, intensity and duration of the formants.

The final approach of the three (until someone thinks of a fourth approach) is known as Linear Predictive Coding (LPC), and is shown in Fig. 3.4.

Fig. 3.4 LPC representations

A more sophisticated method is to make a model, effectively, within the computer of the human vocal organs and to encode the information as changes in the parameters of that model. This has the advantage that the computer, if the model is good, cannot 'hear' things which a human speaker could not physically say. And, when used for speech synthesis, it cannot 'say' things which a human speaker could not say. It also enables speech to be concatenated with greater realism as the transitions from one sound to another must satisfy the parameters of the model and must, therefore, be inherently speakable.

With LPC the fact that the acoustic signal is human speech is taken even further. Effectively, the method consists of creating a model (an electronic model) of the human vocal organs with all of their abilities and limitations. If the model is good then the only sounds it can produce are the sort of sounds a human being could produce and all that is necessary is to specify the parameters for the model to produce speech.

So, of these three methods, which is the best if you want your computer to talk to you? The answer is a trade-off between various items. If you want the best possible quality of speech and only want to produce isolated words or sentences then the best method is still none of these – it is the method we gave originally in which a human voice was effectively 'recorded' digitally. But that gave space problems in storing the message.

It also gave another problem which is in part practical and, in part, more closely concerned with the nature of natural language itself. This is the problem of concatenating sounds with each other and having the end result sound right.

Think back to the example we gave in the previous section concerning the program that warns you when stocks are running low. Displaying the message that you are running out of widgets on the screen was easy and would be made much nicer if 'widgets' was used in its singular form of 'widget' if the computer wanted to tell you that there was only one left.

In BASIC, using string functions, this sort of operation is easy. All you need to do is to hold the string 'Widget' and the string 's' and concatentate the two every time the number involved calls for the plural form. This sort of string operation can be used very readily to help produce natural-looking screen messages. When it comes to producing the spoken equivalent we would obviously like to be able to do the same sort of thing for, apart from anything else, it would save space if we could just pick up standard elements and concatenate them together to form the message we wanted. It would also enable you to produce much more novel – and, hopefully, natural – messages by means of some judicious programming if you could mix the elements of the message together freely.

The snag with natural speech is that it is not as stable as the written word. Sounds run into their neighbours and get merged with them at the boundaries and the overall sound of what is being said depends heavily on the meaning behind it. Thinking of that first point, suppose that you decided to paint your kitchen in an ice-blue colour. Very cool and, to some, tasteful also. But try telling someone, verbally, that you plan to do this. As the words run into each other you will find that most people think you plan to paint your kitchen 'a nice blue colour' – which is more or less true, but not quite what you had in mind. In that example the meaning of what you said got changed to illustrate the point – but the point that was being illustrated was simply that words behave differently depending on the words next to them. 'A lovely ice-blue colour' would not attract anything like the confusion because, here, the word 'ice' has behaved differently with different neighbouring words.

So, for maximum economy and flexibility, we want the method which enables us to mix sounds together to our heart's content and still have the words come out sounding right – and, roughly, this ability occurs in ascending order with the three methods given. Vocoder representations give very poor transitions from one sound to the next, formant representations do better, but best of all are LPC methods because the fact that they are based on a model of the human vocal organs reduces the chances that the model will behave in an unnatural way at word boundaries, abrupt and physically impossible shifts in pronunciation are much less likely to occur, although they are still a problem area.

Typically, most microcomputer users are unlikely to try their hand at getting their computer to talk to them via a loudspeaker unless they happen to be particularly adventurous or particularly fortunate in their choice of machine. The reason for this should be fairly obvious by now. The first method given, that of replaying a straight digital recording, is not too hard as long as you have or can make an A-D and D-A converter – but it uses up a lot of space in memory.

The other three methods all rely on the fact that speech signals occur not just at one frequency but at several simultaneously. And, as most microcomputers currently only allow you to output a signal to the loud-speaker at one frequency at a time this is not sufficient to represent speech accurately – although some people have tried, with limited success, to do so.

More usually, anyone trying to produce a talking microcomputer will obtain a speech-synthesis chip and plug that into their machine. Such a chip will be using one of the methods described here for storing and reproducing speech sounds and you will be able to largely judge how good it is by listening to its performance when you start concatenating elements of speech together. The best are almost certainly using LPC techniques but the state of the art is such that none of them could be described as word perfect yet and this, in the end, is due to a reason at which we have only hinted so far – the meaning of what is being said.

If you want to say something, know what it means and what the words are, then it is very easy to say it in a natural-sounding manner. If, on the other hand, you have to say something and you are not at all sure what it means then, even if you happen to be familiar with the words used, you could be at a loss as to how, exactly, to say it.

Try, for instance, saying:

'The hard green night gently saw the garden rose and fled.'

You should not have a problem with that one – after all, you know all of those words and you know how to pronounce them, you even know how words behave when they occur with other words. You have got a good head start over your computer there. But, if nights can see, maybe gardens can rise and flee. Or, maybe, the garden rose is normal and only the hard green night is doing the seeing and fleeing.

If you knew what it meant then you could say it just right.

And that is the hardest part when it comes to getting your computer to talk to you. If it understood what it was saying then it could, presumably, say it right. But we have not touched on the problem of meaning yet – and neither has the computer.

3.1.3 Talking to the computer acoustically

Of the four types of natural-language problem we outlined at the beginning of this chapter this is the one we labelled 'extremely hard'. In fact, with the current state of the art, it is little short of impossible but, rather than leave it until last, it is worth examining some of the basics of the problem because of the way they follow on from the last section.

Essentially, to talk to a computer acoustically means speaking to it via a microphone. By some means what is said is represented as a varying voltage to the machine and the machine has to make sense of that. The first half of the problem then is to take this varying voltage which represents the acoustic signal and convert it into something that the computer can work on – and the methods of doing that are, generally, very similar to the methods used when the computer has to produce an acoustic signal because it wants to talk to you. Unlike talking to the computer via the keyboard (which we shall come to next) talking to the computer via acoustic signals involves one extra processing stage simply because the incoming acoustic signal is subject to a wide range of variation that does not occur with keyboard input. Press the letter 'A' on your keyboard and an exact ASCII representation of that character is sent into the machine. It will be exactly the same representation whoever presses the key and in whatever context the key is pressed. The 'a' in 'bat' is the same as the 'a' in 'danger' and, for the computer, this makes the first part of the problem so much easier. But, when it comes to spoken input, there are no such absolutes. In a similar way to that discussed under the previous section the incoming signal varies depending on who is speaking and the context in which the spoken signals occur and in the meaning attached to the message.

The problem is how to extract some common, invariant aspects of the speech signal from the very different signals which initially arrive at the machine. In general, the problem is very much that faced by the computer when it tries to produce speech, but in reverse. And that means that very similar methods can be used.

Starting at the beginning, the obvious method is simply to take the entire speech waveform and try to match that against something which the computer already knows – but, even apart from considerations of memory space, this is obviously going to be very hard to achieve. If you should happen to tell the computer that you are unable to read drive A (to reverse roles for a moment) we have already worked out that this method is going to require the computer to examine some 6 kbytes of memory – and that is a lot of matching to do.

So the methods proceed very much as before, with vocoder representations, formant representations and LPC representations being used in the hope of extracting from the speech signal something shorter and easier to process and, also, in the hope that some invariant aspects of speech will be uncovered which will enable the computer to make the correct identification of what you said irrespective of the context in which you spoke, the inflection in your voice or even if it was someone other than yourself speaking at all.

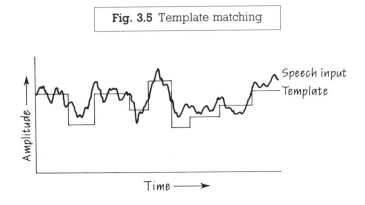

Fig. 3.5 Template matching

Speech is often recognized by the computer as a process of template matching in which the computer stores an internal template of various speech sounds which it attempts to match against the input signal in the hope of finding the best (correct) match. The templates are often built up by training the system on several spoken utterances and may be unique to one single human speaker.

As the number of templates increase, the chance of finding the correct match will decrease as there will be an increasing number of similar templates in store. Also, the time taken to check all templates will increase as the number of templates increases and response time will drop.

All of these methods ultimately rely on some form of pattern matching being carried out. The computer stores a template of speech sounds corresponding to different units of speech and, when it receives a spoken message, it searches through its existing templates in the hope of finding one that represents the best match (Fig. 3.5). A typical method of working, should you buy or construct a speech-recognition device, is to train the computer by repeating some phrase or word several times to enable the computer to construct a template. You let the computer know what this template represents and you repeat this process until the computer has a large number of templates in store, each of which corresponds to some particular signal.

For instance, you can build up a template for the word 'hello' by repeating the word several times and then key in the word 'hello' so that it knows that this is the internal representation it should use when it comes to hearing that particular template again. Likewise, you could do the same with the word 'goodbye' with the end result that you can say 'hello' to your computer and it can make an appropriate response (by, for instance, printing the word 'hello' on its screen) and you can do the same with the word 'goodbye'.

Such systems are commercially available and do work relatively well – but only relatively well.

The most obvious difficulty lies in matching what you say to the template exactly. In general, an exact match will never exist because of chance variations in the way you speak so the computer has to go for the best match, that which gives the least error. But if there are a large number of templates in store then there could, for any spoken message, be a number of quite good matches available. With several close contenders for the title of best match it is obvious that the computer will make mistakes sometimes – and it will be more likely to make mistakes as the number of templates in store increases. So most systems only allow a small and limited vocabulary if they are to work accurately.

The next difficulty that arises will be familiar from the previous section – it is the difficulty of what happens at boundaries between sounds. If you play a game with 'bat and ball' then this is quite clear at the keyboard – but once you start speaking to the computer you will find that you are playing a game with 'batten ball'. And whatever a 'batten ball' might be, it at least contains two words both of which are English (Fig. 3.6).

Fig. 3.6 Phonemes

It is often said that the basic building blocks of speech are phonemes – unique linguistic sounds which correspond in the spoken word to the alphabet in the written word. So phoneme representations would appear to be a good thing. In fact, linguists have their own phonemic alphabet which they use to record speech as it is actually spoken.

For the computer, the situation is a little different as, even though phonemes may exist, they still have to be represented within the computer in some fashion – which brings us back to the three methods of vocoder representations, formant representations and linear predictive coding. In practice, some people feel that phonemes are not quite the linguistic invariants they were once thought to be – or, at least, not sufficiently invariant for computer speech synthesis and recognition without some additional help from other techniques.

The solution which most systems adopt to this problem is to restrict what the speaker says to discontinuous speech – speech in which each spoken unit is a stand-alone item with a distinct gap between each new item. So, to recognize 'bat and ball' you would have to say something like 'Bat. And. Ball.' so that the computer knew where each word started and ended. The snag with this, of course, is that people do not normally speak like that and it goes against the grain to adapt the way in which you speak to suit the computer rather than have the computer listen to you speaking in your own way.

If the computer were able to recognize the way you normally speak it would be capable of recognizing 'continuous' speech – speech in which the words run into each other and vary depending on what precedes and follows them. But the possible variations within continuous speech are such that this problem has not yet been properly cracked by anyone.

Obviously, the computer could do a lot better if it had some idea of what you might be likely to say in any given situation – but although this point is particularly true of acoustic input it is also, in general, true of any attempt to talk to a computer, so it can conveniently be covered in more detail in the next section.

3.1.4 Talking to the computer via the keyboard

Labelled only as a hard problem, rather than extremely hard, talking to the computer via the keyboard is still a long way from being easy.

Certainly, the pressing of keys removes a great deal of uncertainty about the nature of the original signal going to the computer compared with acoustic input, but the basic problems remain the same.

You have a message which you wish to convey to the computer, you encode it in natural language and transmit it to the computer. That bit is easy – you have been doing it all your life to other people. But now the computer has the hard part to carry out. It has to carry out the subsequent decoding of the message in order to find out what it was that you were trying to communicate.

At this point we will draw attention to a let-out which can prove very helpful in some circumstances.

Recall that when the computer was talking to you it had a relatively easy task simply because there were a limited number of things which it might want to say. Well, the same argument can sometimes help out in reverse. After all, what would you want to say to a computer? There might be a wide range of things, but typically there are not – the computer's knowledge of you and your world is so limited that there is not much point in engaging it in a discussion of politics because it knows nothing of the subject. So you could just take the approach that, as the computer can only act upon a small number of possible messages, it need only be able to tell whether the message that you have just given it belongs to any one of this small number.

This approach can be used in some 'trick' systems which can look as if they are processing natural-language input but which, in fact, are just searching the input for key words or phrases from which they can guess which response they should make.

As an example, suppose that you have a system which maintains personnel records. Amongst other things the system holds details of the personnel's names and ages. It would be quite easy to devise a trick system that could answer such questions as 'How old do you reckon John Smith might be?' The question is phrased in natural language and could equally well be phrased as 'What's John Smith's age?' or somesuch. All the program needs to do is to look out for the name of an employee in the input string and a word like 'age' or 'old' and it can guess that it has been asked to print out the age of that employee. Such systems can be made quite convincing with a little thought.

They can also be made to fall over quite readily – try asking 'How old is John Smith's wife?' and, unless you have allowed for something like this you will still get John Smith's age back.

Still, such simple systems as this should not be ignored just because they can not do everything. Where the range of possible responses that the computer could make is limited they can prove helpful. And the system can be made moderately foolproof simply by making sure that any answer the computer gives is clear and unambiguous so that if the wrong response is given at least the user knows it is not the response he wanted. Also, if the input stream contains nothing that the computer can make sense of it can always be programmed to ask the user to rephrase the question until it does get something it can act on.

Listing 3.1 Query program

This is a 'trick' system which does not really understand natural language but, instead, searches for key words in the input stream in order to try to guess the question and make a suitable answer. For all its simplicity, it is possible to have quite a decent conversation with it – albeit about rather a limited field of discourse.

In lines 410 forwards there are a series of personnel records which give the name, age and marital status of various people.

In lines 370–400 are a series of statements which give information regarding the associations that the program is to make between certain words. So, in line 380 the words AGE and OLD are both to be associated with a request for details of a person's age; and, in line 390, there is a whole string of words which are to be interpreted as a request for information concerning a person's marital status.

These DATA statements can be expanded as much as you like as long as each of the language data lines ends with the code '888' and the language data as a whole end with the END1 and the personnel records end with the END2. The system assumes, in line 100, that each personnel record only contains three fields and the first field is always assumed to be the subject of the question – so that the answer to any question will always be JOHN SMITH (for example) IS . . .

The system can give the wrong answers – especially when the subject of the question is not the same as the first field in the record (as, for instance, when you ask about John Smith's wife) but the answers are always unambiguous so that the user would know if he or she had been given the information he asked for or not. If no match is found then the system (in lines 160 or 330) will ask for the question to be re-phrased or admit its ignorance.

The organization of this program should enable you to alter lines 370 forwards, retaining the same format, to cover some other area of discourse. It would be very easy to imagine a pretty run-of-the-mill conversation about the weather being generated in this way, for instance. (Something along the lines of:

'Isn't it chilly today?'
'Cold is not very pleasant, is it?'
'It would be much nicer if it was warm?'
'Hot weather is much more comfortable.'
– should not be too hard to implement!)

As the personnel example shows, though, such a system could have very practical applications as a front end for a database system.

```
10   REM  ********************
20   REM  ** LISTING 3.1    **
30   REM  ** QUERY PROGRAM  **
40   REM  ********************
50   HOME
60   RESTORE
70   READ A$: IF A$ < > "END1" THEN 70
80   I = I + 1: READ A$: IF A$ = "END2" THEN 100
90   GOTO 80
100  P = (I - 1) / 3: REM  P IS THE NO. OF PERSONNEL RECORDS
110   PRINT "I KNOW SOMETHING ABOUT PERSONNEL"
120   PRINT "ASK ME SOMETHING ABOUT SOMEONE"
130   INPUT S$
140  FL = 0:T = 1: REM  FL IS A FLAG TO TELL IF A MATCH HAS BEEN F
     OUND IN THE LANGUAGE DATA AND T SHOWS WHICH FIELD THE MATCH
     WAS FOUND IN
150   RESTORE
160   READ A$: IF A$ = "END1" AND FL = 0 THEN : PRINT "I'M AFRAID
      I DON'T QUITE UNDERSTAND": PRINT "THAT QUESTION": PRINT " -
      COULD YOU REPHRASE IT PLEASE ?": GOTO 130
170   IF A$ = "888" THEN :T = T + 1: GOTO 160
180   FOR I = 1 TO LEN (S$) - LEN (A$) + 1
190   IF A$ < > MID$ (S$,I, LEN (A$)) THEN 210
200  FL = 1
210   NEXT I
220   IF FL = 0 THEN 160
230   READ A$: IF A$ < > "END1" THEN 230
240  M = 0
250   FOR J = 1 TO P
260   READ A$:Q = 0
270   FOR I = 1 TO LEN (S$) - LEN (A$) + 1
280   IF A$ < > MID$ (S$,I, LEN (A$)) THEN 300
```

```
290   PRINT A$;" IS ";: FOR Q = 1 TO T: READ I$: NEXT : PRINT I$:M
      = 1: REM  A MATCH HAS BEEN FOUND IN THE PERSONNEL RECORDS
300   NEXT I
310   IF Q = 0 THEN : READ A$,A$
320   NEXT J
330   IF M = 0 THEN : PRINT "I'M AFRAID I DON'T KNOW THAT"
340   INPUT "DO YOU HAVE ANOTHER QUESTION ?";A$
350   IF A$ = "Y" THEN 130
360   END
370   REM  LANGUAGE DATA
380   DATA    AGE,OLD,888: REM  888 IS THE CODE TO INDICATE END OF
      FIELD
390   DATA    MARRIED,WIFE,HUSBAND,SPOUSE,BATCHELOR,WIDOWER,SPINST
      ER,MARITAL,888
400   DATA   END1
410   REM  PERSONNEL RECORDS
420   DATA   JOHN SMITH,37,MARRIED
430   DATA   BILL BLOGGS,23,SINGLE
440   DATA   JANE HARRIS,25,SINGLE
450   DATA   FREDA BAGGINS,43,MARRIED
460   DATA   JIM JENKINS,67,DIVORCED
470   DATA END2

]RUN
I KNOW SOMETHING ABOUT PERSONNEL
ASK ME SOMETHING ABOUT SOMEONE
?HOW OLD DO YOU RECKON JOHN SMITH MIGHT BE ?
JOHN SMITH IS 37
DO YOU HAVE ANOTHER QUESTION ?Y
?WHAT'S JOHN SMITH'S AGE ?
JOHN SMITH IS 37
DO YOU HAVE ANOTHER QUESTION ?Y
?IS JIM JENKINS MARRIED ?
JIM JENKINS IS DIVORCED
DO YOU HAVE ANOTHER QUESTION ?Y
?WHAT AGE IS FREDA BAGGINS NOW ?
FREDA BAGGINS IS 43
DO YOU HAVE ANOTHER QUESTION ?Y
?DO YOU KNOW IF JANE HARRIS IS DIVORCED ?
I'M AFRAID I DON'T QUITE UNDERSTAND
THAT QUESTION
 - COULD YOU REPHRASE IT PLEASE ?
?WHAT IS JANE HARRIS'S MARITAL STATUS ?
JANE HARRIS IS SINGLE
DO YOU HAVE ANOTHER QUESTION ?Y
?HOW OLD IS BILL BLOGGS ?
BILL BLOGGS IS 23
DO YOU HAVE ANOTHER QUESTION ?Y
?HOW OLD IS JOHN SMITH'S WIFE ?
JOHN SMITH IS 37
DO YOU HAVE ANOTHER QUESTION ?Y
?DOES JOHN SMITH HAVE A WIFE ?
JOHN SMITH IS MARRIED
DO YOU HAVE ANOTHER QUESTION ?Y
```

```
?HOW OLD IS SHE ?
I'M AFRAID I DON'T KNOW THAT
DO YOU HAVE ANOTHER QUESTION ?Y
?DOES JIM JENKINS HAVE A SPOUSE ?
JIM JENKINS IS DIVORCED
DO YOU HAVE ANOTHER QUESTION ?Y
?IS FREDA BAGGINS A WIDOWER ?
FREDA BAGGINS IS MARRIED
DO YOU HAVE ANOTHER QUESTION ?N

]
```

But if we now turn to 'real' natural-language systems, there are two main aspects to the problem – syntactic analysis and semantic analysis.

Syntactic analysis consists of trying to work out the structure of what has been said to the computer; and semantic analysis consists of trying to work out the meaning of what has been said.

It could be argued that syntactic analysis is unnecessary as long as the semantic analysis is right – after all, if the computer understands the message then why should it bother with the structure or the way it was said?

There is some truth in this argument and, in fact, the 'trick' method given above relies on this – all the computer was trying to do was to hit upon the meaning and it made no attempt to analyse the structure of the message. It just tried to get the meaning straight off at one go.

But for much of our language such methods prove inadequate – they are far too simple to enable us to say anything very complex to the computer. And the purpose of introducing syntactic analysis is not an end in itself – it is part of the attempt to get at the meaning of the message.

In one form or another, all syntactic analysis consists of trying to produce a parse tree for the input message – very much as you might have been required to do at school when, for reasons which are forever obscure, you were required to parse sentences in English despite the fact that you understood them perfectly well without a parse tree.

A typical method of producing a parse tree is to assume that English is a context-free grammar – which means that each word in the language occurs in accordance with rules which are not dependent on the context in which the words are used. As an example of a context-free grammar we might have the following units:

Sentence
Noun phrase
Determiner
Adjective
Adjectives
Noun
Verb phrase
Verb
Preposition
Prepositional phrase
Prepositional phrases
Conjunction

which we could then write out as the following rules of grammar:

Listing 3.2 Rules of grammar

```
10   REM    ************************
20   REM    **   LISTING 3.2      **
30   REM    **   RULES OF GRAMMAR **
40   REM    ************************
1000  REM   NOTE THAT NO SPACES ARE ALLOWED EXCEPT WHERE SHOWN
1010  DATA  <SENTENCE>=<NOUN.PHRASE> <VERB.PHRASE-PREPOSITIONAL.P
      HRASES>
1020  DATA  <SENTENCE>=<SENTENCE> <CONJUNCTION> <SENTENCE>
1030  DATA  <NOUN.PHRASE>=<DETERMINER> <ADJECTIVES-NOUN>
1040  DATA  <ADJECTIVES-NOUN>=<ADJECTIVE> <ADJECTIVES-NOUN>
1050  DATA  <ADJECTIVES-NOUN>=<NOUN>
1060  DATA  <VERB.PHRASE-PREPOSITIONAL.PHRASES>=<VERB.PHRASE-PREP
      OSITIONAL.PHRASES> <PREPOSITIONAL.PHRASE>
1070  DATA  <VERB.PHRASE-PREPOSITIONAL.PHRASES>=<VERB.PHRASE>
1080  DATA  <VERB.PHRASE>=<VERB> <NOUN.PHRASE>
1090  DATA  <VERB.PHRASE-PREPOSITIONAL.PHRASES>=<VERB> <PREPOSITI
      ONAL.PHRASE>
1100  DATA  <PREPOSITIONAL.PHRASE>=<PREPOSITION> <NOUN.PHRASE>
1110  DATA  <VERB.PHRASE>=<VERB>
1120  DATA  <DETERMINER>=A,THE,THIS,THAT
1130  DATA  <ADJECTIVE>=GREEN,RED,STRONG
1140  DATA  <NOUN>=ROSE,GRASS,SUN
1150  DATA  <VERB>=GREW,SHONE
1160  DATA  <PREPOSITION>=TO,OF
1170  DATA  <CONJUNCTION>=AND
```

]

Note that this is not a definitive grammar by any means – you could modify it to suit your own ideas about how language should be parsed and add a much larger vocabulary.

But, on looking at it, we see that this is a very formal definition of the language structure and is really no different from the definition given to computer programming languages. In fact, your programming manual may well have an appendix in it defining the language in much the same way as this. The reason for the similarity is that computer programming languages are also context-free grammars and what we are trying to do is to treat natural language as if it were the same. The words are different and the exact structure different, but the idea is the same. This is a contradiction of our earlier statement that natural languages are not, and never can be, the same as formal languages but, as formal languages are the only type of language which is fully understood, the approximation is justified on the grounds that it might prove helpful.

If a sentence is input to this parser the parser works by examining the first word in the sentence and looking for the word in the list of words on the right-hand side of the grammar. When the parser finds the word, the parser replaces the word with the left-hand side of the grammatical rule. The parser then repeats the procedure until it has a correct parse. If the parse is not correct the technique is to back up through the parse tree to date and try a different replacement rule to see if that helps.

An example probably makes things clearer. Consider the following sentence:

'The sun shone'

which produces the following sequence:

```
<DETERMINER> SUN SHONE
<DETERMINER> <NOUN> SHONE
<DETERMINER> <ADJECTIVES-NOUN> SHONE
<NOUN.PHRASE> SHONE
<NOUN.PHRASE> <VERB>
```

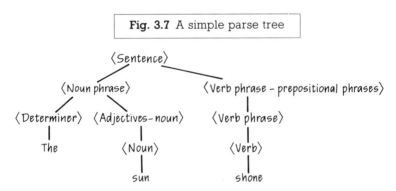

Fig. 3.7 A simple parse tree

This simple parse tree shows that, by parsing a sentence, we can see that 'The Sun' is a noun phrase which applies to the verb phrase 'shone'. This helps to elucidate the meaning of the sentence as it is now possible to ask the system 'What shone?', or, 'What object is mentioned in the sentence?'.

Listing 3.3 First parser

This is a listing of the program which produced the sequence on p. 56 ('The sun shone'). The grammar we described earlier is in lines 1000 forwards and could be modified to suit your own views of the rules of grammar and could be expanded to contain a much larger vocabulary.

The input sentence is placed into S$ and leading and trailing spaces removed. Then the first word is extracted by looking for the first space. This word is then matched against the right-hand side of the rules of grammar and replaced by the left-hand side of the appropriate rule. This process is repeated until there is only one single grammatical unit in S$ (identified in line 330).

If the system reaches a point where no more replacement rules can be applied to the current S$ and there is still not one single grammatical unit then it backs up (lines 360 forwards) by restoring the result of the last replacement rule and then searching the rules of grammar from beyond that rule to see if there is an alternative rule that could be applied. If there is, it applies that replacement rule and carries on as before to see if that produces a successful parse. If not, then it continues to back up until it finds some sequence of replacement rules which actually do give a successful parse or, having exhausted all possibilities, has to give up.

This is a method of searching known as depth-first exhaustive search (see Chapter 7 for more details on searching) and is always guaranteed to work provided a solution exists – although, once it starts backing up, it may prove rather slow.

Arrays LA% and LB% are used to keep track of the route followed so far in terms of the left- and right-hand positions of the string S$ at the point at which a replacement was made. Array R% is used to keep track of which replacement rule was used at each point in the parse so far.

Because of the fact that the program relies on spaces to determine where the units of language are within S$ it is very important to ensure that no spaces are introduced into the DATA statements except between grammatical units. This is why a verb phrase is coded as VERB.PHRASE (with a point between the two words) rather than simply leaving a space there.

The two run time examples shown are relatively straightforward and serve to check that the system is working correctly.

```
10   REM   **************************
11   REM   **  LISTING 3.3         **
12   REM   **  FIRST PARSER        **
13   REM   **************************
20   DIM G$(50),W$(50),R%(50),LA%(50),LB%(50)
30   Z = 0:W = 1:S = W:C = Z
40   HOME : PRINT ,"PARSER": PRINT ,"------": PRINT
50   PRINT "INPUT A SENTENCE AND THEN PRESS RETURN:"
60   PRINT : INPUT S$:S$ = " " + S$ + " ": PRINT : PRINT S$
70   RESTORE
80 R = Z
90 F = Z: READ A$: IF A$ = "999" THEN 170
```

```
100  IF  RIGHT$ (A$,W) = " " THEN :A$ =  LEFT$ (A$, LEN (A$) - W)
     : GOTO 100
110 R = R + W
120  FOR I = W TO  LEN (A$)
130  IF  MID$ (A$,I,W) = "=" THEN :G$(R) =  LEFT$ (A$,I - W):F =
     W:W$(R) =  RIGHT$ (A$, LEN (A$) - I):I =  LEN (A$)
140  NEXT I
150  IF F = Z THEN :G$(R) = G$(R - W):W$(R) = A$
160  GOTO 90
170  REM  IMPLEMENT REPLACEMENT RULES
180  Q = W:F = Z:S = W
190 LS =  LEN (S$)
200  FOR I = Q TO LS
210  IF  MID$ (S$,I,W) < > " " THEN 270
220 I = I + W
230  FOR J = S TO R
240  IF  MID$ (S$,I, LEN (W$(J)) + W) < > W$(J) + " " THEN 260
250 C = C + W:LA%(C) = I - W:LB%(C) = LS -  LEN (W$(J)) - I + W:S
     $ =  LEFT$ (S$,LA%(C)) + G$(J) +  RIGHT$ (S$,LB%(C)):F = W:R
     %(C) = J: PRINT S$:J = R:I = LS
260  NEXT J
270  NEXT I
280 C1 = Z:C2 = Z
290  FOR I = 2 TO  LEN (S$) - W
300  IF  MID$ (S$,I,W) = "<" THEN :C1 = C1 + W
310  IF  MID$ (S$,I,W) = ">" THEN :C2 = C2 + W
320  NEXT I
330  IF C1 = W AND C2 = W AND  LEFT$ (S$,2) = " <" AND  RIGHT$ (S
     $,2) = "> " THEN : PRINT : PRINT "PARSING COMPLETE": GOTO 42
     0
340  IF F = W THEN 170
350  REM  BACK UP THE PARSE TREE
360  PRINT "BACKING UP..."
370  IF C = Z THEN : PRINT "I CANNOT PARSE THIS - SORRY !": GOTO
     420
380 Q = LA%(C):S = R%(C) + W
390 S$ =  LEFT$ (S$,Q) + W$(S - W) +  RIGHT$ (S$,LB%(C))
400 C = C - W
410  GOTO 190
420  END
1000  REM  NOTE THAT NO SPACES ARE ALLOWED EXCEPT WHERE SHOWN
1010  DATA  <SENTENCE>=<NOUN.PHRASE> <VERB.PHRASE-PREPOSITIONAL.P
      HRASES>
1020  DATA  <SENTENCE>=<SENTENCE> <CONJUNCTION> <SENTENCE>
1030  DATA  <NOUN.PHRASE>=<DETERMINER> <ADJECTIVES-NOUN>
1040  DATA  <ADJECTIVES-NOUN>=<ADJECTIVE> <ADJECTIVES-NOUN>
1050  DATA  <ADJECTIVES-NOUN>=<NOUN>
1060  DATA  <VERB.PHRASE-PREPOSITIONAL.PHRASES>=<VERB.PHRASE-PREP
      OSITIONAL.PHRASES> <PREPOSITIONAL.PHRASE>
1070  DATA  <VERB.PHRASE-PREPOSITIONAL.PHRASES>=<VERB.PHRASE>
1080  DATA  <VERB.PHRASE>=<VERB> <NOUN.PHRASE>
1090  DATA  <VERB.PHRASE-PREPOSITIONAL.PHRASES>=<VERB> <PREPOSITI
      ONAL.PHRASE>
1100  DATA  <PREPOSITIONAL.PHRASE>=<PREPOSITION> <NOUN.PHRASE>
1110  DATA  <VERB.PHRASE>=<VERB>
```

```
1120   DATA   <DETERMINER>=A,THE,THIS,THAT
1130   DATA   <ADJECTIVE>=GREEN,RED,STRONG
1140   DATA   <NOUN>=ROSE,GRASS,SUN
1150   DATA   <VERB>=GREW,SHONE
1160   DATA   <PREPOSITION>=TO,OF
1170   DATA   <CONJUNCTION>=AND
1180   DATA   999: REM   STOP CODE
```

```
]RUN
                 PARSER
                 ------
INPUT A SENTENCE AND THEN PRESS RETURN:

?THE SUN SHONE

 THE SUN SHONE
 <DETERMINER> SUN SHONE
 <DETERMINER> <NOUN> SHONE
 <DETERMINER> <ADJECTIVES-NOUN> SHONE
 <NOUN.PHRASE> SHONE
 <NOUN.PHRASE> <VERB>
 <NOUN.PHRASE> <VERB.PHRASE>
 <NOUN.PHRASE> <VERB.PHRASE-PREPOSITIONAL.PHRASES>
 <SENTENCE>

PARSING COMPLETE

]RUN
                 PARSER
                 ------
INPUT A SENTENCE AND THEN PRESS RETURN:

?THE SUN SHONE AND THE GRASS GREW

 THE SUN SHONE AND THE GRASS GREW
 <DETERMINER> SUN SHONE AND THE GRASS GREW
 <DETERMINER> <NOUN> SHONE AND THE GRASS GREW
 <DETERMINER> <ADJECTIVES-NOUN> SHONE AND THE GRASS GREW
 <NOUN.PHRASE> SHONE AND THE GRASS GREW
 <NOUN.PHRASE> <VERB> AND THE GRASS GREW
 <NOUN.PHRASE> <VERB.PHRASE> AND THE GRASS GREW
 <NOUN.PHRASE> <VERB.PHRASE-PREPOSITIONAL.PHRASES> AND THE GRASS GREW
 <SENTENCE> AND THE GRASS GREW
 <SENTENCE> <CONJUNCTION> THE GRASS GREW
 <SENTENCE> <CONJUNCTION> <DETERMINER> GRASS GREW
 <SENTENCE> <CONJUNCTION> <DETERMINER> <NOUN> GREW
 <SENTENCE> <CONJUNCTION> <DETERMINER> <ADJECTIVES-NOUN> GREW
 <SENTENCE> <CONJUNCTION> <NOUN.PHRASE> GREW
 <SENTENCE> <CONJUNCTION> <NOUN.PHRASE> <VERB>
 <SENTENCE> <CONJUNCTION> <NOUN.PHRASE> <VERB.PHRASE>
 <SENTENCE> <CONJUNCTION> <NOUN.PHRASE> <VERB.PHRASE-PREPOSITIONAL.PHRAS
ES>
 <SENTENCE> <CONJUNCTION> <SENTENCE>
 <SENTENCE>

PARSING COMPLETE
```

Listing 3.4 Second parser

This program works in exactly the same way as Listing 3.3 despite its increased length. In principle, it does nothing more than Listing 3.3 does.

The reason for its greater length is that it contains an additional string $H\$$ which holds the original sentence and, as parsing progresses, it introduces left- and right-hand brackets into this string so that you can readily see the tree structure of the parse. So, if two terms are enclosed within a matching set of brackets then they are both branches off the same node.

The first two run time examples with this modified program show the extra information that this program gives you using exactly the same input sentences as in Listing 3.3.

However, the final run time example 'The rose grew to the sun' is more complex because 'The rose grew' could be parsed as a sentence in its own right leaving 'to the sun' hanging out at the end. This, in fact, is what happens and the result is that the program has to work hard, continually backing up as it carries out an exhaustive, depth-first search of the possibilities before it finally finds a correct parse for the sentence as a whole.

```
10   REM   ****************************
11   REM   **  LISTING 3.4        **
12   REM   **  SECOND PARSER      **
13   REM   ****************************
20   DIM G$(50),W$(50),R%(50),LA%(50),LB%(50)
30   Z = 0:W = 1:S = W:C = Z:Q = W
40   HOME : PRINT ,"PARSER": PRINT ,"------": PRINT
50   PRINT "INPUT A SENTENCE AND THEN PRESS RETURN:"
60   PRINT : INPUT S$:S$ = " " + S$ + " ": PRINT : PRINT S$
70   H$ = S$: RESTORE
80   R = Z
90   F = Z: READ A$: IF A$ = "999" THEN 170
100  IF  RIGHT$ (A$,W) = " " THEN :A$ =  LEFT$ (A$, LEN (A$) - W)
     : GOTO 100
110  R = R + W
120  FOR I = W TO  LEN (A$)
130  IF  MID$ (A$,I,W) = "=" THEN :G$(R) =  LEFT$ (A$,I - W):F -
     W:W$(R) =  RIGHT$ (A$, LEN (A$) - I):I =  LEN (A$)
140  NEXT I
150  IF F = Z THEN :G$(R) = G$(R - W):W$(R) = A$
160  GOTO 90
170  REM  IMPLEMENT REPLACEMENT RULES
180  F = Z:S = W
190  LS =  LEN (S$)
200  C1 = Z:Q = W
210  FOR I = Q TO LS
220  IF  MID$ (S$,I,W) < > " " THEN 420
230  I = I + W:C1 = C1 + W
240  FOR J = S TO R
250  IF  MID$ (S$,I, LEN (W$(J)) + W) < > W$(J) + " " THEN 410
260  C = C + W:LA%(C) = I - W:LB%(C) = LS -  LEN (W$(J)) - I + W:S
     $ =  LEFT$ (S$,LA%(C)) + G$(J) +  RIGHT$ (S$,LB%(C)):F = W:R
     %(C) = J: PRINT C;S$
270  C2 = C1 + W
```

```
280   FOR K = W TO  LEN (W$(J))
290   IF  MID$ (W$(J),K,W) = " " THEN :C2 = C2 + W
300   NEXT K
310  C3 = Z:C4 = Z:A$ = ""
320   FOR K = W TO  LEN (H$)
330  A$ = A$ +  MID$ (H$,K,W)
340   IF  MID$ (H$,K,W) < > " " THEN 390
350  C3 = C3 + W:C4 = C4 + W
360   IF C3 > C1 AND C4 < = C2 THEN :A$ =  LEFT$ (A$, LEN (A$) -
     W)
370   IF C3 = C1 THEN :A$ = A$ + "("
380   IF C4 = C2 THEN :A$ = A$ + ") "
390   NEXT K
400  H$ = A$: PRINT H$:J = R:I = LS
410   NEXT J
420   NEXT I
430  C1 = Z:C2 = Z
440   FOR I = 2 TO  LEN (S$) - W
450   IF  MID$ (S$,I,W) = "<" THEN :C1 = C1 + W
460   IF  MID$ (S$,I,W) = ">" THEN :C2 = C2 + W
470   NEXT I
480   IF C1 = W AND C2 = W AND  LEFT$ (S$,2) = " <" AND  RIGHT$ (S
     $,2) = "> " THEN : PRINT : PRINT "PARSING COMPLETE": GOTO 79
     0
490   IF F = W THEN 170
500   REM  BACK UP THE PARSE TREE
510   PRINT "BACKING UP..."
520   IF C = Z THEN : PRINT "I CANNOT PARSE THIS - SORRY !": GOTO
     790
530  Q = LA%(C):S = R%(C) + W
540  C1 = Z:C2 = Z:S1$ =  LEFT$ (S$,Q):S2$ =  RIGHT$ (S$,LB%(C))
550   FOR K = W TO Q
560   IF  MID$ (S1$,K,W) = " " THEN :C1 = C1 + W
570   NEXT K:SP = C1
580   FOR K = W TO  LEN (H$)
590   IF  MID$ (H$,K,W) = " " THEN :C2 = C2 + W
600   IF C1 = C2 THEN :C1 = K:K =  LEN (H$)
610   NEXT K
620  H$ =  LEFT$ (H$,C1) +  RIGHT$ (H$, LEN (H$) - W - C1):C2 = Z:
     A$ =  LEFT$ (H$,C1):F = Z
630   FOR K = C1 + W TO  LEN (H$):M$ =  MID$ (H$,K,W): IF M$ < >
     "(" AND M$ < > ")" THEN 710
640   IF M$ = "(" THEN :C2 = C2 + W
650   IF M$ = ")" THEN :C2 = C2 - W
660   IF C2 < > - W THEN 700
670  C2 = 999
680   IF F = W THEN :K = K + W:F = Z
690   GOTO 720
700   IF C2 = Z THEN :A$ = A$ + M$ + " ":F = W: GOTO 720
710  A$ = A$ + M$
720   NEXT K
730   IF  RIGHT$ (A$,W) = " " THEN :A$ =  LEFT$ (A$, LEN (A$) - W)
     : GOTO 730
740  H$ = A$ + " "
750  S$ = S1$ + W$(R%(C)) + S2$
```

```
760  C = C - W
770   PRINT C;S$: PRINT H$
780  C1 = SP - W:LS =  LEN (S$): GOTO 210
790  END
1000   REM  NOTE THAT NO SPACES ARE ALLOWED EXCEPT WHERE SHOWN
1010   DATA  <SENTENCE>=<NOUN.PHRASE> <VERB.PHRASE-PREPOSITIONAL.P
       HRASES>
1020   DATA  <SENTENCE>=<SENTENCE> <CONJUNCTION> <SENTENCE>
1030   DATA  <NOUN.PHRASE>=<DETERMINER> <ADJECTIVES-NOUN>
1040   DATA  <ADJECTIVES-NOUN>=<ADJECTIVE> <ADJECTIVES-NOUN>
1050   DATA  <ADJECTIVES-NOUN>=<NOUN>
1060   DATA  <VERB.PHRASE-PREPOSITIONAL.PHRASES>=<VERB.PHRASE-PREP
       OSITIONAL.PHRASES> <PREPOSITIONAL.PHRASE>
1070   DATA  <VERB.PHRASE-PREPOSITIONAL.PHRASES>=<VERB.PHRASE>
1080   DATA  <VERB.PHRASE>=<VERB> <NOUN.PHRASE>
1090   DATA  <VERB.PHRASE-PREPOSITIONAL.PHRASES>=<VERB> <PREPOSITI
       ONAL.PHRASE>
1100   DATA  <PREPOSITIONAL.PHRASE>=<PREPOSITION> <NOUN.PHRASE>
1110   DATA  <VERB.PHRASE>=<VERB>
1120   DATA  <DETERMINER>=A,THE,THIS,THAT
1130   DATA  <ADJECTIVE>=GREEN,RED,STRONG
1140   DATA  <NOUN>=ROSE,GRASS,SUN
1150   DATA  <VERB>=GREW,SHONE
1160   DATA  <PREPOSITION>=TO,OF
1170   DATA  <CONJUNCTION>=AND
1180   DATA  999: REM   STOP CODE

]RUN
                    PARSER
                    ------


INPUT A SENTENCE AND THEN PRESS RETURN:

?THE SUN SHONE

 THE SUN SHONE
1 <DETERMINER> SUN SHONE
 (THE) SUN SHONE
2 <DETERMINER> <NOUN> SHONE
 (THE) (SUN) SHONE
3 <DETERMINER> <ADJECTIVES-NOUN> SHONE
 (THE) ((SUN)) SHONE
4 <NOUN.PHRASE> SHONE
 ((THE)((SUN))) SHONE
5 <NOUN.PHRASE> <VERB>
 ((THE)((SUN))) (SHONE)
6 <NOUN.PHRASE> <VERB.PHRASE>
 ((THE)((SUN))) ((SHONE))
7 <NOUN.PHRASE> <VERB.PHRASE-PREPOSITIONAL.PHRASES>
 ((THE)((SUN))) (((SHONE)))
8 <SENTENCE>
 (((THE)((SUN)))(((SHONE))))

PARSING COMPLETE

]RUN
```

```
          PARSER
          ------

INPUT A SENTENCE AND THEN PRESS RETURN:

?THE SUN SHONE AND THE GRASS GREW

 THE SUN SHONE AND THE GRASS GREW
1 <DETERMINER> SUN SHONE AND THE GRASS GREW
 (THE) SUN SHONE AND THE GRASS GREW
2 <DETERMINER> <NOUN> SHONE AND THE GRASS GREW
 (THE) (SUN) SHONE AND THE GRASS GREW
3 <DETERMINER> <ADJECTIVES-NOUN> SHONE AND THE GRASS GREW
 (THE) ((SUN)) SHONE AND THE GRASS GREW
4 <NOUN.PHRASE> SHONE AND THE GRASS GREW
 ((THE)((SUN))) SHONE AND THE GRASS GREW
5 <NOUN.PHRASE> <VERB> AND THE GRASS GREW
 ((THE)((SUN))) (SHONE) AND THE GRASS GREW
6 <NOUN.PHRASE> <VERB.PHRASE> AND THE GRASS GREW
 ((THE)((SUN))) ((SHONE)) AND THE GRASS GREW
7 <NOUN.PHRASE> <VERB.PHRASE-PREPOSITIONAL.PHRASES> AND THE GRASS GREW
 ((THE)((SUN))) (((SHONE))) AND THE GRASS GREW
8 <SENTENCE> AND THE GRASS GREW
 (((THE)((SUN)))(((SHONE)))) AND THE GRASS GREW
9 <SENTENCE> <CONJUNCTION> THE GRASS GREW
 (((THE)((SUN)))(((SHONE)))) (AND) THE GRASS GREW
10 <SENTENCE> <CONJUNCTION> <DETERMINER> GRASS GREW
 (((THE)((SUN)))(((SHONE)))) (AND) (THE) GRASS GREW
11 <SENTENCE> <CONJUNCTION> <DETERMINER> <NOUN> GREW
 (((THE)((SUN)))(((SHONE)))) (AND) (THE) (GRASS) GREW
12 <SENTENCE> <CONJUNCTION> <DETERMINER> <ADJECTIVES-NOUN> GREW
 (((THE)((SUN)))(((SHONE)))) (AND) (THE) ((GRASS)) GREW
13 <SENTENCE> <CONJUNCTION> <NOUN.PHRASE> GREW
 (((THE)((SUN)))(((SHONE)))) (AND) ((THE)((GRASS))) GREW
14 <SENTENCE> <CONJUNCTION> <NOUN.PHRASE> <VERB>
 (((THE)((SUN)))(((SHONE)))) (AND) ((THE)((GRASS))) (GREW)
15 <SENTENCE> <CONJUNCTION> <NOUN.PHRASE> <VERB.PHRASE>
 (((THE)((SUN)))(((SHONE)))) (AND) ((THE)((GRASS))) ((GREW))
16 <SENTENCE> <CONJUNCTION> <NOUN.PHRASE> <VERB.PHRASE-PREPOSITIONAL.PHR
ASES>
 (((THE)((SUN)))(((SHONE)))) (AND) ((THE)((GRASS))) (((GREW)))
17 <SENTENCE> <CONJUNCTION> <SENTENCE>
 (((THE)((SUN)))(((SHONE)))) (AND) (((THE)((GRASS)))(((GREW))))
18 <SENTENCE>
 ((((THE)((SUN)))(((SHONE))))(AND)(((THE)((GRASS)))(((GREW)))))

PARSING COMPLETE

]RUN
          PARSER
          ------

INPUT A SENTENCE AND THEN PRESS RETURN:

?THE ROSE GREW TO THE SUN
```

```
THE ROSE GREW TO THE SUN
1 <DETERMINER> ROSE GREW TO THE SUN
 (THE) ROSE GREW TO THE SUN
2 <DETERMINER> <NOUN> GREW TO THE SUN
 (THE) (ROSE) GREW TO THE SUN
3 <DETERMINER> <ADJECTIVES-NOUN> GREW TO THE SUN
 (THE) ((ROSE)) GREW TO THE SUN
4 <NOUN.PHRASE> GREW TO THE SUN
 ((THE)((ROSE))) GREW TO THE SUN
5 <NOUN.PHRASE> <VERB> TO THE SUN
 ((THE)((ROSE))) (GREW) TO THE SUN
6 <NOUN.PHRASE> <VERB.PHRASE> TO THE SUN
 ((THE)((ROSE))) ((GREW)) TO THE SUN
7 <NOUN.PHRASE> <VERB.PHRASE-PREPOSITIONAL.PHRASES> TO THE SUN
 ((THE)((ROSE))) (((GREW))) TO THE SUN
8 <SENTENCE> TO THE SUN
 (((THE)((ROSE)))(((GREW)))) TO THE SUN
9 <SENTENCE> <PREPOSITION> THE SUN
 (((THE)((ROSE)))(((GREW)))) (TO) THE SUN
10 <SENTENCE> <PREPOSITION> <DETERMINER> SUN
 (((THE)((ROSE)))(((GREW)))) (TO) (THE) SUN
11 <SENTENCE> <PREPOSITION> <DETERMINER> <NOUN>
 (((THE)((ROSE)))(((GREW)))) (TO) (THE) (SUN)
12 <SENTENCE> <PREPOSITION> <DETERMINER> <ADJECTIVES-NOUN>
 (((THE)((ROSE)))(((GREW)))) (TO) (THE) ((SUN))
13 <SENTENCE> <PREPOSITION> <NOUN.PHRASE>
 (((THE)((ROSE)))(((GREW)))) (TO) ((THE)((SUN)))
14 <SENTENCE> <PREPOSITIONAL.PHRASE>
 (((THE)((ROSE)))(((GREW)))) ((TO)((THE)((SUN))))
BACKING UP...
13 <SENTENCE> <PREPOSITION> <NOUN.PHRASE>
 (((THE)((ROSE)))(((GREW)))) (TO) ((THE)((SUN)))
BACKING UP...
12 <SENTENCE> <PREPOSITION> <DETERMINER> <ADJECTIVES-NOUN>
 (((THE)((ROSE)))(((GREW)))) (TO) (THE) ((SUN))
BACKING UP...
11 <SENTENCE> <PREPOSITION> <DETERMINER> <NOUN>
 (((THE)((ROSE)))(((GREW)))) (TO) (THE) (SUN)
BACKING UP...
10 <SENTENCE> <PREPOSITION> <DETERMINER> SUN
 (((THE)((ROSE)))(((GREW)))) (TO) (THE) SUN
BACKING UP...
9 <SENTENCE> <PREPOSITION> THE SUN
 (((THE)((ROSE)))(((GREW)))) (TO) THE SUN
10 <SENTENCE> <PREPOSITION> THE <NOUN>
 (((THE)((ROSE)))(((GREW)))) (TO) THE (SUN)
11 <SENTENCE> <PREPOSITION> <DETERMINER> <NOUN>
 (((THE)((ROSE)))(((GREW)))) (TO) (THE) (SUN)
12 <SENTENCE> <PREPOSITION> <DETERMINER> <ADJECTIVES-NOUN>
 (((THE)((ROSE)))(((GREW)))) (TO) (THE) ((SUN))
13 <SENTENCE> <PREPOSITION> <NOUN.PHRASE>
 (((THE)((ROSE)))(((GREW)))) (TO) ((THE)((SUN)))
14 <SENTENCE> <PREPOSITIONAL.PHRASE>
 (((THE)((ROSE)))(((GREW)))) ((TO)((THE)((SUN))))
BACKING UP...
```

```
13 <SENTENCE> <PREPOSITION> <NOUN.PHRASE>
 (((THE)((ROSE)))(((GREW)))) (TO) ((THE)((SUN)))
BACKING UP...
12 <SENTENCE> <PREPOSITION> <DETERMINER> <ADJECTIVES-NOUN>
 (((THE)((ROSE)))(((GREW)))) (TO) (THE) ((SUN))
BACKING UP...
11 <SENTENCE> <PREPOSITION> <DETERMINER> <NOUN>
 (((THE)((ROSE)))(((GREW)))) (TO) (THE) (SUN)
BACKING UP...
10 <SENTENCE> <PREPOSITION> THE <NOUN>
 (((THE)((ROSE)))(((GREW)))) (TO) THE (SUN)
BACKING UP...
9 <SENTENCE> <PREPOSITION> THE SUN
 (((THE)((ROSE)))(((GREW)))) (TO) THE SUN
BACKING UP...
8 <SENTENCE> TO THE SUN
 (((THE)((ROSE)))(((GREW)))) TO THE SUN
BACKING UP...
7 <NOUN.PHRASE> <VERB.PHRASE-PREPOSITIONAL.PHRASES> TO THE SUN
 ((THE)((ROSE))) (((GREW))) TO THE SUN
8 <NOUN.PHRASE> <VERB.PHRASE-PREPOSITIONAL.PHRASES> <PREPOSITION> THE SU
N
 ((THE)((ROSE))) (((GREW))) (TO) THE SUN
9 <SENTENCE> <PREPOSITION> THE SUN
 (((THE)((ROSE)))(((GREW)))) (TO) THE SUN
10 <SENTENCE> <PREPOSITION> <DETERMINER> SUN
 (((THE)((ROSE)))(((GREW)))) (TO) (THE) SUN
11 <SENTENCE> <PREPOSITION> <DETERMINER> <NOUN>
 (((THE)((ROSE)))(((GREW)))) (TO) (THE) (SUN)
12 <SENTENCE> <PREPOSITION> <DETERMINER> <ADJECTIVES-NOUN>
 (((THE)((ROSE)))(((GREW)))) (TO) (THE) ((SUN))
13 <SENTENCE> <PREPOSITION> <NOUN.PHRASE>
 (((THE)((ROSE)))(((GREW)))) (TO) ((THE)((SUN)))
14 <SENTENCE> <PREPOSITIONAL.PHRASE>
 (((THE)((ROSE)))(((GREW)))) ((TO)((THE)((SUN))))
BACKING UP...
13 <SENTENCE> <PREPOSITION> <NOUN.PHRASE>
 (((THE)((ROSE)))(((GREW)))) (TO) ((THE)((SUN)))
BACKING UP...
12 <SENTENCE> <PREPOSITION> <DETERMINER> <ADJECTIVES-NOUN>
 (((THE)((ROSE)))(((GREW)))) (TO) (THE) ((SUN))
BACKING UP...
11 <SENTENCE> <PREPOSITION> <DETERMINER> <NOUN>
 (((THE)((ROSE)))(((GREW)))) (TO) (THE) (SUN)
BACKING UP...
10 <SENTENCE> <PREPOSITION> <DETERMINER> SUN
 (((THE)((ROSE)))(((GREW)))) (TO) (THE) SUN
BACKING UP...
9 <SENTENCE> <PREPOSITION> THE SUN
 (((THE)((ROSE)))(((GREW)))) (TO) THE SUN
10 <SENTENCE> <PREPOSITION> THE <NOUN>
 (((THE)((ROSE)))(((GREW)))) (TO) THE (SUN)
11 <SENTENCE> <PREPOSITION> <DETERMINER> <NOUN>
 (((THE)((ROSE)))(((GREW)))) (TO) (THE) (SUN)
12 <SENTENCE> <PREPOSITION> <DETERMINER> <ADJECTIVES-NOUN>
```

```
(((THE)((ROSE)))(((GREW)))) (TO) (THE) ((SUN))
13 <SENTENCE> <PREPOSITION> <NOUN.PHRASE>
(((THE)((ROSE)))(((GREW)),)) (TO) (THE)((SUN)))
14 <SENTENCE> <PREPOSITIONAL.PHRASE>
(((THE)((ROSE)))(((GREW)))) ((TO)((THE)((SUN))))
BACKING UP...
13 <SENTENCE> <PREPOSITION> <NOUN.PHRASE>
(((THE)((ROSE)))(((GREW)))) (TO) ((THE)((SUN)))
BACKING UP...
12 <SENTENCE> <PREPOSITION> <DETERMINER> <ADJECTIVES-NOUN>
(((THE)((ROSE)))(((GREW)))) (TO) (THE) ((SUN))
BACKING UP...
11 <SENTENCE> <PREPOSITION> <DETERMINER> <NOUN>
(((THE)((ROSE)))(((GREW)))) (TO) (THE) (SUN)
BACKING UP...
10 <SENTENCE> <PREPOSITION> THE <NOUN>
(((THE)((ROSE)))(((GREW)))) (TO) THE (SUN)
BACKING UP...
9 <SENTENCE> <PREPOSITION> THE SUN
(((THE)((ROSE)))(((GREW)))) (TO) THE SUN
BACKING UP...
8 <NOUN.PHRASE> <VERB.PHRASE-PREPOSITIONAL.PHRASES> <PREPOSITION> THE SU
N
((THE)((ROSE))) (((GREW))) (TO) THE SUN
9 <NOUN.PHRASE> <VERB.PHRASE-PREPOSITIONAL.PHRASES> <PREPOSITION> <DETER
MINER> SUN
((THE)((ROSE))) (((GREW))) (TO) (THE) SUN
10 <SENTENCE> <PREPOSITION> <DETERMINER> SUN
(((THE)((ROSE)))(((GREW)))) (TO) (THE) SUN
11 <SENTENCE> <PREPOSITION> <DETERMINER> <NOUN>
(((THE)((ROSE)))(((GREW)))) (TO) (THE) (SUN)
12 <SENTENCE> <PREPOSITION> <DETERMINER> <ADJECTIVES-NOUN>
(((THE)((ROSE)))(((GREW)))) (TO) (THE) ((SUN))
13 <SENTENCE> <PREPOSITION> <NOUN.PHRASE>
(((THE)((ROSE)))(((GREW)))) (TO) ((THE)((SUN)))
14 <SENTENCE> <PREPOSITIONAL.PHRASE>
(((THE)((ROSE)))(((GREW)))) ((TO)((THE)((SUN))))
BACKING UP...
13 <SENTENCE> <PREPOSITION> <NOUN.PHRASE>
(((THE)((ROSE)))(((GREW)))) (TO) ((THE)((SUN)))
BACKING UP...
12 <SENTENCE> <PREPOSITION> <DETERMINER> <ADJECTIVES-NOUN>
(((THE)((ROSE)))(((GREW)))) (TO) (THE) ((SUN))
BACKING UP...
11 <SENTENCE> <PREPOSITION> <DETERMINER> <NOUN>
(((THE)((ROSE)))(((GREW)))) (TO) (THE) (SUN)
BACKING UP...
10 <SENTENCE> <PREPOSITION> <DETERMINER> SUN
(((THE)((ROSE)))(((GREW)))) (TO) (THE) SUN
BACKING UP...
9 <NOUN.PHRASE> <VERB.PHRASE-PREPOSITIONAL.PHRASES> <PREPOSITION> <DETER
MINER> SUN
((THE)((ROSE))) (((GREW))) (TO) (THE) SUN
10 <NOUN.PHRASE> <VERB.PHRASE-PREPOSITIONAL.PHRASES> <PREPOSITION> <DETE
RMINER> <NOUN>
```

```
((THE)((ROSE))) (((GREW))) (TO) (THE) (SUN)
11 <SENTENCE> <PREPOSITION> <DETERMINER> <NOUN>
(((THE)((ROSE)))(((GREW)))) (TO) (THE) (SUN)
12 <SENTENCE> <PREPOSITION> <DETERMINER> <ADJECTIVES-NOUN>
(((THE)((ROSE)))(((GREW)))) (TO) (THE) (SUN))
13 <SENTENCE> <PREPOSITION> <NOUN.PHRASE>
(((THE)((ROSE)))(((GREW)))) (TO) ((THE)((SUN)))
14 <SENTENCE> <PREPOSITIONAL.PHRASE>
(((THE)((ROSE)))(((GREW)))) ((TO)((THE)((SUN))))
BACKING UP...
13 <SENTENCE> <PREPOSITION> <NOUN.PHRASE>
(((THE)((ROSE)))(((GREW)))) (TO) ((THE)((SUN)))
BACKING UP...
12 <SENTENCE> <PREPOSITION> <DETERMINER> <ADJECTIVES-NOUN>
(((THE)((ROSE)))(((GREW)))) (TO) (THE) ((SUN))
BACKING UP...
11 <SENTENCE> <PREPOSITION> <DETERMINER> <NOUN>
(((THE)((ROSE)))(((GREW)))) (TO) (THE) (SUN)
BACKING UP...
10 <NOUN.PHRASE> <VERB.PHRASE-PREPOSITIONAL.PHRASES> <PREPOSITION> <DETE
RMINER> <NOUN>
((THE)((ROSE))) (((GREW))) (TO) (THE) (SUN)
11 <NOUN.PHRASE> <VERB.PHRASE-PREPOSITIONAL.PHRASES> <PREPOSITION> <DETE
RMINER> <ADJECTIVES-NOUN>
((THE)((ROSE))) (((GREW))) (TO) (THE) ((SUN))
12 <SENTENCE> <PREPOSITION> <DETERMINER> <ADJECTIVES-NOUN>
(((THE)((ROSE)))(((GREW)))) (TO) (THE) ((SUN))
13 <SENTENCE> <PREPOSITION> <NOUN.PHRASE>
(((THE)((ROSE)))(((GREW)))) (TO) ((THE)((SUN)))
14 <SENTENCE> <PREPOSITIONAL.PHRASE>
(((THE)((ROSE)))(((GREW)))) ((TO)((THE)((SUN))))
BACKING UP...
13 <SENTENCE> <PREPOSITION> <NOUN.PHRASE>
(((THE)((ROSE)))(((GREW)))) (TO) ((THE)((SUN)))
BACKING UP...
12 <SENTENCE> <PREPOSITION> <DETERMINER> <ADJECTIVES-NOUN>
(((THE)((ROSE)))(((GREW)))) (TO) (THE) ((SUN))
BACKING UP...
11 <NOUN.PHRASE> <VERB.PHRASE-PREPOSITIONAL.PHRASES> <PREPOSITION> <DETE
RMINER> <ADJECTIVES-NOUN>
((THE)((ROSE))) (((GREW))) (TO) (THE) ((SUN))
12 <NOUN.PHRASE> <VERB.PHRASE-PREPOSITIONAL.PHRASES> <PREPOSITION> <NOUN
.PHRASE>
((THE)((ROSE))) (((GREW))) (TO) ((THE)((SUN)))
13 <SENTENCE> <PREPOSITION> <NOUN.PHRASE>
(((THE)((ROSE)))(((GREW)))) (TO) ((THE)((SUN)))
14 <SENTENCE> <PREPOSITIONAL.PHRASE>
(((THE)((ROSE)))(((GREW)))) ((TO)((THE)((SUN))))
BACKING UP...
13 <SENTENCE> <PREPOSITION> <NOUN.PHRASE>
(((THE)((ROSE)))(((GREW)))) (TO) ((THE)((SUN)))
BACKING UP...
12 <NOUN.PHRASE> <VERB.PHRASE-PREPOSITIONAL.PHRASES> <PREPOSITION> <NOUN
.PHRASE>
((THE)((ROSE))) (((GREW))) (TO) ((THE)((SUN)))
```

```
13 <NOUN.PHRASE> <VERB.PHRASE-PREPOSITIONAL.PHRASES> <PREPOSITIONAL.PHRA
SE>
 ((THE)((ROSE))) (((GREW))) ((TO)((THE)((SUN))))
14 <SENTENCE> <PREPOSITIONAL.PHRASE>
 (((THE)((ROSE)))(((GREW)))) ((TO)((THE)((SUN))))
BACKING UP...
13 <NOUN.PHRASE> <VERB.PHRASE-PREPOSITIONAL.PHRASES> <PREPOSITIONAL.PHRA
SE>
 ((THE)((ROSE))) (((GREW))) ((TO)((THE)((SUN))))
14 <NOUN.PHRASE> <VERB.PHRASE-PREPOSITIONAL.PHRASES>
 ((THE)((ROSE))) ((((GREW)))((TO)((THE)((SUN)))))
15 <SENTENCE>
 (((THE)((ROSE)))((((GREW)))((TO)((THE)((SUN))))))

PARSING COMPLETE

]
```

At this point you could be forgiven for wondering what the point of it all was – after all, the net result is that the parsing process tells us we have a sentence! That, we already knew.

The answer is that the parsing can reveal something of the meaning of that sentence by virtue of the structure of the parse tree that is produced whilst all this was going on.

Consider the sentence:

'The garden rose and the grass grew.'

Now, if the grammar we defined specified 'rose' to be a noun and made no mention of the fact that it can also be a verb then the apparent ambiguity of the sentence can be removed because only the parse tree which shows both the garden rose and the grass growing will be generated, showing that growing is something that both of them are doing (see Fig. 3.8).

If we had also defined rose to be a verb in our grammar then two possible parse trees could be generated and the syntactic analysis could draw our attention to the fact that there is ambiguity here – or, more precisely, it could draw its own attention to the fact, and the program could set about trying to resolve that ambiguity.

Also, because 'grew' applied both to the rose and the grass it would be possible, in theory, for the program to answer a question like 'What is growing?' simply by reference to the parse tree, to say that the rose and the grass were growing. To do this, it would not need to know what either grass or roses were or what constituted growing. The structure of the sentence would reveal a correct answer – even if the words were nonsense words. A parse tree applied to Lewis Carroll's lines:

> Twas brillig, and the slithy toves
> Did gyre and gimble in the wabe;
> All mimsy were the borogoves,
> And the mome raths outgrabe.

Fig. 3.8 A good parse tree can aid understanding

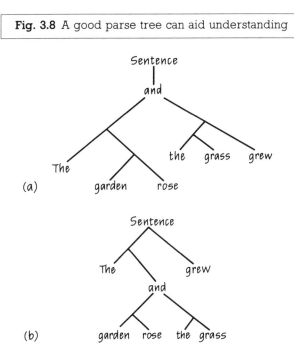

The sentence 'The garden rose and the grass grew' is shown parsed in two distinct ways. In (a) the garden is rising and the grass is growing. In (b) both the garden rose and the grass are growing. Although this is an extreme example whose main ambiguity is due to the fact that 'rose' may either be a noun or a verb it does show that a correct parse tree can help in resolving ambiguity either by itself or simply by drawing attention to the fact that such ambiguity exists. This can be a considerable help towards resolving the meaning of input sentences.

enables the program to give rudimentary answers to such questions as 'What did gyre and gimble in the wabe?' or 'What were the borogoves like?'

So, although parsing might seem incidental to the problem of natural-language understanding it does enable the computer to do something with the language which can suggest that it more or less understands what is going on and can make some responses accordingly.

In order really to make sense of what is being said to it though, the computer has to carry out some semantic analysis – it has to be able to assign real meanings to what is being said so that it really understands the matter. Or, at least, it would be a good thing if it did.

The problem is that when we are speaking we know so much about the subject matter and related items and the computer knows nothing at all. We know that there are no such things as borogoves and that, if there were, they would not be mimsy. We also know that gardens do not rise but garden roses might well grow. The problem is in getting this information into the computer.

One method of doing this is to use thematic role frames which are, to some extent, rather like syntactic analyses except that they describe possible meanings rather than possible structures.

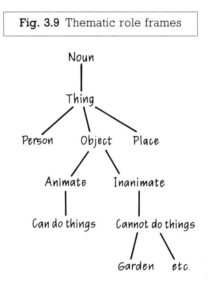

Fig. 3.9 Thematic role frames

Thematic role frames can be used in much the same way as a parse tree but, in this case, they are used to store semantic information about the world and the objects therein. They can be carried to almost any level of detail but here, for instance, we see that a Noun is a Thing and a Thing can be a Person, a Place, or an Object. An Object can be either Animate or Inanimate. Animate Objects Can Do Things but Inanimate Objects Cannot. A Garden is an Inanimate Object and, therefore, it could clearly not rise. So, when parsing the sentence 'The garden rose' it is impossible to interpret 'rose' as a verb if garden is a Noun and, as the construction noun-noun is not possible then the parser must conclude that 'garden' is not being used here as a noun and will use it in its adjectival sense.

For instance, as shown in Fig. 3.9 a noun can be a thing and a thing can be a person, an object or a place. An object can be animate or inanimate. Inanimate objects can not do anything but an animate object can.

This process of defining thematic roles within which language must be understood can be taken to almost any level of detail (and, almost invariably, still results in something being left out). But it can be very useful in understanding language. If our frame has 'garden' defined as an object which remains static then, even if the parser knows that 'rose' could either be a verb or a noun, it will be able to avoid making mistakes simply because it knows that gardens do not rise and it will then only generate the one correct parse tree.

In splitting the discussion up into syntactic and semantic analysis you might have gained the impression that the two are quite separate and distinct operations. Hopefully, you have not got that impression too strongly. We have seen that syntactic analysis can give clues to meaning and that semantic analysis can give clues to the correct syntactic analysis. In fact, the tendency is to think that the two are inextricably intertwined with each feeding from and to the other. So semantic analysis is used in carrying out a correct parse and the parsing is used to feed the semantic analysis. This approach applies whether we are trying to get the computer to understand what we key in or what we say acoustically. In fact, when it comes to the matter of acoustic input the need for the various parts of the analysis to assist each other is even stronger because of the initial uncertainty about the nature of the input signal itself.

At the start we said that talking to a computer was a very hard problem and, on a quick reading of this, you might think that potential solutions are there and all they need is implementing. There is some truth in that – but beware of that phrase 'all they need is implementing'.

It is the very size of the problem which gives rise to difficulties. If computers are going to understand what we say to them they have to have semantic knowledge equivalent to our own. So, whereas for a limited application it might be possible to construct frames which give semantic information to an adequate level, if you really want to talk to the computer about anything under the sun you have to be prepared to write a program with all of that information in it. And, as soon as you have done that, someone will think of a new word or a new meaning for an old word, and the program will need modifying.

The theoretical difficulties are enormous – but, even if they were not, the practical difficulties in implementing a solution would be.

3.2 Natural language

It could be said that what we have been looking at is not really natural language at all – it is simply a very complex formal language with, hopefully, enough complexity in it to be able to mimic a natural language. To a very large extent this is true. People do not get programmed in language to any noticeable extent – they just pick it up as they go along and do very nicely with that method.

So, maybe that is what computers should do? After all, it would make life so much simpler if, instead of having to program in these complexities and define everything in the finest detail, the computer were able to acquire the language for itself.

In fact, some attempts have been made to develop parsers which will build up their own parsing rules as they go along and it is fairly easy to see that a program could be written which would gradually build up its own semantic frames. Both of these approaches start off by programming the computer with some knowledge and allow it to modify this knowledge gradually as it goes along. But the emphasis is very much on modifying – not creating from scratch – which means that some basic structure has to be given to the machine in the first place and it cannot, in general, modify itself in a way that is outside that basic structure.

There are essentially two schools of thought concerning natural language. The first is that natural language is, more or less, a very complicated formal language – all we need to do is to work out the rules which govern it and work out a way of programming them into the machine. The second argues that natural language is inherently too complex for us ever to be able to write down all of the rules that govern it and the only ultimate way forward is to devise a method by which the computer can acquire language for itself, allowing it to develop in directions which we may have been unable to think of for ourselves.

At present, the first school of thought is winning – because that school is developing programs which, to a limited extent, seem to work using some of the methods described here. The idea of a computer which can acquire language for itself is certainly attractive and may, in the end, prove to be the right approach. But, as yet, no very striking, workable results have really materialized.

But there is something so attractive about the idea of talking to a computer that, eventually, substantial progress must be made. When enough people want to do something badly enough then it is only a matter of time before they get what they want. Although how much time will pass before you can have a quiet chat with your own computer is rather hard to say.

4

Computer vision

Of all the human senses most people would readily agree that sight is the most precious. The blind can often achieve remarkable feats of adjustment to the world, feats which do them outstanding credit, but for all their achievements there is a gulf between the sighted and the blind which can never fully be crossed.

When we have a concept which we believe will never, ever, be understood by some other person we might make use of the saying that 'it's like trying to describe colour to a blind man' as an indication of just how wide the conceptual gap is. For a congenitally blind man can never, we feel, truly understand the meaning of colour – or of a great many things in our world which the rest of us take for granted.

Naturally, therefore, if we want our computers to exist in, and fully understand, the world that we live in and take for granted it follows that the gift of sight is something that we would very much like to bestow on our machines.

Even apart from the attractiveness of the idea itself, it would be extremely convenient if machines could see in the same way that we can. If, for instance, one wanted to write a program which made use of the concept of trees (those wooden things with leaves stuck on them) then it would save a great deal of arduous programming if you could just point the computer at a tree, tell it to take a look, and then assume that it knew what you were subsequently talking about.

To some extent, computers can be made to see – but the extent to which they can do so is limited and depends, to a large measure, on what it is that we mean by 'seeing'.

This point can be made clearer if we consider three broad classes of computer vision: image processing; image analysis; and image comprehension.

Naturally, as with most subjects in the field of AI, there is considerable overlap between these three categories – in particular, each category depends to some extent on abilities developed in the preceding categories in the list – but the division into categories can be a useful aid to thought.

4.1 Image processing

In some sense, most people have a mechanical device which can 'see' long before they ever acquire a computer. That device is a camera and it can 'see' whatever you point it at, evidence of which is the simple fact that, upon pressing the shutter release and processing the film, it can show you a pretty good representation of what it saw. That may sound a long way away from computer vision but the analogy between a camera and the human eye has been made so often that most people would accept that some process of this sort at least makes a valid starting point for the study of vision as a whole.

As we shall eventually come to see, it does not make a starting point which is entirely free from criticism, but it does get us started.

For most computer-vision systems the front end of the process actually does consist of a camera which has an arrangement of lenses and a focusing screen little different from an ordinary camera. Obviously, for the computer to get involved in the seeing, the image from the camera has to get into the computer somehow and, typically, this is done by using a video camera and mapping the output from the camera into an area of memory within the computer.

If you wanted to get involved with computer vision yourself you could purchase a monochrome video camera and an interface which would map the image into memory for something like £500 – which seems a lot (and is) but if you already had a video camera the cost would come down as only an interface would be needed and these typically cost £100–200 (which is not that much for anyone who already has enough money to purchase a video camera).

Given such a set-up the image seen by the camera would be mapped into memory in the form of a two-dimensional array with each element in the array representing 1 pixel (picture element), as shown in Fig. 4.1. Often the number of pixels would be made to correspond to the high-resolution graphics display of the computer in use and each pixel would be stored as a number which represented the light intensity at that point.

So, the picture might be represented as a 1000-element × 1000-element array with each element represented by 1 byte. One byte can hold the numbers 0–255 so the pixels can represent light intensities on a 256-point scale. If you were taking the image from a TV video camera then you might want to preserve the definition of the TV picture which, in the UK, means a 625-line image. For a square picture the horizontal resolution equals the vertical resolution when there are the same number of pixels across the screen as there are lines in the image, i.e. 625. For most microcomputers 625-pixel resolution vertically is only slightly optimistic nowadays which means that a video camera connected to a microcomputer would be able to give a monochrome image which would be nearly as good as the image that you see on your TV set when watching a normal transmission. The only snag is the amount of memory needed to store this image. If, for the sake of calculation, you were going to display an image 625 pixels × 625 pixels with 1 byte representing each pixel then this would use up 390 625 bytes of memory – which is more than most people have.

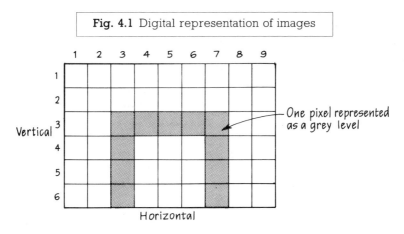

Fig. 4.1 Digital representation of images

The computer may represent a visual image as a series of squares each known as a pixel (picture element) and the whole scene may be held in a two-dimensional array with the value of each element in the array corresponding to the brightness level of that pixel in the image area. This is known as the grey-scale value of the pixel.

In this figure, the picture has 9-pixels horizontal resolution and 6-pixels vertical resolution.

But, to take a typical example of the Apple II computer, this has a high-resolution graphics area of 280 pixels × 192 pixels and if we assigned just 4 bits to each pixel this screen information would be capable of being stored in 26 880 bytes of memory – just over 26K which is comfortably within the range of the machine. In return you would get an image which had only one-third the resolution of a TV picture, because the resolution is determined by the number of pixels used (and 192/625 is about one-third), and the range of brightness levels which could be displayed would be 0–15, i.e. sixteen brightness levels. In short, a rather poor-quality picture compared with a good black-and-white TV set receiving trans-missions from the BBC, but certainly good enough to be worth looking at with the bulk of the detail discernible.

In case you happen to be wondering just how manufacturers enable the high-resolution graphics area to fit into a relatively small portion of memory within your computer (in the case of the Apple II it fits into 8 kbytes of memory) then the reason is that 280 pixels × 192 pixels equals a total of 53 760 pixels which, with 1 bit per pixel, fits into just over 6 kbytes. High-resolution graphics on most microcomputers typically consist of only 1-bit resolution per pixel which gives either black or white at that pixel location. Obviously, the image you could theoretically display would be better than your current high-resolution graphics.

So, at this stage, the image is in computer memory and it is not a bad image, the question then remains: What can you do with it next?

The two most common activities in image processing are image stretching and grey-scale modification.

Both of these techniques can be illustrated by thinking in terms of space satellites which use the same techniques to 'photograph' objects from space and send the picture back to Earth.

Think of the weather satellite – now, some of these are placed directly over the area of the Earth they happen to be looking at, so a view of the British Isles would look fine if the satellite was directly over the Midlands, as in Fig. 4.2. But, due to the varying orbits of these satellites, it frequently happens that the area of interest is some way away from the satellite – the British Isles may, for instance, be viewed by a satellite which is in an equatorial orbit. This means that England will be seen with a considerable amount of perspective on it with Scotland narrowing to a point as it recedes into the distance.

This effect can be corrected by image stretching in which the picture array is stretched and compressed until the final result is a view of the British Isles as if it had been seen from directly above the Midlands. The technique is not particularly complicated and simply involves stretching out each row in the array until it is the length it should have been had the image been viewed from above. Typically, the image is stretched, rather than compressed, to get the shape right because this does not involve any loss of information from the original array.

The basic point to note about image stretching, as described here, is that in order to stretch the image to the right shape you must know what the right shape is. With a satellite viewing the Earth from a known position this information is fairly readily to hand. Further, the 'right shape' is not determined by the computer directly on the basis of what it sees – it is determined by the human operators and programmers and applies only to the one object currently being viewed, i.e. the Earth.

If the computer were looking at a scene and did not know what that scene contained then the matter of working out what shape the image should be would be very much harder.

When we mentioned the number of bits used to store information about the brightness level of each pixel we were talking about the 'grey scale'

Fig. 4.2 Image stretching

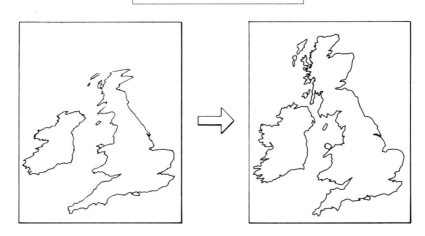

Image stretching can be used to overcome problems of perspective. A good example is the picture of the British Isles taken from a weather satellite to the south of us – the image will appear to show Scotland as much narrower than it really is. By stretching the image it is possible to produce a picture that looks much as it would had the satellite been directly over the Midlands. To do this, however, requires that the computer shall know exactly how much the image should be stretched and where. This information can be supplied by human operators as far as satellite pictures are concerned – but if the computer was working by itself with images it had not seen before then it might not know just how much stretching it should carry out. It is a chicken-and-egg situation in many cases inasmuch as the computer cannot stretch the image until it knows what it should look like and it doesn't know what it should look like until it knows what it is. And as the main task of computer vision is often to determine the identity of an object in the first place that takes the problem back full circle!

of the image – the number of levels of grey, from pure white to pure black, in which the picture is encoded.

This grey scale can be altered easily. At its simplest, all of the elements of the array could be increased or decreased by a constant amount, thereby making the picture lighter or darker overall.

A more sophisticated approach is to take a narrow band of grey-scale values and ignore all values above or below this band and then to stretch the values within the band to fill the full scale again. This might take the form of removing all values which were definitely black and all of those values which were definitely white in our original 4-bit grey scale to leave the two remaining grey bits which represented intermediate tones. These two intermediate bit values can then be expanded so that the dark-grey bit becomes black and the light-grey bit becomes white and the result displayed on the screen. The effect of this is to show up the fine detail which might have been present in the midtones but which was previously hard to see because they were so close together.

Essentially, grey-scale manipulation consists of altering the grey scales used so that that part of the scale which, for some reason, is thought to be the most interesting shows up most clearly on the screen.

These techniques have been used with considerable success by NASA in its analysis of images sent back to Earth by spacecraft orbiting other planets.

In many ways the techniques are simply ultra-sophisticated methods of doing on the computer what was once done in a photographic darkroom where the shape of an image could be changed by tilting the head of a photographic enlarger and the grey scale could be manipulated by careful selection of photographic printing paper.

At this point, most people will feel that image processing, as we have used the term here, has very little to do with computer vision. The computer is not really 'seeing' what is before it, it does not understand what it is seeing, and it did not even decide of its own accord exactly what modifications it should carry out on the images it received.

A sophisticated camera-cum-darkroom would seem to be all that we have got here.

Whilst these criticisms are, in general, true they must not be allowed to mask the fact that computer vision has to start somewhere. The image must be brought into the computer somehow and, if it is to be 'seen' by the computer this might become a lot easier at some later stage if the image was presented in a favourable way.

So what we have done is to present some techniques which can be used as a starting point in getting the computer to see – and which have a very real usefulness, in a more limited context, in their own right.

4.2 Image analysis

The difference between image processing and image analysis, as the terms are used here, is that image processing is largely a passive operation. What is done to the image will be done to all of the image and it will be largely specified by a human operator in some detail. This detailed specification may be encoded into a computer program but it is not up to the computer to decide which specification to use – it will carry out the processing it is told to carry out.

Image analysis occurs when the computer gets to have a say in what processing should take place and when it makes its decisions on the basis of what it sees before it. Even confining ourselves to the operations discussed earlier we can see that the computer could be programmed to ignore midtones in an image and that the decision as to what constituted a midtone could be left largely to the computer itself – it could work out which were the lightest and darkest tones in an image and ignore the tones in between, so the processing it carried out would depend on the image it was given at any given time.

It could also make decisions about stretching the image – although the criteria it might use to decide exactly how to stretch any given image would be much harder for it to determine.

But, if we are to make any headway at all with the subject of image analysis, we need to ask ourselves why the computer is analysing the image at all. The answer is obvious – because it is trying to 'see' what is in the image, it is trying to find things there which make sense. So what makes sense in an image? What is there in an image which is worth analysing out?

The general answer to these questions stems from the fact that, typically, the images we give the computer will be images of something that exists in the real, three-dimensional world. If the computer can genuinely see we would like it to be able to see well enough to be able to describe (in some sense or another) what it sees. So the analysis consists of trying to find items in the image which correspond to real-world entities.

This does not mean that when we show the computer an image of a cat it can say that it sees a cat – that would take us on to the next section on image comprehension. It just means that it must be able to analyse those items in the image which would enable it to move one step further down the chain towards full computer vision. Essentially, it is going to try to analyse the image in order to find some suitable descriptors of the image – features which it can extract from the image which would help it to carry out image comprehension and which correspond to something a little more real than merely, say, grey-scale levels.

Of all the features which it might extract the most fundamental features are the line and the surface. Given that the image the computer is studying is an image of something in the three-dimensional world then the objects in that world all have shape, extension and boundaries associated with them and, if they did not, it would not only be the computer that failed to make sense of the image – we could not make sense of it either.

So the computer now has the task of analysing an image in order to find surfaces, and lines denoting the boundaries of those surfaces.

4.2.1 Lines and surfaces

Recognizing lines and surfaces represents something of a chicken-and-egg situation for the computer – for, in order to recognize a line which denotes the boundary of a surface, the computer must by implication also have been able to recognize the surface and, in order to be able to recognize a surface, the computer has to know that it is unbroken by any lines.

In practice, the process of line (or edge) analysis proceeds hand-in-hand with surface analysis.

The basic assumption is that on a surface the image varies very little whereas at an edge the image varies very rapidly. In theory this is fine – surfaces are smooth and uniform, whereas edges represent sharp discontinuities – but in practice, using real images, the process involves quite a bit of computation in order to get an analysis which is even approximately right.

The first stage of the analysis consists of smoothing out the image to remove irregularities on a small scale such as might be observed in a moderately smooth surface. This can be done by working through the array which holds the image and giving each pixel a new value which is the average of its original value and that of its nearest neighbours.

So, if the image were held in the two-dimensional array $I(I, J)$ then a smoothed array $A(I, J)$ could be formed by simply calculating:

```
FOR X = -1 TO 1
FOR Y = -1 TO 1
A(I,J) = A(I,J) + I(I+X,J+Y)
NEXT:NEXT
A(I,J) = A(I,J)/9
```

for each pixel element I, J in the array. This can then be stored back into the original array I or work can proceed on the new array A. In many ways, this is simply a process of blurring the image to remove small variations which have little value.

The process can be repeated more than once to give successively greater degrees of blurring – the end result being, if it is carried out often enough, that the whole picture will become blurred and quite uniform, all of the information in the image having been lost.

The idea behind the blurring though is that surfaces only contain small, irregular variations in the light intensity which they emit but edges – lines – have very great local variations associated with them which will still show up even after the image has been blurred quite considerably.

It is these large, local variations that the computer looks for next.

The obvious way to proceed is to look for a large variation from one pixel to the next and, when it exists, decide that this may denote an edge. Assuming that the blurred array A has been placed back into the original array I each element of I can be assigned a value according to the difference in brightness that occurs at that point:

S(I,J) = (I(I−1,J) − I(I+1,J))/2

where, clearly, $S(I, J)$ has the greatest absolute value if the pixel at I, J represents a point at which the light intensity varies greatly on either side of it. The obvious snag with this method is that it might not locate an edge – it might just locate an isolated point of some kind because it is only working in one dimension in the array. To be sure of a line we might want to work in two dimensions and only reckon there to be evidence of a line when $S(I, J)$ has a high absolute value in one dimension but a low value in the other dimension – a technique which might work well for horizontal and vertical lines, but which might be fooled by lines which cross the image area at an angle.

Another problem is the fact that the computer has to decide just how big a value it should take notice of – it has to have some kind of internal threshold which must be crossed in order to decide that there is a line there.

The solution might typically take something of the form of

S(I,J) = SQR(((I(I−1,J)−I(I+1,J))/2)↑2 + ((I(I,J−1)−I(I,J+1))/2)↑2) for each pixel

and the computer would decide that an edge was there if $S(I, J)$ exceeded some threshold value which was determined by reference to the range in brightness levels in the image as a whole. Further clues to the analysis can be obtained from the fact that an edge, to be an edge, has to go some-where. As we have already mentioned, we do not want the system to pick up odd points and call them edges so it has to look at both dimensions in the image array. But having done this and established new values for $S(I, J)$ throughout the array it could then use its threshold criteria in conjunction with the fact that if any given pixel denotes an edge then one of the pixels next to it must denote an edge also. In this way the program is looking for a plausible-seeming way to draw a line through the image following a path of large changes in brightness levels.

The end result of all this should be that the computer has been able to find the edges in the image and can draw a series of lines into the original picture in order to show where it thinks these edges are.

So, given a picture of someone standing against a fairly uniform background, it ought to be able to draw an outline of that person and their main features which, even if the computer hasn't a clue as to what a 'person' is, still constitutes valuable evidence that it has done something fairly intelligent when it looked at the picture (Fig. 4.3).

Fig. 4.3 Smoothing and edge detection

Starting with a normal digitized image the computer first smooths out any minor variations in intensity in the image and then works over the image again looking for sudden, strong, changes in intensity. Assuming these strong changes to be edges the computer can then proceed to carry out edge detection on the picture – looking for lines which give some clues as to the outline of the object. The result is an image with a lot of the 'noise' removed from it leaving, hopefully, only those features that are genuinely important for recognition.

Of course, there are other cues which human observers use to interpret images when looking for information about surfaces and edges and there is no reason why the computer should not do the same.

Two of the most useful techniques are stereoscopic vision and illumination levels. Unfortunately, neither of these techniques are readily within the reach of even the well-heeled amateur, mainly on the grounds of cost, but they are still worth mentioning for completeness.

Stereoscopic vision (Fig. 4.4) involves using two cameras separated by a distance to record images of the same scene. By comparing the displacement of the images from the two cameras it is possible to work out the distance from the cameras of each object in the image. So, once each camera's image has been analysed for edges the distance of the edges from the cameras can be determined by measuring their shift in the image area as a whole. The advantage of doing this is that it enables the computer to form some kind of 'solid' appreciation of the scene before it which might enable it to build up a three-dimensional model of what it sees. The technique obviously doubles the cost of the equipment needed because you need two of everything (including two computers

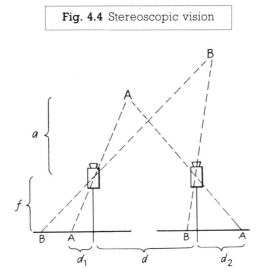

Fig. 4.4 Stereoscopic vision

Two vision systems can be used together to give stereoscopic vision which provides valuable information about the distance of objects in the external world. In this case the system can work out that object B is further away from the cameras than object A simply by working out the intersection point of the two lines to each object. Specifically, the distance to object A can be worked out using the formula: $a = fd \div (d_1 + d_2)$, where a = distance of object from camera lens; f = focal length of camera; d = separation of cameras; d_1, d_2 = displacement of images from focal axes of cameras. The only problem that arises is when the vision system cannot work out which is object A in one 'eye' and which is the same object in the other 'eye' – when this happens it is by no means certain what the computer should be measuring. Essentially, the problem consists of the computer having to recognize the objects for each 'eye' before it can work out their distance – although it may make tentative distance assessments as an aid to recognition in the first place.

if the process is to run at the same speed as it did before) but it also raises a rather more subtle problem.

Suppose that both cameras have produced images which show an edge in them and that the two cameras give a displacement of the image from which the distance of the edge can be computed. That is fine – but only as long as both cameras are looking at the same edge! In a complex scene with very many edges in it and a method of edge detection which is not infallible there might be no great certainty as to just which edge in one image corresponded to which edge in the other image. And mis-identifying the edges between the two pictures could lead to some very weird results as the computer tried to work out the shape of the scene before it.

The second technique uses surface illumination to determine the position and orientation of surfaces. It assumes that the program has found its edges and that the area between edges represents a surface. The problem is: What is the orientation of the surface?

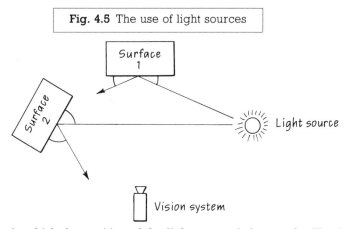

Fig. 4.5 The use of light sources

In situations in which the position of the light source is known the illumination of the surfaces can provide useful information on their position and orientation. In this figure surface 2 will appear much brighter than surface 1 because of its orientation and a nearer surface will appear, in general, brighter than a more distant surface.

This can be tackled by analysing the surface illumination on the assumption that the light is coming from a single source and the direction of that light source is known. As Fig. 4.5 shows those surfaces facing the light source directly will have the greatest brightness levels and the brightness level in the computer's image will depend on the angle of the light source and the angle of the surface to the camera. Using this technique it is possible to draw a map of the surface and represent this within the computer as a solid object. The snag is that the position of the light source may be unknown, there may be several light sources or the light may even be quite diffuse, as occurs on a cloudy day.

Even if the light source has a known position and there is only one light source this can give rise to fresh problems of its own making, namely shadows which, if they have sharp enough edges, will be picked up by the edge-detection techniques and help to confuse the picture even further.

By and large, the use of the light source as a means of image analysis is confined to fairly closely controlled situations in which more can be gained from the technique than is lost through the added complications involved in the analysis of the image in this way.

4.3 Image comprehension

So far we have seen the computer do something useful with the images it receives but we have not yet seen the computer do anything which definitely suggests that the computer understands what it sees. This is the problem of image comprehension.

Suppose that the image has been processed and analysed to show an edge-map of the scene – an outline drawing of the main objects in the picture – surely it is just a short step from there to image comprehension, understanding what it is that the computer has just drawn an outline of?

In some ways this is true.

Consider a computer looking at a simple scene made up of toy blocks. The most striking feature of such a scene is that all of the lines are straight so image analysis could extend itself a little by adding the constraint that each edge it found had to be a straight line. That would help to clean up the edges it had found and would help to eliminate some edges which it had 'found' but which were not really there. Having done that these straight lines would have to follow certain rules. For instance, no blocks are suspended in midair and no lines disappear into thin air either. This is the well-known 'blocks world' which computers have come to know and love because it is so easy (relatively speaking) to understand.

Together the collection of lines has to add up to something meaningful in this blocks world and the position, orientation and relationships between these lines can enable the computer to determine quite an exact internal understanding of what it is looking at.

But the important point to note is that the computer, of its own accord, cannot comprehend even a blocks world simply by image analysis – it has to apply some comprehension to the problem. It has to have within it some knowledge of the type of things which it is likely to see in order to be able to make sense of what it sees.

To some degree it had within it this internal knowledge when it carried out image processing and analysis – for instance, when it was looking for lines and surfaces it had to be programmed to do so and, in the act of carrying out that programming, the computer was tacitly given the information that the world at which it was looking contained surfaces and lines and that these were, for some reason, significant.

But as we move closer towards image comprehension the need for the machine to know more about the world at which it is looking grows. Even if it only happens to be a blocks world the computer can only make

Fig. 4.6 Top-down and bottom-up image understanding

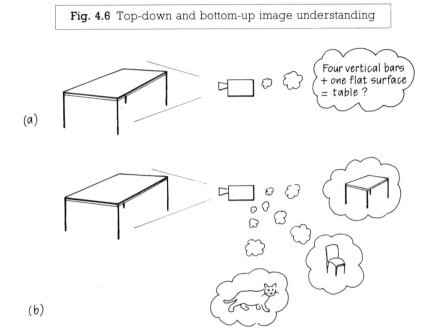

(a)

Four vertical bars + one flat surface = table ?

(b)

In the bottom-up approach (a) the computer examines the image, finds its component parts and works out what these might all add up to. So, four vertical bars plus a flat surface could well equal a table. This approach is also called 'analysis by synthesis'. In the top-down approach (b) the computer succesively imagines that it is looking at any one of a series of objects and examines the image to see how well they accord with that idea. So, it might wonder if it was seeing a table, a chair, or, even, the cat. The idea that gives the best match will be what the computer finally decides it has seen. This approach is also known as 'controlled hallucination'.

The bottom-up approach enables the computer to synthesize images of objects it has never seen before whereas the top-down approach requires the computer to 'know' an image in the form of an internal model before it can see it at all.

progress in comprehension if it is given some explicit information concerning the likely appearance and nature of blocks in that world.

The way in which the computer is given its knowledge about the world at which it is looking falls roughly into two categories.

In the first, the computer is given information in small, fairly general-purpose, units. It is told, for instance, that lines in a blocks world have a beginning and an end, are always straight and always intersect with other lines and that the objects represented have a real existence in three-dimensional space which must conform to the laws of physics. Using this information the computer is able to extend its image analysis into image comprehension to build up an internal model of what it sees.

In the second method, the computer is given substantial, specific information about what it is likely to see at any given moment. So, in the blocks world, the computer might have programmed into it an internal model of blocks and the different ways in which they can appear in a digitized image and all it has to do is to examine the current image to see which of its internal models agrees best with it.

The first method is often called 'bottom-up' comprehension because it works by building up its knowledge of what it sees from the small constituent parts of the image to form a comprehensive whole. It is sometimes also called 'analysis by synthesis' because it synthesizes what it sees into a whole (Fig. 4.6).

The second method is often called 'controlled hallucination' because this is, effectively, what the computer is doing – hallucinating. It is taking each of its internal models in turn, examining the incoming digitized image, and asking itself if what it now sees could actually be the object it is 'thinking' of from its set of possible internal models. This approach is sometimes called, less memorably, 'top-down' comprehension – because it starts with a high-level assumption about what it is seeing and then works down from there to check out the fine detail to either confirm or deny this assumption.

If you continue to think in terms of a blocks world you may find that there is not an awful lot to choose between the two methods. This is because the blocks world is so easy to define, either as a complete internal model or as a set of internal rules which any scene must obey, that either approach can be made to work. If anything, though, the bottom-up approach may have some advantages simply because it enables the computer to 'see' and understand things which it has never seen before – as long as they conform, in general, to the strictures of the blocks world. For instance, a rectangular block could be recognized as such because its basic constituent parts and their possible relationships (edges, surfaces, etc.) had been adequately specified in the program even though this particular shape and size of rectangular block had never been seen before by the computer.

But when we pass outside of simple blocks worlds and come up against more complex images the bottom-up approach has difficulties. It is very hard, for instance, to specify the rules by which a computer might be able to build up a picture of a tree and make sense of that picture. In these more complex cases it can be better to give the program an internal model of all the things it might be likely to see and let it 'hallucinate' these models onto the scene before it, in order to try to determine whether any of them match that model – rather like taking a series of photographic transparencies and laying them in turn on top of a new transparency to see which matched the best, with the added advantage that the computer holds an internal three-dimensional model of the things it might see and can therefore rotate them, alter their size and orientation and generally play around with the image in a rather more comprehensive fashion than would be possible with a photographic slide. The price to pay for this approach is that the computer can never 'see' anything which it has not already been told about. A system using this method which was used, for instance, to identify aircraft from internal models of different aircraft types would always try to see aircraft in the sky. If a bird should fly across its field of gaze then, unless it also had internal models of birds, it would attempt to identify what it saw as an aircraft and would either give up in the attempt (if the match seemed poor) or go around pronouncing that it had seen a jumbo jet everytime a seagull came into view – this being another reason why the approach is called 'hallucinating'.

In summary, a computer can only carry out image comprehension if it is given enough information to enable it to build up a sensible interpretation of the scene before it (and this is exceptionally hard to do for all possible types of scenes); or if it is given information on each and every object which it might see (which precludes the possibility of the computer ever 'understanding' new objects on which it has no information).

However the comprehension of simple scenes or the comprehension of a finite number of more complex scenes is rapidly becoming possible.

4.4 Computer vision

We have seen how computer vision can range from sophisticated image processing, through image analysis, to some degree of image comprehension. None of the techniques used are outstandingly difficult in their own right but, paradoxically, getting a system that works well *is* difficult.

One reason for this is the sheer processing power involved in full image comprehension. It is all very well to define a simple operation to be carried out on the pixels in the image array and it would not be hard to write a program in BASIC to carry out these operations. The real problem is that there are so many pixels involved. Consider the example we gave earlier of a 280-pixel × 192-pixel image area using a 4-bit grey scale – this fits in about 26K of memory which, on a 48K machine, leaves a fair bit of room for the program. That would seem to offer hope to the enthusiast.

But suppose that you wanted to hold two image arrays – one for the untransformed scene and another to hold the scene after processing and analysis had been carried out – at once you have exceeded your 48K of memory. The image size can be reduced and the number of grey-scale levels can be reduced – but doing this reduces the resolution of the image, where 'resolution' refers to the amount of detail that can be discerned in the picture.

There is also the problem of processing time. Each single operation carried out on each pixel may be fairly simple but, in the example we cited, there are 53 760 pixels and, as will be clear, there is not just one operation to be carried out but several. Initial processing, analysis and, then, comprehension all require further operations to be performed on the image.

One experiment carried out by researchers into computer vision found that the computer could accurately recognize certain objects, such as a person walking down the street, but that the images had to be presented to the computer in the form of colour transparencies, for the simple reason that each frame took approximately 15 min to process – and that was using a DEC VAX computer which is an extremely powerful, large machine.

If the same computer had wanted to be able to see and understand a real-time image of the same person walking down the street it would have had to be connected directly to a video camera and would have had to be capable of processing each image 25 times per second – 22 500 times faster than it was processing images at the present time.

This is not to say that the task is impossible – just that it requires considerable effort to achieve a working solution to the problem of understanding images in real time.

Like most tasks in computer science the problem of recognizing and understanding images is greatly helped by the application of a little controlled laziness – trying to think of ways of avoiding doing things which you do not have to do. In the case of image comprehension in real time consider first of all the very simplest case – that of a series of incoming images each of which is exactly the same as the others. In this case there may be 25 or so images arriving at the computer each second but the computer only ever has to do anything with one of the images and it has done the job on the lot, so it would not matter if it was a little slow about it.

This principle can be applied to a series of images even if each one actually is different from the one preceeding it and the one following it. The reason for this is that we live in a, comparatively, stable world in which things do change but, by and large, they do not change a lot.

The most basic illustration of this can be seen next time you watch the news on TV. Look at the newscaster reading the news and ask yourself just how much of the picture on the TV screen is actually changing. The

Fig. 4.7 Image redundancy

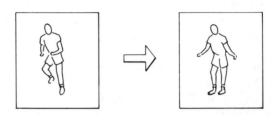

Although to process images in real time may require the computer to process and understand up to 25 separate images each second the processing involved can be greatly reduced by means of image redundancy. Each successive image will only differ slightly from the preceding image and so the computer need only concentrate on those parts of the image which have changed.

Also, real-world constraints can be utilized to reduce the work the computer has to do. If the first image contained a man then the second image is unlikely to reveal that he has turned into a table lamp, or somesuch. More likely, the image will still be of a man, the same man, in a slightly different position which will be constrained by the positions into which men can move themselves in a short space of time. This is another aspect of redundancy in the images which the computer can use to ease its processing task.

answer is: very little. Each picture is, strictly speaking, different but the differences are very small.

Consequently, the computer need only look at those items in the image area which have changed since the last image was presented and this can reduce the amount of work which the computer must do. This can be thought of as image redundancy (Fig. 4.7) – a situation in which some of the image is redundant as a consequence of the previous image – and it has been used in image-processing systems which have nothing at all to do with computer vision simply in order to reduce the amount of data which need to be encoded in order to transmit a series of moving pictures.

The next technique for reducing the amount of work the computer has to do if it is to understand moving pictures involves the fact that, ultimately, we want the computer either to have or develop some internal model of what it sees and that this internal model must be a representation of the real world around it. The real world, fortunately, is governed by very firm physical laws which do not change and it is possible to make use of this fact to reduce the processing which the computer has to carry out.

For instance, the computer may, after a great deal of work, come to the conclusion that what it sees in the first of a series of images is someone walking down the street. Well, physical laws being what they are, it is extremely unlikely that the next image to arrive will show that this person has suddenly turned into a double-decker bus or any other object. The next image will almost certainly be of the same person walking down the street, just as before, but in a slightly different position.

These physical constraints on what can be seen enable the computer to ignore a lot of interpretations of the image which might, in the first scene, have been possible. Instead, having decided in general what it is that it is looking at the computer can concentrate on the simpler task of deciding in what ways the image has changed and can use its internal knowledge about the way in which change is possible for the objects in that particular image in order to reduce the different number of possible interpretations it can place on what it sees.

One final example of controlled laziness in computer vision is very similar in principle to the 'trick' system which we discussed in the chapter on natural language. In that chapter we mentioned that some systems can be made to appear pretty intelligent, not by carrying out full natural-language processing (which is hard) but by simply looking for key words and phrases to enable it to sidestep the full scope of the problem and make an intelligent guess as to what is being said to the computer quite quickly.

The same principle can be applied to computer vision. It may not be necessary in all systems to go through the whole gamut of image processing, analysis and comprehension so that the computer really understands every aspect of the scene before it. Instead, it could just look for key features which will give strong clues about what it sees and use these to guess the correct interpretation. This approach is of most use when there are a small number of significant items which the computer might see and a small number of responses which it might make to what it sees.

As an example, consider a computer which was programmed to watch out for intruders in some security-conscious area. The system uses computer vision and is intended to detect intruders and inform the user where the intruders are. A problem like this can, in part, be tackled using a 'trick' system in which an intruder is defined as a moving object that was not there before. All the computer has to do is to scan the image and look for something that changes. If nothing changes there are no intruders. If there is a change then it probably is an intruder. If the intruder interpretation is correct then the area of the image over which change is taking place will slowly move as the intruder moves around. By working out the approximate location of the changing part of the image the computer can work out where the intruder is by reference to an internal map of the area. At no stage does the computer actually carry out full image analysis and comprehension but it still does a good enough job to be useful. Of course, like the trick systems used in natural language, this type of system can be fooled – it might report a lorry or a stray dog as being an intruder because it does not really understand what it sees. But the ease with which such a system could be implemented to carry out a useful task could well outweigh any such disadvantages.

In many ways it is similar to the 'vision' systems used to identify bad peas in a pea-processing plant. Good peas are green, but bad peas are black. So, if all the peas are passed in front of a sensor which is able to measure their colour bad, black peas can be knocked out of the stream of peas very easily. Maybe that hardly sounds like true computer vision – but what would you expect of a system that only had to detect bad peas? There is no point in designing computer-vision systems that are more complex than they need to be for the task in hand and, if the task is simple and well defined, then a very simple computer 'vision' system might well prove not only possible but actually desirable.

The analogy with natural-language systems is actually quite strong when we consider computer vision. To date, both problems have proved extremely hard to crack completely and, yet, some distinct progress can be made in both fields if we are prepared to accept a solution that is less than perfect. With both problems we ourselves carry out the tasks of speaking, hearing and seeing with no conscious effort whatsoever but exactly how we do it is by no means clear – or, at least, not quite clear enough to be directly programmable onto a machine.

The real key to the matter almost certainly lies in the fact that all of these acts are so intimately bound up with our knowledge of the world and the sort of 'objects' we ourselves are that to get a computer to perform these tasks as well as we can could practically involve the transference of every aspect of our make up and knowledge to the machine – an enormous task. So enormous, in fact, that it is not at all apparent how or where we should make a start. The best we can do at the moment is to try various approaches and see how we get on in the hope that, one day, we will find we have arrived at our destination.

Listing 4.1 Perceptron-type vision system

In this chapter so far we have been very much concerned about top-down and bottom-up vision systems but, in the systems we have looked at so far, the emphasis in both approaches has still been on vision systems which rely on items which we, as humans, are able to recognize for ourselves.

For instance, in the top-down approach we assumed that the vision system had an internal image of, say, a table. And, in the bottom-up approach we assumed that the vision system was able to detect edges.

But historically the bottom-up approach goes much deeper than this. In the early days of AI it was often thought that a true bottom-up approach would be one in which the basic building blocks were not items which we could immediately recognize but were occurrences at the level of the individual nerve cells in human beings. The belief was that, to produce good AI programs, all that was necessary was to produce a model of the neural structure of the human brain and then leave this model to get on with the task of seeing. Including learning to see. One of the first examples of this was the Perceptron system which was a computer model of a simple neural network in the brain which could be trained to recognize objects by sight simply by being shown them. Since then, neural network models of computer vision have wavered in their fortunes with the methods described so far in this chapter being those most often used nowadays. But there are still adherents of the Perceptron type of model of computer vision and there are beginning to appear commercially viable vision systems which do utilize these principles. So, it only seemed right to produce a program for you which uses some of these principles.

Obviously, you are going to have difficulty in doing anything much with a program for computer vision unless you have some method of inputting a visual image into your computer – which most of you may not have. But, as a substitute for a proper image input system, you will find in lines 2000 forwards a simple routine for 'painting' an image into the computer. When the program wants an input image you can draw one for it by pressing the *, space, U, D, L, R, X keys. The * key draws a point at the current location, the U, D, L, R keys make the drawing extend up, down, left or right, the space key draws a blank space (useful if you want to erase something) and the X key exits from the painting routine. Once you have pressed X the routine at line 2200 will re-draw the image using colons (:) to show you what you have drawn. To get the feel of how it works the best thing to do is to play with it and see what happens. This routine is called from lines 120 and 260, so if you have a better method of inputting a visual image, that is where you should insert it.

Array $I\%$ will be familiar because it is a 16-pixel by 16-pixel image area with two grey levels – white and black. A 1 in $I\%$ signifies white and a 0 signifies black. Each time you input an image you have to think of it as belonging to one of two classes – class 0 or class 1 – and the task of the program is to distinguish between objects from either of these two classes. So you might want to get it to learn the difference between a horizontal line or a vertical line – or you might draw something rather more complicated for it to choose between.

You will first of all have to train the program by presenting it with a few examples from each of the two classes and, after that, you will be able to let it loose on some new examples for classification without telling it in advance what class the objects belong to. You can tell whether or not it has made a successful classification by looking at the two scores for the classes, output in lines 390 and 400. If it got it right then the class of object to which the new example belonged should have the higher score.

The way the program manages to work is by examining each input image and taking a random sample of eight points from the image area (in lines 160–200). It uses these eight points to form an 8-bit address (remember that each point was either a 0 or a 1) and it then uses this address to find a location in array $D\%$ which it sets to 1. This process is repeated 32 times so that most of the image area has been covered by the process and has effected a change in $D\%$. After several training sessions on the same class of object $D\%$ then effectively holds a 'signature' of the type of object it has been shown and if, later, it is shown the same type of object it will tend to produce the same signature in $D\%$ again if the image area is sampled in the same way. Lines 360 and 370 are looking for the extent to which the signature of a new object matches the signatures of existing learned objects which the system has seen.

As it stands this program can learn two distinct signatures and, hence, can classify two distinct types of object (for instance, horizontal lines versus vertical lines).

The system may look a little haphazard but it is based on current systems which actually do work well in some areas of computer vision.* They are particularly useful in areas of computer vision where feature extraction of itself is difficult (making more common methods of bottom-up processing difficult) or where the image to be recognized is so difficult to define that it is hard to specify an adequate model for top-down methods to be used. A good example is the problem of recognizing human faces in which it is very hard to specify a rigid model in advance for top-down processing due to the extreme variability of people's appearance, and in which bottom-up feature extraction is also hard because of the lack of many very well-defined edges and surfaces.

In a way though you could think of it as an example of feature extraction and simply argue that, as you are not sure in advance what features you should extract, the program simply extracts features at random in the general hope that there must be some similarities between different objects of the same class somewhere in the image area.

Note, however, that in lines 130 and 270 seed values are set for the random number generator that extracts the features so that, although the image area is sampled randomly, it is sampled in exactly the same random pattern each time – which means that any two identical images will always trigger the same effects in array $D\%$. The process is not totally random!

Effectively, $I\%$ is supposed to be a model of the retina at the back of the eye in which each receptor cell at the back of the retina is connected permanently, although with no particular pattern, to a selection of other receptors at the back of the retina. Together, these connections, when simultaneously stimulated by an image, send a signal back up the optic nerve to some particular nerve cell within the brain's visual cortex, as represented by array $D\%$. If a particular pattern of cells within the visual cortex is stimulated (a particular pattern in $D\%$) then the brain will recognize the object it sees before it as an object belonging to some particular class and, if in doubt as to what it is seeing, it will make its decision on the basis of the greatest number of nerve cells firing in favour of each out of several interpretations.

That, in brief, is the rationale behind this particular listing.

---

*For example, Professor Igor Aleksander's WISARD system.

```
10   REM   ****************************
20   REM   ** LISTING 4.1           **
30   REM   ** PERCEPTRON-TYPE       **
40   REM   ** VISION SYSTEM         **
50   REM   ****************************
60   DIM I%(16,16),D%(8192,1)
70   REM   I% IS IMAGE ARRAY,D% IS ADDRESS ARRAY
80   REM  NOTE THAT I% CONTAINS EITHER 0 OR 1
90   HOME : VTAB 17: HTAB 1: INPUT "WHICH CLASS IS IT (0/1) ?";C
100  FOR I = 1 TO 16: FOR J = 1 TO 16:I%(I,J) = 0: NEXT : NEXT
110  REM  INPUT AN IMAGE INTO I% AT THIS POINT
120  GOSUB 2000
130  R =  RND ( - 1): REM  THIS IS THE SEED VALUE
140  FOR I = 1 TO 32
150  A = 256 * (I - 1)
160  FOR J = 0 TO 7
170  R1 =  INT ( RND (1) * 16 + 1)
180  R2 =  INT ( RND (1) * 16 + 1)
190  A = A + I%(R1,R2) * 2 ^ J
200  NEXT
210  D%(A,C) = 1
220  NEXT
230  INPUT "ANOTHER TRAINING SESSION (Y/N) ?";A$: IF A$ = "Y" THEN
     90
240  FOR I = 1 TO 16: FOR J = 1 TO 16:I%(I,J) = 0: NEXT : NEXT
250  REM  INPUT AN EXAMPLE FOR CLASSIFICATION AT THIS POINT
260  GOSUB 2000
270  R =  RND ( - 1): REM   THIS IS THE SEED VALUE
280  C0 = 0:C1 = 0: REM  THESE ARE THE SCORES
290  FOR I = 1 TO 32
300  A = 256 * (I - 1)
310  FOR J = 0 TO 7
320  R1 =  INT ( RND (1) * 16 + 1)
330  R2 =  INT ( RND (1) * 16 + 1)
340  A = A + I%(R1,R2) * 2 ^ J
350  NEXT
360  IF D%(A,0) = 1 THEN :C0 = C0 + 1
370  IF D%(A,1) = 1 THEN :C1 = C1 + 1
380  NEXT
390  PRINT "CLASS 0 HAS A SCORE OF ";C0 / 32
```

```
400   PRINT "CLASS 1 HAS A SCORE OF ";C1 / 32
410   INPUT "DO YOU WANT TO CLASSIFY ANOTHER ITEM (Y/N) ?";A$: IF
      A$ = "Y" THEN 240
444   END
2000  REM  -- IMAGE-MAKING ROUTINE:
2010  HOME : VTAB 17: HTAB 1: PRINT "*,SPACE,U,D,L,R,X"
2020  T = 0:A$ = " "
2030  H = 1:V = 1:C$ = ""
2040  REM  CHECK FOR KEY DEPRESSION:
2041  X =  PEEK ( - 16384): IF X > 127 THEN :C$ =  CHR$ (X - 128):
      POKE  - 16368,0
2042  SV = V:SH = H: VTAB SV: HTAB SH: INVERSE : PRINT " ";: NORMAL

2043  FOR I = 1 TO 200:X = 0: NEXT : REM     DELAY
2050  IF C$ = "U" THEN :V = V - 1
2060  IF C$ = "D" THEN :V = V + 1
2070  IF C$ = "L" THEN :H = H - 1
2080  IF C$ = "R" THEN :H = H + 1
2090  IF H > 16 THEN :H = 1
2095  IF H < 1 THEN :H = 16
2100  IF V > 16 THEN :V = 1
2105  IF V < 1 THEN :V = 16
2110  IF C$ = " " THEN :T = 0:A$ = C$
2120  IF C$ = "*" THEN :T = 1:A$ = C$
2130  I%(H,V) = T
2140  IF I%(SH,SV) = 0 THEN : VTAB SV: HTAB SH: PRINT " ";
2141  IF I%(SH,SV) > 0 THEN : VTAB SV: HTAB SH: PRINT "*";
2145  VTAB V: HTAB H: PRINT A$;
2150  IF C$ = "X" THEN 2155
2151  GOTO 2040
2155  GOSUB 2200: REM  RE-DISPLAY
2160  RETURN
2200  REM  -- DISPLAY ROUTINE:
2210  FOR H = 1 TO 16
2220  FOR V = 1 TO 16
2230  IF I%(H,V) > 0 THEN : VTAB V: HTAB H: PRINT ":";" ";
2240  NEXT : NEXT
2250  VTAB 17: HTAB 1
2260  RETURN
```

5
Machine learning

There is one aspect of computers which has caused disquiet and unrest ever since they were first invented – and this is that programming them is hard work. Every single aspect of their operation has to be defined in the minutest detail and this takes time and considerable thought. And, at the end of the day, the computer does exactly what it was told to do, no more and no less – which is bad news for those who programmed it and did not mean it to do exactly *that*. For, whatever you want a computer to do, it is quite certain that you start off with some generalized idea of what it should do and then find that the hard work comes in 'explaining' this to the computer.

It would be much better by far if the computer could work out what to do for itself without the need for laborious programming on your part. If you could just say to the computer 'Do this', where 'this' was just a general indication of the task, and then the computer would proceed to figure out the rest for itself.

This is the basis of machine learning – which is AI's ultimate in laziness – the attempt to get the machine to learn for itself how it should act without the need to be explicitly told.

And, like every other attempt by computer scientists to be as lazy as possible, the result has been that researchers have worked pretty well night and day in order to develop programs which will enable machines to learn. In many ways that is the rub – that to get a machine to learn you have to write a program which will enable it to do so and, of course, writing a program was the very thing which you were trying to avoid in the first place. So why bother to try? What are the advantages of trying to write a program which will carry out machine learning?

Basically, there are two advantages. The first is that, hard as it may be to write a program to carry out machine learning, it can be a good deal easier than writing a program which is intended to carry out some task and which has no learning capability. The second is the age-old AI excuse for doing anything – that it is interesting to do it – and that in the course of doing it you find out more about computers and more about learning which may turn out to be useful knowledge in its own right at some stage.

But first, if we are going to discuss machine learning, we have to have some kind of definition of the subject. We need to know exactly what is machine learning.

This is rather awkward because, if you consider human learning, you will find that definitions of that are pretty hard to come by. Psychologists, for instance, usually give a definition something along the lines of 'learning is the process by which an organism modifies its responses to stimuli as a result of experience'. Which sounds fine, but can lead to a few problems.

Take, for instance, the wall thermostat which controls your central heating. You could say that the thermostat was modifying its responses (the setting of a control valve) in response to stimuli (the temperature of the room) as a result of experience. And the only part at which most people would quibble is that the thermostat seems to have little in it which corresponds to 'experience'. But maybe it has, in some limited way. After all, it will raise the temperature by a large amount when the room is very cold and lower it by a large amount when the room is very hot. The adjustments that the thermostat makes are much smaller when the room is nearly at the required temperature – and maybe this corresponds, to a small degree, to experience. A sort of built-in experience derived from the way it was made.

Clearly, it will be helpful if we pin things down a little more closely and we can do this by thinking in terms of three levels of learning which we can think of as long term, medium term and short term.

In humans long-term learning can be applied to learning that takes place over several generations. The fact that successive generations of individuals modify their responses to external stimuli as a result of experience gained over the generations. This modification may be transmitted culturally, by means of word of mouth or books; or it may be transmitted genetically, in which case the learning that takes place is evolutionary in nature.

Translating this down into machine learning, it is easy to see that computers are learning and they have always been learning ever since they were invented – simply because they are being constantly modified in the light of the experience of successive generations of machines. This may seem, at first glance, to be a false argument because, in machine terms, it is not the machine that is learning but the designers of the machines. But a little closer thought tends to reveal that the difference is more apparent than real – after all, human beings are not always consciously aware of modifying their own behaviour over periods of whole generations – the changes are largely wrought by the action of the environment upon them. So, for machines to be modified by the action of their environment on them is in many ways similar – simply because, from the machines' point of view, the designers are a part of their environment.

Now turning to the other end of the scale we consider very-short-term learning – the kind of thing that a wall thermostat might be said to carry out. Humans too can learn short-term responses of this sort – you might even think of your own internal thermostat which tells you to start shivering when it is cold so that the action of shivering helps to warm you up again. Like the thermostat this might be said to fall a long way short of true learning because the conscious element of experience is lacking – but it does help to fix the middle ground of medium-term learning which we are most interested in.

This middle ground is learning which takes place within a single individual (in the case of people) or a single machine (in the case of computers). And it is not of a very short duration. It is a modification of the system's behaviour as a result of experience and we can expect this modification to remain present for some time.

An important part of learning which we must mention specifically is this matter of 'experience' though. As humans we all know what experience is – it is an accumulation of everything we have experienced to date. But you can not just tell a computer to accumulate everything it has experienced and expect it to make something of it – we have to be a little more precise about the matter. This extra precision is obtained by thinking in terms of feedback in which information concerning the results of a particular course of action are fed back into the system as an aid to modifying the same action next time (Fig. 5.1). If the feedback loop is rather short in duration and simple in nature we get something like the thermostat which never gains any really substantial experience. If the feedback loop is very long we tend towards a situation in which the machine, or person, learns so slowly that it may never be aware of learning at all – such as may occur over several generations.

Fig. 5.1 The importance of feedback in learning

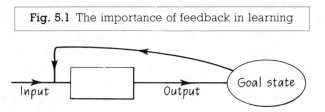

A machine can only learn if it has some form of feedback as a result of its actions. Without feedback it would proceed in the same course of action either without changing or without changing in any predictable fashion. With feedback the system can compare what it was trying to do with what it actually has done and adjust its actions accordingly.

But whatever form of learning takes place there must be some form of feedback into the system to let it know exactly how it should modify its behaviour in the future.

In the early days of machine learning a lot of effort was made to develop machine-learning programs which would be able to learn anything. Like the human brain, which can learn anything, it was thought that it would be possible to develop computer programs which had the same ability. And, of course, it would have been nice if that had turned out to be the case – after all, a program that could do that would be immensely valuable. Any problem in the world could be tackled by it and, eventually, it would learn how to solve that problem – even if its human creators could not!

There is, as yet, no good reason why such a general-purpose learning machine could not be built – the very existence of the human brain suggests that such a thing might one day be possible. But, in practice, most practical attempts at machine learning have now acknowledged that the different things which we might want a machine to learn are so disparate that different methods and, hence, different programs are required for different kinds of machine-learning problems.

For instance, if we develop a program which can learn to recognize objects as a form of computer vision then we are unlikely to find that this same program can learn to parse sentences for us. It is not that there seems to be any strong theoretical reason why this should be the case – it is just that machine-learning problems are most easily solved by writing programs to concentrate on just one particular type of learning problem.

What does remain as a general-purpose principle is the concept of feedback. Every machine-learning program consists of showing the machine a set of examples, telling the machine what these are examples of and then letting the machine learn what it is that distinguishes between these examples. This is feedback. If we just gave the machine a set of examples and told it nothing about what these examples represented then it would learn nothing about them which would be of any use to us.

From this there emerges another general-purpose principle – which is that the machine can only learn things which it very nearly knows already. This follows from the fact that the programs which are written to carry out machine learning are written with some particular field of learning in mind and they are written in such a way that they very nearly do whatever it is that we ultimately want the machine to do. The machine's task when the program is running is to home in, using the feedback we give it, on the precise behaviour which we require of that machine.

This is tied in very closely with the concept of a description language – the language in which we present the learning problem to the machine. Consider, for instance, a situation shown in Fig. 5.2 in which you are

Fig. 5.2 Necessary conditions for learning

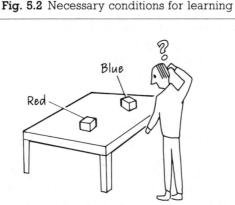

Placed before you on a table are two objects. Their colours can vary and they can be placed either on the left or the right of the table. You have to select which object is the 'right' object to win a prize. In fact, we suppose that the red object is the correct one to choose.

If you are never told when you are right then you will never learn that the red object is the right object – this is the importance of feedback.

If the problem is presented to you in a badly-worded fashion then you might make the mistake of thinking that you could choose both objects, or none of them, or, even, the table itself! This emphasizes the importance of expressing the problem in a suitable description language.

If you happened to be colour blind then you would never learn the problem correctly – this is because the information presented to you was insufficient.

Machine learning requires that the machine should be programmed in such a way that the program has feedback, a suitable description language, and sufficient information for learning to take place.

asked to learn the difference between two objects placed on the table in front of you. One object is red, the other is blue, sometimes the object is placed on the left of the table and sometimes on the right. To make things interesting you get offered a prize if you can learn which is the 'correct' object to choose every time they are placed on the table.

Well, you have two variables there – colour and position – and with a bit of trial and error you could quickly learn what the important difference was between choosing the right object and choosing the wrong one. But suppose that the right object to choose was always the red one and you happened to be colour blind – you would never be able to learn to solve that problem correctly. And the reason is that the description language which you have of the situation was inadequate to solve the problem because the description language did not include the crucial variable of colour.

The same applies to machine learning. If a machine is to learn what it is that you want it to learn then it can only do so if it has all of the information it needs concerning the problem. This information has to be encoded in some way so that the machine can understand it and, as the nature of the information changes from one type of problem to another, also the way that this information is encoded changes.

In summary, then, we get three important points to remember in every case of machine learning.

The first is that the program must have feedback – it must be told what it is that it is supposed to learn and be told how well it is doing at learning it.

The second is that the problem must be presented to the machine in a description language which is closely suited to the nature of the problem that the machine is to learn so that the machine is set up to learn that particular type of problem.

The third is that the machine must be given enough information to enable it to learn the task you require of it.

In order to break down the problem of machine learning a little further we will consider two broad categories of machine learning – the black-box approach and the cognitive model.

5.1 The black box

The idea behind a black box – any black box – is that there are a set of inputs to the box, a set of outputs from the box and nobody knows or cares what happens inside the box itself. This concept is not strictly confined only to machine-learning situations – it is used frequently when we want to describe what a system does in functional terms but are not particularly interested in how it does it in any great detail.

As far as learning theory is concerned the black-box approach has been used in many psychological theories of human and animal learning. In stimulus-response models of learning the psychologists suppose that an organism is exposed to certain stimuli to which it makes certain responses. The effects of these responses are fed back to the organism as additional stimuli (this being feedback) and, in the light of this feedback, the organism adjusts its responses to subsequent stimuli.

As an example, suppose that you knew nothing about fire and, by some chance, you happened to put your hand in a fire. Naturally, you would get burned and would, thereafter, not put your hand in fires anymore. Roughly analysing this as a stimulus-response learning situation, you could say that seeing the fire was a stimulus and your initial response was to reach out and touch it. Getting your hand burned then provided an additional stimulus to you which you incorporated with the original stimulus of seeing the fire and you modified your behaviour so that, next time, on seeing a fire your response was different – you avoided it.

This is a simple example of a group of theories which can get much more complex than this – but it does get across the idea. The basic idea being that the theory says very little about what actually goes on inside your head when you touch the fire and get burned. You may, in fact, form all manner of theories concerning things that glow, temperature, and the effect thereof on human flesh. But, as far as the learning theory is concerned, you are just a black box. At its strongest, this approach is typified by the behaviourist psychologists who argue that the behaviour of humans and animals can be explained solely in terms of the stimuli they receive and the responses they make with no reference to any internal processes that might take place. And, as such, the ideas have a lot to recommend them. After all, if you wanted to know that an organism, or a machine, had learned something you could only be sure that it had learned by looking at what it did to see if learning had taken place. If the machine never altered its behaviour then you would be reasonably justified in saying that the machine had not learned anything – and the fact that, possibly, quite complex processes were going on inside its main memory would count for nothing if these processes did not manifest themselves in action.

Now, obviously, we cannot build a black box into a computer for the very simple reason that, as we have to program the machine, we must know something about what is going on in that machine – so computers are never completely black boxes. But we can write programs which mimic this kind of learning and the way that this is done is by saying that we do not mind too much what method we use to get the machine to learn as long as the machine actually does learn. The essence of the approach is that we do not expect to be able to look inside the program, after learning has taken place, and find anything remarkably human-like by way of learned intelligence. If we did look inside the machine all we might find is that some mathematical formula or other had changed in some way.

An example of this is the Markov-chain approach which is very easily implemented in BASIC. For those who are uncertain about what, exactly, is a Markov chain: it is a sequence of events in which the probability of each event occurring depends only on the previous event that occurred. So, if you think of a two-dimensional array M, we could have S rows and R columns to give DIM $M(S, R)$ and think of the rows as the stimuli to the system and the columns as its responses. Initially, all of the elements of the array are set to zero.

The machine is then confronted with a certain stimulus (input) and this consists of specifying one of the stimulus rows in the array. As a result of this the machine has to make some response which it will choose from the R columns associated with that row. In the beginning each element of the array is set to zero so there is no reason to choose any one response over any other and, most likely, the machine will make the wrong response.

But then you tell the machine it was wrong and tell it what the right response should have been. The program can then add some value to that element of the array which connects that stimulus with that response so next time that stimulus is received the machine can make the correct response simply by choosing the response with the largest value associated with that stimulus.

Fig. 5.3 Markov chains

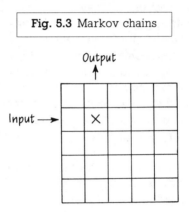

Effectively, the array becomes a Markov chain (Fig. 5.3) in which the probability of any event is dependent solely upon the preceding event and these probabilities are learned by adjusting the values in each element of the array.

Obviously, this is fairly easy to program and it might sound a little too simple to be of any great use. But from this simple model you can build up quite a complex behaviour pattern by bearing in mind two things: first, the array can be quite large; and, second, the columns could in many cases be identical to the rows so that, having made a response to some stimulus, the program could then take this response as a stimulus to make some further response building up quite a complex stimulus–response (S–R) chain of behaviour.

As an example, think of the psychologist Pavlov and his dogs which were trained to salivate when they heard a bell ring. The way Pavlov achieved this was by ringing a bell every time he gave them food. The dogs salivated when food was presented to them and, in the course of time, they learned that a bell was associated with food so they began to salivate when they heard the bell ring even though food was not present.

You could build this into a learning program using a Markov chain. On the stimulus side of the array would be 'food' and 'bell' and on the response side of the array would be 'food' and 'salivate'. Either by training or by inserting a value into the array right at the beginning you could ensure that every time you keyed in 'food' the computer output the word 'salivate'. And then, by training the machine, you could get the program to alter the values in the array so that every time you input 'bell' the computer learned to output 'food'. Then, when running the program, by going around the array twice 'bell' could cause the output 'food' which would then be used as input to produce the output 'salivate' – and the computer would have learned to salivate every time it heard the bell ring, as it were.

Although this method might be interesting as an example of modelling some kinds of human and animal behaviour it can be used for more serious applications as well. In general, the responses consist of choosing any one out of a given number of outputs on the basis of an input and, by using multi-dimensional arrays the behaviour can be made quite sophisticated.

But you see why this is a black-box approach. The array is really a closed box in which you have little, if any, intrinsic interest. As long as the system learns and behaves correctly you do not really mind what is in the array at all – and if, by some extra programming, you were to ask the machine to explain why it did what it did then you could not get a very sensible answer. The best it could say was that it did what it had done because experience had taught it that this was the right thing to do. It could not explain why it thought it was the right thing to do in any more detail than that.

A similar approach is the learning algorithm shown in Fig. 5.4 which, again, uses a two-dimensional array in which the rows of the array represent the inputs and the columns represent a choice of possible outputs. This approach differs from the Markov-chain approach inasmuch as more than one input can be activated at the same time. Typically, all of the inputs are activated simultaneously by means of a 'description vector' – a one-dimensional array which contains values for each of the possible inputs. This description vector is multiplied by each column of the array to produce a single figure and that column of the array which gives the greatest figure represents the chosen output. If this is the correct output then the array is unchanged, and if it is the wrong output then the values in the description vector are subtracted from the incorrectly chosen column in the array and added to the column which would have been the correct choice.

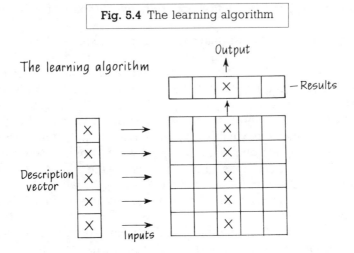

Fig. 5.4 The learning algorithm

More complex situations can be dealt with using the learning algorithm in which a description vector contains all of the information about the current problem to be learned. This vector (a one-dimensional array) acts as input to the two-dimensional array and is successively multiplied by each column of that array. The column which gives the highest result 'wins' and the output corresponding to that column will be selected. If the system makes a mistake the main array can be adjusted by subtracting the description vector from the column that was incorrectly chosen and adding it to the column which should have been chosen. This method will only work totally correctly on problems which are linearly separable.

To make this clearer, consider the following code (we assume all variables set to zero at the start):

```
FOR I=1 TO R
FOR J=1 TO S
D(I)=D(I)+ V(J)*M(I,J)
NEXT:NEXT
```

In this, the array V contains the description vector and the response of the system is determined by that value in the array D which is the largest. If the response is correct then the array M remains unchanged, and if the response is incorrect then the contents of array V are subtracted from that column of array M which was incorrectly chosen and added to that column of M which should have been chosen.

The result is that M gradually becomes adjusted so that the system will make the correct response to whatever input vector V it is provided with.

Essentially, the method consists of finding a linear equation of the form

$$d_i = m_{i,1}v_1 + m_{i,2}v_2 + m_{i,3}v_3 + \ldots + m_{i,s}v_s$$

which will separate out all the possible responses by adjusting the values of $m_{i,j}$ until it does so.

Being a linear equation the method will only work if the various responses are, in fact, linearly separable – which means that, roughly speaking, you would be able to plot the positions of each of the description vectors on a piece of paper and be able to draw a set of straight lines between them in such a way that each description vector was allocated to its correct response.

Both of these methods make clear use of feedback in order to learn. You must be able to tell the program when it is right and what the correct response should have been if it is wrong.

They also have their own description language. In the case of the Markov-chain approach this consists of a single item which says, in binary yes/no terms, just which stimulus the machine is receiving at this precise moment. And, in the case of the learning algorithm, this consists of a set of values (the description vector) which describe each one of a set of variables being input to the system. These need not be binary, or even integer values but can be any real number.

And in order for the methods to work, the input must contain sufficient information to enable the system to actually make a correct choice and, usually, this simply consists of ensuring that there are enough relevant variables present and enough examples to 'train' each system on.

In general, black-box methods rely heavily on mathematical approaches to the problem of learning and these two example methods are really only scratching the surface of the subject.

5.2 Cognitive models

There are two disadvantages to black-box models of learning. The first is that, in human terms, we do not always know how they work and the second is that, to a large extent, they can tell us nothing new about the problem that they are working on. In a way both of these criticisms link together with each other and both derive from the fact that most black-box models rely on a mathematical formulation.

Considering the first of these problems, suppose that we set up one of the black-box models mentioned in the earlier section, and got it working on some learning problem. After a bit of practice, the machine might well have learned the task assigned to it and it might even be able to carry out that task better than we could. But now, because the system is a black box, we cannot readily open it up to see how it adapted itself to learn the task. If we did open it up all we would find would be an array of numbers with no particular indication as to how, precisely, these numbers got there. If we were mathematically inclined we could work out something from these numbers but, for the most part, it would be very hard to say whether the system had come up with the best solution or, in extreme cases, even to say what solution it had come up with.

This is very much to do with the fact that, although mathematicians and computers think in terms of numbers and equations, people, generally, do not. And this is at the core of the second problem – that if we had a black-box system we might have difficulty learning from it ourselves. After all, suppose that the machine did learn well – better, perhaps, than we could have learned the same problem – in that case it would be to our advantage to be able to ask the computer to explain what it had learned so that we could benefit from its experience too. It would also provide a very useful check that the machine was functioning properly – because, if its explanation was hopelessly ridiculous, we would then know that the procedures the machine had used were, in some respect, wrong.

To solve these problems, what we really want is a machine-learning system which not only learns, but learns in a way which is understandable in normal human terms.

This is what cognitive models try to do. Instead of postulating a black box as the mechanism which carries out the learning they attempt to produce a mechanism which might, conceivably, model the way in which that box works on the inside and make this model open to inspection.

In psychological terms, the difference is largely between the stimulus–response, behaviourist approach to learning and the cognitive theorists. The cognitive theorists argue that, maybe, a dog learns to salivate when he hears a bell ring by some unconscious internal mechanism – but that people most definitely do not learn very much this way. When we learn something we do so by using much higher levels of thinking in which we are conscious of some particular train of reasoning which we apply in the learning process. We are not 'just' machines, the cognitive theorists say, we are thinking machines which know what we are doing.

Naturally, there is considerable overlap between these two points of view. At one level, people do learn things in a black-box fashion. If you look at your wristwatch at around lunch time your stomach will doubtless begin to rumble a little – and the mechanism by which that particular piece of learning takes place might as well be modelled as a black box. And, looking at the matter from the other angle, when Pavlov's dogs began to salivate on hearing the sound of a bell ringing there is little evidence to suggest that the dog is not thinking something along the lines of 'There goes the dinner bell – must be time for food!' and starts to salivate.

In other words, the simplest learning may have a cognitive element to it and the most complex learning might have a black-box element in it somewhere.

However, in machine-learning terms, there is some advantage to be gained by having the machine learn in a fashion that is at least vaguely reminiscent of the way in which people might be thought to learn – and this is what the cognitive approaches attempt to achieve.

As an example of a machine-learning program of this sort consider a very simple robot – one that is designed to learn its way around a maze. It can do this by trying every path it comes to and sensing around to see where the walls are and where there are open pathways. At the end of its exploration it will (hopefully) have learned to find its way around the maze without having to use its sensors again because it will have learned the layout of the maze. Now, if we add a bit of extra programming to that robot, we can ask it what it has learned about the maze and it will be able to tell us in terms that we understand – it could, in fact, be made to print out an actual map of the maze which would correspond exactly to the map we ourselves would draw of the maze if we had to. That is evidence that the machine has learned the maze and it is an illustration of the fact that the machine has a cognitive model of the maze. It still had to have all of the other ingredients of a learning machine. It needed feedback from its sensors to tell it when it had run into a wall, it needed an adequate description language and sufficient information about the problem, all of which came from the programming that was used to get it to interpret the input from its sensors.

But the end result is not a black box – it is something we can open and immediately understand.

Listing 5.1 Robot maze learner

This is a program which simulates a robot moving around in a maze in an attempt, not only to find its way out, but also to learn something about the maze so that next time it encounters it, it will be able to do much better.

In lines 50–130 the maze is drawn on the screen using block graphics. The main points to note are that, apart from drawing the borders of the maze and clearing an area around the entrance and exit to increase the chances that there actually is a path through the maze, the maze is drawn entirely at random. What is more, the actual design of the maze is not held anywhere within the program. It is not contained in any of the arrays – it only exists on the screen, so there is no chance of the robot having access to information about the maze unless it goes looking for it.

In array $V\%$ the robot keeps track of how many times it has already visited each cell in the maze and in array $M\$$ it keeps information about the position of walls in the maze for each cell that it has already visited. The scheme is that the robot starts at the top left of the maze and always tries to move first downwards, then to the right, then upwards, then to the left (in that order) so that its overall direction will tend towards the exit. Its progress through the maze is stored in array $R\%$ with $R\%(M, 1)$ holding one coordinate of the current position and $R\%(M, 2)$ holding the other.

Now, if the robot comes to a cell it has visited before $V\%$ will contain a value other than 1 and, in lines 200–220, $R\%$ will be modified simply by changing the value of the marker M to remove from the robot's memory all recollection of the route it followed since it last visited that cell. Effectively, to re-visit a cell the robot must have followed a path which constituted a redundant loop and these lines of code remove the memory of that loop so that the robot will have learned that this was a bad route to follow. And, to make sure that it does not follow the same route again, line 220 uses the value in $V\%$ to decide which direction it should travel in next (a different route, obviously, to the route it followed last time it was in this particular cell). In fact, it always follows the next route in the down–right–up–left cycle.

Once the robot has successfully completed the maze it will then re-run it from its memory of $R\%$ – so, in the re-run, it will only visit each cell on its route a maximum of once.

The search strategy used by the robot is a brute-force, exhaustive search (see Chapter 7) and it would be possible to modify the program using some of the more sophisticated methods outlined in Chapter 7 in order to improve its ability to plan and solve this maze problem. In particular, you might consider the 15-puzzle program (the 'tile puzzle') which contains many similar features (and, consequently, some very possible methods of enhancing the robot's performance). For example, you might consider what a simple application of the concept of Manhattan Distance could do for the robot's choice of path from each cell.

Finally, in array $M\$$ the robot holds a character string of four binary numbers for each cell which represent what it knows about the maze so far (each binary number is 1 for a wall and 0 for an opening) which it learned by using its 'sensors' (in the form of the FNSCRN function) to 'feel' whether or not there was a wall on each of the four adjacent cells.

This means that the program could be readily modified to make it print out a partial map of the maze showing those areas it had visited and what it knew about them.

Then, if you are feeling adventurous, some of the problem-solving methods of Chapter 7 could be applied to this map in order to try to get the robot to follow an optimal route through the maze given its current knowledge rather than by using its present method of simply following the first successful route through the maze with redundant loops removed. Obviously, if this approach were used then the robot would benefit from being able to make several runs through the maze in order to add to its knowledge rather than one, single run – and each of these successive runs should try to cover new ground each time. Possibly, for a robot which simply wanted to find out as much as it could about the maze prior to attempting to solve it efficiently, the Drunkard's Walk of Chapter 7 might be as good a method as any (if you do not mind having a robot that drinks a little, that is). Figure 5.5 shows the screen output of this listing.

```
10   REM   ***************************
11   REM   **   LISTING 5.1       **
12   REM   **  ROBOT MAZE LEARNER **
13   REM   ***************************
20   SW = 40:SH = 40: REM   SW IS SCREEN WIDTH AND SH IS SCREEN HEI
     GHT
30   DIM M$(SW,SH),V%(SW,SH),R%(2000,2)
40   TEXT : HOME : GR : COLOR= 15: REM   WHITE
50   FOR I = 3 TO SW: PLOT I - 1,0: NEXT
60   FOR J = 2 TO SH: PLOT SW - 1,J - 1: NEXT
70   FOR I = SW - 2 TO 1 STEP  - 1: PLOT I - 1,SH - 1: NEXT
80   FOR J = SH - 1 TO 1 STEP  - 1: PLOT 0,J - 1: NEXT
90   FOR I = 2 TO SW - 1
100  FOR J = 2 TO SH - 1
110  IF  RND (1) < .25 THEN : PLOT I - 1,J - 1      } Rand walls
120  NEXT : NEXT
130  COLOR= 0: FOR I = 2 TO 4: FOR J = 2 TO 4: PLOT I - 1,J - 1: PLOT   } clear Entrance
     SW - I,SH - J: NEXT : NEXT : COLOR= 15                              & exit
140  REM   SEARCH MAZE USING SENSORS
150  VTAB 24: HTAB 1: PRINT "EXPLORING..."; SPC( 10);
160  I = 2:J = 1: REM  POSN ROBOT AT START
170  GOSUB 390:M = M + 1:R%(M,1) = I:R%(M,2) = J:V%(I,J) = V%(I,J
     ) + 1: IF M$(I,J) = "" THEN : GOSUB 470: REM   REMEMBER THE
     ROUTE,HOW OFTEN YOU VISIT EACH CELL AND USE SENSORS IF YOU H
     AVEN'T BEEN THERE BEFORE
180  B$ = M$(I,J)
190  IF V%(I,J) = 1 THEN 230
200  FOR K = 1 TO M - 1: IF R%(K,1) = I AND R%(K,2) = J THEN :M =
     K: REM  IF YOU'VE BEEN HERE BEFORE FORGET THE ROUTE THAT BRO
     UGHT YOU BACK HERE
210  NEXT
220  ON V%(I,J) -  INT ((V%(I,J) - 1) / 4) * 4 GOTO 230,240,250,2
     60
230  IF  MID$ (B$,1,1) = "0" THEN : GOSUB 430:J = J + 1: GOTO 270
240  IF  MID$ (B$,2,1) = "0" THEN : GOSUB 430:I = I + 1: GOTO 270
250  IF  MID$ (B$,3,1) = "0" THEN : GOSUB 430:J = J - 1: GOTO 270
260  IF  MID$ (B$,4,1) = "0" THEN : GOSUB 430:I = I - 1
270  IF I <  > SW - 1 OR J <  > SH THEN : GOTO 170
280  GOSUB 390:M = M + 1:R%(M,1) = I:R%(M,2) = J
290  VTAB 24: HTAB 1: PRINT "GOT THERE !"; SPC( 10);
300  REM   RE-RUN MAZE
310  GOSUB 430
320  FOR K = 1 TO M
330  I = R%(K,1):J = R%(K,2)
340  GOSUB 390
350  FOR Q = 1 TO 25:X = X + 1 - 1: NEXT : REM     DELAY
360  GOSUB 430
370  NEXT : GOSUB 390
380  VTAB 24: HTAB 1: PRINT "HOW'S THAT !"; SPC( 10);: END
390  REM   SUBROUTINE TO POSITION ROBOT AT I,J
400  COLOR= 7
```

Fig. 5.5 Typical screen output from ROBOT MAZE LEARNER (Listing 5.1)

This figure is an actual reproduction of the screen output produced by Listing 5.1 – so you could use it as a guide to ensure that your program is working correctly. You should note though that, as the walls of the maze are placed by the random number generator, the exact positions may not be the same as you get on each run of your program.

In general, a robot placed in this maze (which would be represented by a square of a different colour) can find its way around by 'feeling' for walls. It can then learn a route through the maze by remembering what it has learned and storing it as an internal cognitive map. If we wanted to we could program the robot to print out its internal map of the maze – thereby showing that the machine had learned and had learned in a way that we could understand and criticize. If we had no knowledge of this particular maze then we too could learn about it – from the robot.

```
410   PLOT I - 1,J - 1
420   RETURN
430   REM  SUBROUTINE TO DELETE ROBOT FROM I,J
440   COLOR= 0
450   PLOT I - 1,J - 1
460   RETURN
470   REM   USE SENSORS TO BUILD UP MAP AT POSN I,J AND PLACE IN A
      RRAY M$
480 X = I - 1:Y = J - 1
490 M$(I,J) = "0"
500   IF  SCRN( X - 1,Y) = 15 THEN :M$(I,J) = "1"
510   IF M = 1 THEN :M$(I,J) = "1" + M$(I,J): GOTO 540
520   IF  SCRN( X,Y - 1) = 15 THEN :M$(I,J) = "1" + M$(I,J): GOTO
      540
530 M$(I,J) = "0" + M$(I,J)
540   IF  SCRN( X + 1,Y) = 15 THEN :M$(I,J) = "1" + M$(I,J): GOTO
      560
550 M$(I,J) = "0" + M$(I,J)
560   IF  SCRN( X,Y + 1) = 15 THEN :M$(I,J) = "1" + M$(I,J): GOTO
      580
570 M$(I,J) = "0" + M$(I,J)
580   RETURN
```

Once we get onto more general learning tasks we find that the most usual form of a cognitive model is in the form of rules which the machine must develop for itself if it is to solve the learning problem and which, if we wish, we can ourselves examine and understand to see exactly how it has solved the problem.

In fact, many machine-learning programs rely on rule-based systems and the aim of the learning program is to develop rules which can then be executed by the rest of the program to solve the problem.

By way of example, think of a specific learning problem – suppose, for instance, that you yourself wanted to learn how to figure out what had gone wrong with your car. Now, when you first start to drive you will not have much of an idea what might go wrong with it but, as time passes, you will gradually start to build up an internal set of rules rather like:

If there is no petrol then the thing will not go.

If the battery is flat the thing will not go.

If there is a flat tyre and no spare then the thing will not go very far.

These are all very *ad hoc* and, also, very understandable. What we want is a computer which can learn things like that in much the same way so that we can understand what it has learned and comment sensibly on it.

There are a number of ways of doing this but they all rely on the same basic methods as the black-box systems – you have to give the machine some examples of what it has to learn, described in some particular way and containing enough information for it to learn. And, for the most part, this means that the information you give the machine will be very similar in kind to the information you would give the machine for a black-box system – all that varies is what the machine does with this information.

The most common approach is for the program to examine the information you give it and work through each of the variables in turn to build up a tree structure – a decision tree which will enable the program to make correct decisions concerning its future output when it gets confronted with new, but similar, problems. It is the building of this tree structure that is the learning process.

At its simplest the program takes the first variable and finds some value of that variable which best discriminates between all of the different courses of action which it could take. So, if the problem was to learn what might go wrong with a car, as shown in Fig. 5.6, the first variable might be petrol and the program might note that cars never go if they do not have petrol, but even when they do have petrol they sometimes do not go either.

So the first node in the decision tree would be formed on the basis of the simple question of whether or not the car had any petrol in it – because if it did not that would lead the computer to assert that the car will not go.

However, the fact that the car has or has not any petrol will not solve all problems – there will still be some instances in which the car does have petrol but still will not go. So the program passes on to the next variable which might be the matter of whether or not the battery is flat and, by adding another node to the tree at this point, it can refine its knowledge about what can go wrong with cars.

In its basic form this approach to machine learning can work well – but there is plenty of scope for refinement. Just a moment's thought will reveal that a good decision tree is better than a bad one and that a good decision tree is one in which the most important items are considered first so that the tree does not become too complicated. There are various ways of tackling this problem, possibly the simplest being to scan all of

Fig. 5.6 Learning by decision trees

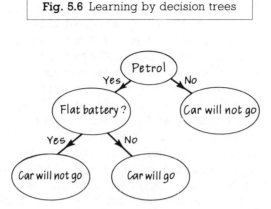

A machine can learn by gradually building up a decision tree in its memory on the basis of the information presented to it. This has the advantage that the machine can explain exactly what it is that it has learned by expressing it in a series of rules which we can understand. In this example, the program has learned that:

If a car has no petrol then it will not go.

If a car has petrol and a flat battery then it will not go.

If a car has petrol and does not have a flat battery then it will go.

Had we given the program some more complex problem it might well be that the rules the program developed were unknown to us and, again, we could then learn from the computer.

the variables right at the start and to choose that variable which seems to get the best overall discrimination between different courses of action right at the beginning. Then the procedure can be repeated when the program tries to establish the next node in the tree, and so on.

Methods can also be used to refine the decision tree after it has been formed to make it rather more generally applicable, or simpler. One such method is to try relaxing the conditions in the decision tree a little so that instead of taking one variable at a time, and applying a strict yes/no criteria to that variable, the program might try taking pairs of variables and seeing if an adequate decision tree can be built using rather looser criteria such as 'If x OR y then ...'

In the example given above it would be much clearer to say that:

If there is no petrol or the battery is flat then the car will not go.

If there is petrol and the battery is not flat then the car will go.

In the first rule the conditions have been relaxed and, in the second rule they have been made more stringent by adding an AND condition.

Many of these methods work by, first, establishing a basic decision tree and then trying out various forms of relaxation and specialization (making the rules more stringent) to see if they either improve the performance of the system or enable it to achieve the same performance but with rather less effort on its part. In every case the actual learning involves the development of a good set of decision rules to work from – and it could be argued that this is how we ourselves learn in many instances.

When we run such a system, if it has learned correctly, not only will it be able to produce the right output but, by backing up its decision tree, it will be able to tell us why it produced that output – which is a very useful check that all is well with the system.

There are, of course, many other methods that can be used to develop cognitive models of machine learning and, in the main, these other methods are heavily dependent on the particular way in which the information is presented to the machine. In terms of machine learning this depends on the particular form of the description language used to describe the problem to be learned and, more generally, it is tied in with the idea of particular forms of knowledge representation within the machine – a subject which is dealt with in a separate chapter.

5.3 The scope of machine learning

One of the biggest problems in producing a short introduction to machine learning is the sheer scope of the subject. Man may possess many in-built abilities – but he does not possess very many of them. To all intents and purposes everything we do is something that we have learned to do by one means or another.

This does not mean that we have necessarily been formally taught everything that we know – for the most part we just learn it as we go along. But we have still learned it – and this applies to such basic abilities as seeing, hearing, walking, talking and moving as well as the more complex intellectual tasks which we carry out.

So, obviously, the subject of machine learning could legitimately be applied to every human activity there is in the hope of getting the computer to learn as well as we have done (or better).

In the field of computer vision, machine-learning systems have been developed which will help the computer to recognize objects simply by being shown the object and being told what it is.

In the field of natural language understanding, machine-learning systems have been developed which can be trained to recognize particular fragments of speech spoken by a human being; and have been developed to help develop new rules for language parsers.

In the field of expert systems, machine-learning systems have been developed which can work from examples in order to simplify the task of building up a knowledge base in some specific field of expertise.

The problem is then: Is machine learning a subject in its own right or is it just an adjunct to every other subject? There is no general agreement on this question because sometimes it is one thing and sometimes it is more usefully regarded as another. To look at machine learning without reference to the type of problem that the machine might be required to learn places the subject in rather too much isolation but, as there are certain common elements in any machine-learning situation, it might be wasteful to simply tack a section on machine learning onto the end of every single chapter in this book. Hopefully, this chapter has given rise to some thoughts which might be useful when applied in a more specific context than simply the study of machine learning for its own sake.

5.4 Machine learning

Machine learning can be applied to an enormous variety of problems and, in general, the nature of the problem tends to suggest, or even dictate, the methods used to carry out the learning.

But certain key elements are common to all machine-learning situations.

The most basic is that learning consists of the ability to correctly select some particular output from a number of possible outputs. The basis upon which this selection is made will be the inputs that the system receives at the time. In the final analysis, all systems which learn can be said to have learned to discriminate between two choices of output – a binary choice. Even if, ultimately, several possible outputs are to be considered these several outputs can be expressed as a series of binary choices.

In order for learning to take place on some particular problem a suitable description language must be chosen which contains all of the necessary information needed by the system to learn to make the correct choices. The description language and the information may be, simply, numeric data or, in some applications, may describe other features of the learning situation. For instance, a learning system for computer vision might use a description language which was expressed in terms of edges and surfaces; a description language for natural-language parsing might be expressed in words.

Most important of all, the system must be provided with feedback – information to let it know how it is getting on so that it can adjust itself accordingly. This 'feedback' does not have to come after the system has already produced a response – it could be incorporated in the set of input information on which the system was initially trained – the 'learning set'. So, a machine-learning system could be provided with a set of examples of different items which typified the sort of inputs it would receive once it was running for real. This set of examples would contain information concerning the correct choices to be made by the machine and this would enable the machine to learn something about the situation without the need for an operator to be standing by to comment on its performance all the time.

There are a vast number of methods which might be used in machine-learning situations and whole books have been written covering just small subsets of these methods. In general, though, they tend to fall into two categories – black-box systems, which rely on some precise mathematical formulation of the learning system, and cognitive systems, which attempt to more closely mimic the way that people learn. The mathematical systems often have a big advantage inasmuch as, when they are applicable, they can often yield results which have known mathematical properties which makes it possible for mathematicians to make very definite statements about what these methods can and cannot do.

The cognitive systems have the big advantage that when the machine learns something it is better placed to explain to the average person exactly what it has learned, which makes it easier to assess and debug these systems using common sense rather than mathematics. It is also true that many problems which we would like machines to learn are not always well enough formulated to be sure that a black-box, mathematical approach will work. The cognitive-model approach may give difficulties too on occasions – but at least we can see and understand more readily any problems which do arise.

Machine learning is applicable to most fields of AI and some people will argue that if machines are ever to become truly intelligent, then they are going to have to learn how to do so by themselves anyway.

6

Knowledge representation

Normally speaking, the last thing that you think about when writing a computer program is the particular knowledge representation you will use. Typically, you write a program to process some data and then arrange the data to suit the program. Or, if you happen to have had difficulties using that approach before, then you might have the foresight to write the program bearing in mind the actual format that the data come in.

But that is data – not knowledge – and the questions that spring to mind are: What is the difference between data and knowledge? How should you go about organizing an appropriate representation for either?

For the moment we will make life easy by thinking only of data and, to make life easier still, we will consider as an example a program which is supposed to process a small payroll. Now, we might want to work out how much each employee is paid and we do this by considering their rate of pay and the number of hours they have worked. Clearly, the program is simply a matter of multiplying these two numbers together. So we could write a program to do just that:

```
10   READ H: READ P
20   PRINT H*P
30   END
```

Obviously, this has to go into a loop of some kind so that a large number of employees can be processed but, in essence, we have already written the program and the data could be held as DATA statements, like

```
1000   DATA 40,5
```

which might indicate that this particular employee has worked 40 hours that week for a rate of £5 per hour.

Obviously, though, we have forgotten something – the employee's name. It is easy enough to add it though. Insert another READ at the end of line 10 to bring in a string variable representing the employee's name and alter the DATA statement to be

```
1000   DATA 40,5,JOE BLOGGS
```

and we now have everything just as we want it.

The only snag is that next week Joe Bloggs may not work 40 hours – in which case we want to be able to alter that particular item in the DATA statement. Now, if you look at the way that the data are held you will see that we have everything almost exactly the wrong way around for our purposes, because the last thing that any employee changes is his name; most frequently he changes the number of hours that he works; and, less frequently, he changes his rate of pay. So it would have been better if the DATA statement had been

1000   DATA JOE BLOGGS,5,40

because that way we could have amended the data much more readily each week as the payroll program is run.

In the course of writing the payroll program this fact will probably have dawned on us and, consequently, we will have amended the program from its original form so that, eventually, both the program and the data represent the information we have on that employee in the most convenient fashion possible – both for us and for the computer.

Of course, on a full-scale payroll program we would be unlikely to hold employee data in DATA statements – most likely, we would have used disc files and there would have been much more information present than the very spartan details shown here.

But the general principle remains – that it is easier to solve a problem if the data are represented in the right way and it is easier to program a solution to the problem if you have thought out in advance just how the data should best be represented within the machine. This is true whether we are talking about AI or about relatively common commercial problems.

So, if we now turn to problems in AI, it is obviously a good idea to work out exactly how our data are to be held within the machine at an early stage because that way we avoid having to re-program the computer every time we find out that the original scheme was not much good when it came to actual practice.

Notice though that we are still talking about data, rather than knowledge. Is there a difference between the two things?

6.1 Data and knowledge

Data are what we are all used to when programming computers. It is the variable information which the program acts upon. Everyone knows what a program is and everyone knows just what data are. For the reasons given above, it makes sense to work out exactly what data a program needs to solve a given problem well in advance and to organize those data, and the program, so that they act together on the problem in the best possible fashion.

But, in large part, the reason why data are so obviously data is due to the nature of the programming languages that we are used to. Most procedural languages, such as BASIC, allow only very limited types of data – typically, numbers, strings and arrays. With such limitations on data types there is very little incentive to think in terms of anything else. So if you have a number, a string or an array, then you can safely reckon that to be data and you will not go far wrong.

But, traditionally, computers have been used for tasks which only ever involve numbers, strings or arrays as data. They calculate payrolls, they print out names and addresses, they carry out mathematical operations – and all of these problems can be represented quite simply and conveniently by numbers, strings or arrays.

However, when AI started to gain ground, people started to realize that there were a large range of problems which could not be expressed simply in this way. Suppose, for instance, that you wanted to write a program to carry out natural-language processing – maybe the data for that could be expressed in terms of strings, but the structure of those strings would get rather complex. Or, maybe, you wanted to write a program which would carry out some task in computer vision – that could possibly be dealt with by the use of arrays as data, but as the task expands into image recognition then there might be limitations there.

More telling, perhaps, would be the situation in which you wanted to write a program which could carry out some kind of common-sense reasoning. You want it to be able to think in much the same way as people think. Well, how do people store their data? Do they use numbers, strings or arrays for their everyday data representations?

Just asking the question makes the matter appear somewhat silly – because common sense tells us that people do not store data in any of these ways. They have much broader, rather 'fuzzier' methods of storing their data, and yet we can not ignore the way people store data because they happen to be such good examples of thinking machines. It was for this reason that AI workers first started to talk about knowledge rather than data – to make it clear that the information which the program was to work on might not be represented in the traditional methods used by computers. In a sense, they just wanted to make it clear that they were prepared to use other methods than the traditional means for getting the information into a computer. So, when we talk about knowledge, rather than data, it is really just to indicate that everyone has a pretty open mind as to how, exactly, the data should best be held.

6.2 Programs and knowledge

One aspect of this is that, in AI, there is seldom the clear dividing line between programs and knowledge that there is between programs and data in more traditional fields of computer activity. Turn back to the best example we have of an intelligent mechanism – man – and again ask yourself where the dividing line is between man and the data that are input to man. You might be able to answer that question in part but the snag is that man, to some extent, is the sum of all his experience. Everything that has ever happened to you has played some part, however small, in making you the kind of person you are. Now, that is not the case with a typical computer program. Every payroll that a payroll program has ever processed has not contributed one iota to making the payroll program what it is today – it is the programmer who has been solely responsible for the program and the program merely chews its way mindlessly through the data.

People do not chew mindlessly through data – they modify the data and the data modify them – which makes it very hard to draw a line strictly between the two. And the same may hold true for programs which attempt to display intelligence. It may be that it is very hard to draw a strict line between the program and the data because there may be such close interaction between the two. At its most extreme this might be seen in programs which carry out machine learning – because the very concept of machine learning suggests that the program will actually be modified by the data it receives. So, which is the 'real' program – is it the original, unmodified, untutored program, or the same program after it has modified itself and learned something? And, are the data totally separate from the program or are they, in some way, an inherent part of the program once some degree of machine learning has taken place?

Even apart from the paradigm of machine learning, it is obvious that 'knowledge' is not something that just exists in the 'data' itself. Going back again to the payroll program, this program obviously has quite a bit of knowledge about how payrolls are structured and how they should be processed – it is implicit in the actual program itself. And, as computers are applied to ever more complex and 'intelligent' tasks the amount of knowledge inherent in the program will grow.

This, then, is another good reason for thinking in terms of knowledge rather than data – that 'knowledge' can encompass the whole program *and* its data if we want it to. It is just a more general term to describe what the computer knows and what it can do as a result of that knowledge.

6.3 Knowledge and programming languages

One of the reasons why knowledge and knowledge representations have been relatively ignored outside of AI so far lies in the nature of the languages we use to program computers. For the most part, everyone programs in procedural languages – languages which are executed step by step following some pre-ordained algorithm. These languages do, in general, separate data from programs very clearly and are equally clear about the different forms which the data can take. Typically, these forms are the traditional ones of numbers, strings and arrays.

And this fact has a strong effect on the way most people write their programs. Because you are brought up to think in terms of the procedural languages you find that there are certain things which these languages do well and certain data formats which they handle best. So it is only natural to program the computer to make best use of the available languages. It is rather like the theory propounded by some linguists to the effect that we can only think what our language enables us to express. This theory has a rather uncertain following, but most people would agree that it is easier to think in terms of easily expressed aspects of the language with which the person who is doing the thinking is working. So, for instance, it is very hard for a person with no knowledge of the language of mathematics to grasp some mathematical ideas – and it may even be that some people, having been immersed in the language of mathematics for a long enough time, have difficulty expressing ideas, or even having ideas, which are best expressed in the common-sensical form of everyday speech.

In terms of computer languages, it may be that if your background is in BASIC then when confronted with a programming problem you solve that problem using, say, FOR loops. This may not be a bad idea because the FOR loop is a very powerful aspect of the BASIC language. But it can lead to a blinkered approach in which, when confronted with a problem, you start off by writing a solution using FOR loops and try to force the problem into a form which can be solved by using FOR loops even if the problem itself is not really best solved in that way. This is just an example, of course. There is nothing inherently wrong with the use of FOR loops as such and, often, they are an ideal construction for certain types of problem (they would not have been invented if they were not). But you do, perhaps, see that the programming languages you are used to can modify the approach you instinctively choose when trying to program a solution for some task.

In principle, of course, any computer language can be used for any operation you care to name. As long as that language is inherently capable of reading from and writing to every location in memory then that language is capable of making the computer do anything of which the computer is theoretically capable. And BASIC fits that particular bill simply because, if all else fails, you can always get the machine to do exactly what you want by using PEEKs and POKEs.

But the pitfall still exists because particular programming languages can suggest (if not dictate) particular methods of programming and, as we have already decided that knowledge is a part of the program itself, the language you are used to can have a tremendous influence on the type of knowledge representations you choose to use when tackling a particular problem.

This is one of the main reasons why different programming languages have been developed – to suggest ways in which different types of problem might usefully be tackled and to make it easier to tackle those types of problem.

Just to give a couple of examples, LISP (List Processing Language) has been developed to make it easier to program problems in which the knowledge is best represented using lists; and PROLOG (Programming in Logic) has been developed to make it easier to program problems in which the knowledge is best represented using statements in formal logic. Many other languages could be mentioned but, for the time being, these two will be sufficient – and they are both languages which figure large in the world of AI.

If you want to stay with BASIC then there is no real reason why you should not do so – and the same is true of almost any other language. But it is important to remember that a particular language can channel your thoughts into a particular direction – and that may or may not be a good thing, depending on the type of problem which you want to solve.

6.4 Why knowledge representation matters

Before we get onto some specific examples of different types of knowledge representation it is worth asking exactly why the subject matters at all. Certainly, we have seen that some problems are best expressed in one form than in another – but that really only scratches at the surface of the matter.

The really important point is that the particular knowledge representation which you choose has a very strong effect on the way you can actually solve the problem.

Consider, for example, the problem of having to add two numbers together. In BASIC you can simply write

10 A = B + C

and that will do the job nicely. But it does it nicely because you chose to represent the knowledge about the numbers as the numeric variables A, B and C.

If, instead, you had chosen a different knowledge representation you might still have solved the problem but it could have been a great deal more difficult. Consider, for example, the following start to the program:

```
10   B$ = STR$(B)
20   C$ = STR$(C)
```

so that the numbers are now represented as string variables. The knowledge is still there but the problem is now to add the number represented by the string $B\$$ to the number represented by the string $C\$$ and to place the result in the numeric variable A.

The problem can be solved and, if you feel like a puzzle to work on, you could try to write code which will solve it (try working through the two string variables from the right using $MID\$$ to take one character at a time and apply the normal, primary-school rules for addition and carrying). The snag is that this method is slow and difficult to program – and the reason why that is the case is because the knowledge representation that was used was not very well suited to the problem in hand.

The same reasoning applies to problems in AI. A good, appropriate, knowledge representation can help enormously in the solution of a problem. Almost, it tends to suggest a solution of its own accord, if you are lucky. A bad, or inappropriate, choice of knowledge representation can be a tremendous handicap, but a good knowledge representation can amount to winning half the battle.

So, now we will turn to a few common knowledge representations used in AI work and sketch out their bare essentials. They might not all be right for what you want to do but, hopefully, they will give you some ideas which might help when developing AI programs of your own.

6.5 Internal maps

Imagine that you had a robot which was designed to move around a maze, learning the layout of the maze using its sensors, and gradually able to find its way through the maze. In a situation like this the most obvious and natural form of knowledge representation would be an internal map. By making a map of the maze, such as that shown in Fig. 6.1, the robot would know exactly where it was and, by printing out the map, it would be able to prove to you that it actually did understand the layout of the maze in terms that you could understand.

Fig. 6.1. Internal maps

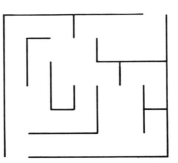

Knowledge can be represented as an internal map – the classic example being that of a maze-solving robot. The map can be held in a two-dimensional array in which each element contains a number which indicates where the walls are for each cell in the maze.

The approach can be extended for more complex maps by, effectively, thinking of them as a maze but with more, and smaller, cells.

Specifically, you could go so far as to represent the maze as a two-dimensional array, say DIM $M\%(20, 20)$ for a maze 20 cells deep by 20 cells wide, and let each element of the array contain an integer number which would denote exactly which parts of each cell consisted of walls and which were open to other cells. So, if we used a binary representation, we could have each element of the array containing a binary four-digit number in which 1 would denote a wall and 0 would denote an opening. If this representation was ordered then it would be possible for the first binary digit to refer to the north direction, the second to refer to the east direction, and so on until each of the important aspects of the four directions had been encoded.

So the binary number 1111 would denote a completely closed cell (into which, of course, the robot could never get) and 0000 would denote a completely open cell. A cell which had a wall to the north and was open on all other sides would be denoted by 1000. So to examine the characteristics of each cell all that would be needed would be to convert the integer into a binary pattern and examine the bit positions.

This may seem like rather a specialized application of knowledge representations – after all, not everyone wants to build a robot – but it does have some useful general aspects and also makes some useful points.

The general aspects are that, when describing something in the real, three-dimensional world, a map is actually a pretty good knowledge representation to use. You do not have to confine yourself to robots for this to be true. You might be simply telling your computer about something that exists in the outside world (outside of the computer, that is) and the simplest way for the computer to understand what you are saying and to be able to prove that it understands it would be for it to draw a map. This map need not be quite like the highly ordered map used in a regular maze – it could be more complex, giving the details of the varied shapes of objects and their positions – or it could be very much the same only with many more elements to it so that everything was approximated by a model in which a large number of equal-sized cells existed.

The second point is that knowledge representation does not have to be hard. A map is about the most obvious way of representing spatial knowledge that you could think of – and, yet, it is still a good way. A method which can be used by both the computer and yourself. And, in line with any other good method of knowledge representation, when you have settled on the right representation to use and programmed that then the actual problem facing the computer (that, say, of finding its way through a maze) becomes so much easier to solve because a good knowledge representation was chosen.

Finally, an internal map does not have to be confined to the three-dimensional world of physical objects. It can be used to describe other relationships as well. If we wanted to describe relationships amongst people we could equally well draw a map in which the distance between people on the map was a measure of the closeness of the relationships between them. And, to express complex relationships, we do not even need to confine ourselves to three dimensions – you just use as many dimensions as the problem seems to require. We have already done that with the maze map in which, although we were thinking of the three-dimensional world, all of the important items could be represented in two dimensions and there was no point in adding a third. It is possible to go the other way and start adding dimensions to make a map of whatever complexity the problem requires.

6.6 Rules

In many problems which humans solve the knowledge they use does not seem to be encoded in any particularly rigorous fashion. It is not, for instance, encoded in the form of a sequence of instructions analogous to a computer program.

What people often seem to do when thinking about problems is to apply a series of rules of thumb, or heuristics, to guide them in their actions. These can often be represented as rules.

A typical example is the person who takes a glance out of the window, notes that the sky is pretty overcast and decides that it is likely to rain. This might be formalized as the rule:

If the sky is overcast *Then* it will probably rain

This is not a knowledge representation that is used very often in traditional computer programming but its use in AI is growing, largely as a result of the work on expert systems. Human experts appear to represent a large amount of their knowledge in this way so, if we wish to design computer programs which will mimic the human experts, then it makes sense to try to adopt a similar style of knowledge representation for the computer. This style of knowledge representation is often known as 'rule-based programming' and consists of representing the knowledge in the form of rules and then writing a program which can interpret and act upon these rules. In expert-systems terminology the rules are the 'knowledge base' and the program which acts on them is called the 'inference engine'.

The usual format of the rules is to have an antecedent part and a consequent part. Sometimes the antecedent part is called the 'condition' and the consequent part called the 'action'. Which means that the rules may be called condition–action rules and sometimes, just to confuse things even further, they are called 'production rules'.

In general, though, the first part of the rule is that bit which follows the 'If' and the second part of the rule is that bit which follows the 'Then'.

This may sound like a conventional If . . . Then statement in a procedural programming language and it is possible to write a program using this form of knowledge representation in that way by making the bulk of the program consist of If . . . Then rules inside a main loop which constantly scans the conditions to see which are true at any one time, acting on those that are true and ignoring those that are not. Obviously, if the program is to do anything interesting, then some of the consequences of the rules must match the antecedents of other rules – otherwise only a very small set of rules would ever 'fire' and one pass through the program would result in the program doing everything it was ever going to do.

Although rules are almost always spoken of as if they actually did consist of If . . . Then statements there is no compelling reason why the knowledge should actually be embodied in this precise form. For instance, any program which tests for some condition and then acts on the basis of the result of that test could be said to be following a rule-based course of action and representing its knowledge in a rule-based fashion.

How explicit you want to make the rules in the program is up to you and also depends on the nature of the problem you are trying to solve.

But if you have knowledge like that of the car mechanic who says 'If the electrics are dead and no fuses are blown then the battery must be flat' then you have a likely candidate for representing that knowledge in the form of rules.

6.7 Trees

There may be plenty of good things in this world which do not grow on trees but knowledge is not one of them. A great deal of computer information is held in the form of tree structures and this is especially the case in the field of AI.

Unlike real trees, computer trees do not grow upwards, they grow downwards looking more like the roots than the branches of a tree as Fig. 6.2(a) shows. But, for all that, most of the terminology derives from normal trees which grow upwards.

Fig. 6.2 Trees

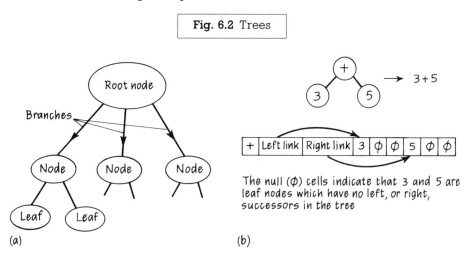

The null (φ) cells indicate that 3 and 5 are leaf nodes which have no left, or right, successors in the tree

(a) (b)

Knowledge can be represented as trees which are traditionally shown 'upside down' compared with normal (wooden) trees.

The points where the branches meet are known as nodes. The root node is always at the top and the bottom nodes, which lead nowhere, are called leaf nodes. Trees are particularly useful for representing hierarchical knowledge with large numbers of branching options.

In (b) a tree structure is used to represent a mathematical formula with the operator at the root node and the branches leading to the operands.

Tree structures can be held in one-dimensional arrays. For instance, a binary tree (one with only two branches from each node) can be represented by showing the contents of each node followed by the link address to the left branch and the link address to the right branch out of this node.

The tree starts off with a root which (given that everything is upside down) is at the top of the tree. This root has branches attached to it, each of which either terminates at a node or at a leaf. A node is that part of the tree from which further branches can arise and a leaf is that part of the tree which goes no further – like leaves on normal trees.

Obviously, a tree structure is very good for storing knowledge of a hierarchical nature and, as such, it has been used in commercial data processing for a long time to denote the various levels, say, in data hierarchy – such as files, records and fields.

But there is a lot of hierarchical knowledge in AI too. You might want to represent a family tree (one of the better-known uses of a tree structure) or any other knowledge which, starting from a single point, branches out into a large number of options. Game playing is AI's best-known example of this, in which the knowledge a computer might have of the state of a game of chess can be represented in the form of a tree structure which branches out rapidly as the computer considers the effects of making any one out of a variety of different moves (see Chapter 8).

The point about game playing is that although there is an intrinsic hierarchy in the knowledge which the computer uses (because each move has to be made before some other moves and after another set of moves) the essence of the matter is that the knowledge has a structure which can be best represented as a sequence of branches and nodes.

To give another example, mathematical formulae can be represented as a tree structure with the operators being placed at the nodes and the operands (the variables on which the operators act) being placed below them in the tree. This way the hierarchical, branching structure of the formula can be represented as a tree structure.

One of the big advantages of representing knowledge in the form of trees is that the theory of trees is so well understood. In the chapter on planning and problem solving you will see in more detail how trees can be used to represent knowledge and how they can best be searched in the most efficient manner for solutions to problems.

For the moment it is probably sufficient to note that you do not have to have an actual, physical, representation of a tree inside the machine to make it work. Trees can be represented within a computer quite simply by having each node consist of the contents of that node and a list of addresses pointing to the location of any other nodes which lead from that node further down in the tree. So, if you were programming in BASIC, you could easily represent a tree as a one-dimensional array in which each element in the array either contained the contents of a node or the pointer to that element in the array which contained the next node down from there.

6.8 Graphs

Graphs might sound a little like those things that you draw on paper in order to display some information which is usually of a mathematical nature. But, in the context in which we are using the word here, graphs are probably best thought of as nets or networks. They are a series of interlinked nodes, as shown in Fig. 6.3, which illustrate the way in which different items of knowledge are related to each other.

Because of this, it is very easy to think of them as trees – but the big difference is that whereas trees are intrinsically hierarchically ordered, graphs are not. There is no root node in a graph – in a sense, all nodes are equal. Also, the control of knowledge does not just flow downwards as it does in a tree. It may flow in any direction between two nodes which are linked. This linking takes place through arcs connecting the various nodes and it is even possible to have one node linked by an arc to itself so that it can continue doing whatever that node says it is doing for as long as it wants.

Also, unlike most trees, the arcs between the nodes can be labelled to show not only that there is a link between two nodes but what that particular type of link is called. This makes it possible for the program to store knowledge and also to be able to say something about the nature of the knowledge that it has stored.

A good example of knowledge representation using graphs is in the field of language in which the nodes might correspond to individual words and the arcs connecting them might be used to show which words can follow which in order to form a grammatical sentence. By labelling the arcs it is possible for the program to know something about the nature of the grammar it is using. So, for instance, the program might contain a graph which showed that the sentence 'The strong young man lifted the weight' was grammatical and then, by reference to the labelled arcs, it would be able to justify this statement on the grounds that the linkage between 'young' and 'man' was an adjective–noun linkage.

Not only language can be represented in this way. We might want to represent some other kind of knowledge within the computer – such as the fact that tables are a kind of furniture and chairs are a kind of furniture and both are found in dining rooms. This could be achieved by defining a linkage called 'a kind of' and another linkage called 'is found in' and using the graphs to show how tables, chairs and dining rooms relate to each other. At this point, by searching through the graph the computer would be able to answer questions like 'What kinds of furniture do you know about?' and 'What is found in dining rooms?'

In general, graphs can be represented within the machine in a language such as BASIC in much the same way as trees – using a one-dimensional

Fig. 6.3. Graphs

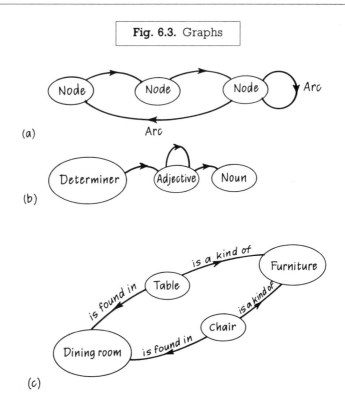

Knowledge may be represented as graphs in which the nodes are linked by arcs. The arcs may be directed to indicate that there is only one direction in which the program may travel along the arc. Arcs can be made to point to any node in the structure, even to the node that they originated from. Arcs may also be labelled so that the arc itself has a name and stands for something.

In (b) the language structure Determiner–Adjective–Noun is represented with an additional arc referencing Adjective to itself to allow for multiple adjectives. So, this may represent the knowledge that the following form is allowable: 'The strong young man'. (Determiner–Adjective–Adjective– Noun).

In (c) the graph represents the knowledge that both tables and chairs are a kind of furniture and are both found in dining rooms using labelled arcs.

array, each element of which is either the contents of a node or the pointer to some other node which connects to it. However, if the arcs are to be labelled, there is some advantage in using string arrays because these make it easier to insert the labelling information. So the array might contain the sequence:

contents of node; name of arc; pointer to node that this arc connects to;

For more complex structures, you might want to adopt a format such as:

name of node; contents of node; number of arcs leading from this node; name of first node connected; name of second node connected; etc.

And then the whole graph can be traversed by matching the names of the nodes connected against their actual occurrence further on in the array.

6.9 Lists

Lists are precisely what their name implies they are – lists of objects, very much like a shopping list – and it is surprising just how many different knowledge representations can be subsumed under the heading of 'lists'.

Think for a start of a very simple list. The list itself has a name and in the list are a number of objects. Suppose, for a start, that there are only two objects on the list.

Now that makes the list very much like a simple binary tree structure. The name of the list is the root node of the tree and the two items on the tree are the two leaf branches that come out of that root node.

Add more items to the list and the same basic structure remains – it is just that more leaf branches appear out of the root node.

Now make the list a little more complex by making some of the items in the list not single items but the names of further lists. See, for example, Fig. 6.4. Immediately, it appears that we have constructed a tree structure because the naming of each extra list effectively adds another node to the tree which will have more branches descending from that. So tree structures can be represented as lists.

Now make the list a little more complex by allowing the sublists to contain items which are either elements in lists higher up in the structure or are the names of lists higher up in the structure and, immediately, the hierarchical nature of the tree structure disappears and you are left with a graph structure, or a network.

This all goes to show just how powerful lists can be for representing knowledge. So powerful, in fact, that a specific language LISP (for List Processing Language) has been invented solely to handle lists.

It is not necessary, though, to move to a new language if you want to represent knowledge as lists – as will have been obvious from the discussion on trees and graphs. If you did try a new language you might find life got a little easier, once you had got used to the language, but there is nothing to stop you doing the same things in a language such as BASIC.

In many ways this helps to illustrate the point that, although some knowledge representations are better than others for specific purposes, there

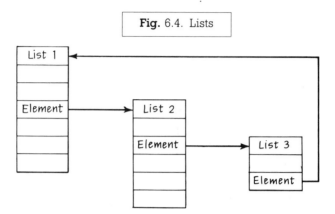

Fig. 6.4. Lists

Knowledge can be represented as lists. Usually, the first element of the list is the name of the list and subsequent elements are items on the list. Lists may be connected together into lists and sub-lists by making elements in the lists the names of other lists. Working in this way, very complex structures can be represented, including trees and graphs.

is considerable overlap between many of the methods used to represent knowledge. So much so that a useful guideline is to study the knowledge you wish to represent and think out how you, personally, would be happiest to represent that knowledge. After all, it is not just the computer which has to make sense of the representation – you have to be able to make sense of it too!

6.10 Frames

A frame is a form of knowledge representation with which everyone is familiar because, in its simplest form, it is identical to a questionnaire. It consists of a list, or table, of items each of which has a specific purpose and each of which is associated with a blank which must be filled in to get the complete picture.

Much knowledge exists which is tightly enough defined to be able to fit into this format – the important point about it being that, in general, it is not the relationships between the items which matter so much (as they do in trees and graphs) but the sum total of all of the entries.

An example of this is the typical newspaper story, much of which could be represented as frames. Consider the following story:

PQR Computers today went bust leaving 10 000 unsatisfied customers. The Receiver said he had never seen management like it and that he was going to lie down for a while and think about it.

This story, and many others, could have the knowledge it contains represented in a frame, such as shown in Fig. 6.5, in which the entries would be items like: Who is the story about? What did they do? Who else was involved? What did they feel? What did they do?

By making up a complete frame and filling in the blanks the computer could represent the complete story and, if it had any blanks left unfilled, it would know that it did not have all the knowledge it needed and could ask for more. It could also answer questions about the knowledge it had by looking up the entry in the appropriate space.

Obviously, frames are fairly easy to implement in a language like BASIC, because all that is really needed is a string array which holds the labels for each entry and is also able to hold the entries for the blanks themselves.

Equally obviously, the matter can become more complex than this because a part of the computer's task might be to decide exactly which frame, of several it held in its memory, would be applicable to any given situation. But, if the computer was asking the user for information (or receiving information anyway) then it could check through all of its possible frames to see which one best matched the information it was

Fig. 6.5. Frames

Who is the story about ?	········PQR Computers
What did they do ?	········ went bust
Who else was involved ?	········10 000 customers
What did they feel ?	········ unsatisfied

Knowledge may be represented as Frames – questionnaire-like structures that contain a blank form for a standard situation. An example is the news story which might have the above frame. When the blanks are filled in the computer has the knowledge that PQR Computers went bust involving 10000 customers who all felt unsatisfied.

A computer is then able to know when it has all the knowledge it needs (because all of the blanks on the questionnaire are filled) and it is able to answer questions about the knowledge it has, such as: Who is the story about?

A program may contain several different types of frame for different situations and a task of the program is then to decide exactly which frame is appropriate to the current situation. When it has done that it is a long way forwards in understanding the situation.

receiving and, when it had found the best match, it would then have selected the right 'line of thought' which it should be following. It would have cottoned on to the type of situation in which it had found itself.

Some people think that this is very much how people store their knowledge on some occasions. They have a series of frames which are applicable to particular situations and their first task is to select the right frame. After that they can proceed to deal with the situation quite effortlessly because they are then following a pre-specified plan in acquiring and accessing their knowledge.

6.11 Programming languages

In theory (and for the most part in practice too) you can program any form of knowledge representation in any language you choose. All of these knowledge representations can be programmed, if you wish, in BASIC.

But there are other languages, such as LISP and PROLOG, which are widely used by AI workers. LISP is used for representing knowledge as lists and PROLOG is used for representing knowledge in a form of logic known as the predicate calculus (if that sounds a little daunting do not worry, it is rather like representing knowledge as rules, and there is nothing too daunting in that).

As most people have BASIC on their computers there is a lot to be said for using it, rather than splashing out good money on extra languages. Also, whenever you tackle a programming problem, there is a lot to be said for tackling it in a language you understand well – that way you only have to concentrate on the problem itself and not on an unfamiliar language at the same time.

But it is worth bearing in mind that different languages, even though they may not actually dictate the way you think, can be very suggestive. Consider, for instance, COBOL. This was designed to enable commercial programmers to solve problems easily and allowed them to represent commercial knowledge in a way that seemed natural in commerce. Or FORTRAN, which was designed to enable programmers to represent the knowledge contained in formulae and to solve problems concerning those formulae easily.

So, although most languages may be able to do most things in principle, in practice you will find that the language you use tends to steer you in particular directions and it can take a positive effort of will to avoid being oversteered in a direction that may not be best suited to the problem.

If, for instance, you are using BASIC, then the temptation will be enormous to represent your knowledge in the form of numbers, arrays and strings – because that is what BASIC handles most easily. You will have to apply some real thought (not too much, but a little) to represent knowledge in the form of rules, trees, graphs, lists or frames using BASIC. But it is important to remember that it can be worth it. Not only do you find out more about these knowledge representations by trying to construct them in a language you know, but you also find out more concerning what they can and cannot do for you.

Think about the problem that you would like to tackle and think about the way that knowledge might best be represented – then try to make your computer represent that knowledge in that way. Even if that is not the way that comes most naturally to the language you are using. It is just a matter of not letting your computer steer you away from what you really want to do. After all, the ultimate aim you have in mind is to make your computer intelligent so that it, eventually, can take over some intelligent tasks on its own – but you do not want it to take over from you too soon in the game!

7
Problem-solving methods

It is a still, moonless night. Somewhere in southern England a man with a metal detector is criss-crossing a stretch of waste ground, hoping to uncover buried treasure in the form of a golden hare. Not far away, another man is pacing up and down a dimly lit room, trying to prove a theorem in algebraic topology. What do the two men have in common?

They are both *searching* for something. One is engaged in a literal search for a tangible object. The other's search is more abstract and metaphorical. But when we speak of 'searching' for a solution or 'finding' the answer we recognize that both kinds of search have important common features.

AI scientists have taken the search metaphor very seriously, as we saw in Chapter 1. In this chapter we examine some of the methods they have developed for solving a variety of problems by a searching process. In doing so we will show how some of the tree-like and graph-like data structures described in the previous chapter can be utilized.

Problem solving can be treated as a search process if there is a 'space' of potential solutions and some means of traversing or exploring that space. The space may have a geographical basis (e.g. finding a route on a map) or, as we shall see, it may be highly abstract (e.g. proving a theorem in propositional calculus).

In either case, the key to *intelligence* in the search is to do as little work as possible. (Yes, idleness is a virtue in AI!) That is to say: one method of search is said to be more 'intelligent' than another if the former examines fewer potential solutions than the latter, but still succeeds.

7.1 Hunt the thimble

To clarify some of these notions, we will consider the children's game of Hunt the Thimble – a classic search process. One player hides a thimble under a carpet, behind a cupboard or wherever and then the other player or players attempt to locate it. As a seeker gets closer to the object, the other player is supposed to say 'warm', 'warmer', 'hot' and so on. If the seeker goes away from it, the other player says 'cool', 'cold', 'colder', etc. The fun arises because the feedback about warmth is usually rather inaccurate; but it is certainly better than no feedback at all.

If there were no one to tell you when you were nearing your goal (or receding from it), you would have to perform an exhaustive search – for instance, by dividing the area up into thimble-sized sectors and examining each one in turn. An exhaustive search will eventually succeed, unless the problem setter has cheated, but it cannot be regarded as very clever. To put it simply, you cannot search intelligently without knowledge.

In fact it is useful to distinguish three levels of intelligence in problem solving by searching:

(0) Dumb search, e.g. the Drunkard's Walk.
(1) Blind search, e.g. systematic enumeration.
(2) Heuristic search, e.g. guided exploration.

'Blind' or 'brute-force' search will be our baseline for comparison: it is simply an orderly and exhaustive enumeration of all the possibilities. For interesting problems, however, it is likely to prove far too slow. Still, it is possible to do worse.

The so-called Drunkard's Walk consists essentially of choosing a direction at random and moving one pace in that direction, then doing the same again, until success or exhaustion. The Drunkard's Walk is studied in connection with the behaviour of stochastic processes. A Drunkard's Walk approach to Hunt the Thimble would be to wander around aimlessly until you happened to stumble on it. (Many of us resort to such methods in moments of stress.)

The objective of all heuristic-search techniques (level 2) is to do better than this, and better than systematic enumeration. This is only possible by exploiting additional knowledge about the problem domain. If there is no way of telling whether you are getting 'warmer' or 'colder', you just have to fall back to level 1 (and if the problem is very complex, to level 0).

7.2 Terminology

At this point, let us review some of the terminology of problem solving viewed as a search process.

Search space	The set of possible solutions.
State	A potential solution.
Operator	Some way of getting from one state to another.
Heuristic	Information about the quality of a proposed solution.

There is, typically, a goal state or destination (sometimes several) and a starting-point or initial state. In terms of Hunt the Thimble the search space is the area in which it is hidden. The goal state is discovering the thimble. The initial state is being where you happen to be without the thimble. Available operators include moving from one place to another; and the source of heuristic information is the 'temperature' messages.

Alternative terms are sometimes used: a state may be called a node and an operator may be called an arc, i.e. a link from one node/state to another.

7.3 Route finding

Now we are ready to consider our first search problem. Our example is spatial (indeed hyper-spatial!).

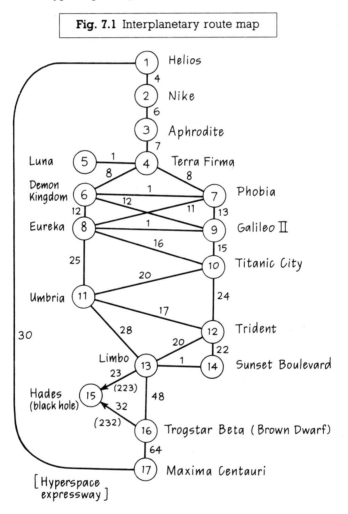

Fig. 7.1 Interplanetary route map

You are sitting quietly in the lounge bar of the Snark Inn on Trogstar Beta, the inconspicuous Brown Dwarf companion of a totally hypothetical yellow star in the third galactic arm when your radionic modem emits a beep. You assume it is merely some promotional data-frame that has somehow evaded the junk-mail filtering algorithms, but you examine it out of curiosity anyway.

Surprisingly it turns out to be an invitation to a party on Terra Firma, the third planet of your local system. So you whip out the galactic gate-crasher's map of the vicinity (Fig. 7.1) and ask your portable computer to work out the quickest way to get there.

We will look at some of the ways the computer can do that job.

But first we must decide a data structure for the map, which defines a network (see Chapter 6). Since the structure is static – i.e. no new inter-space highways are due to be built before the party – a pair of fixed-length lists will suffice. One is a list of all the locations with a pointer from each to a second list of its neighbours and how far away each one is (in time units rather than distance).

Thus, to take your current location as an example, Trogstar Beta is represented as shown in Fig. 7.2.

Fig. 7.2 A node and its connections

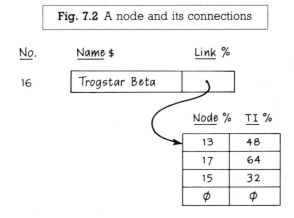

This states that Trogstar Beta is node 16 and that it takes 48 time units to get from there to node 13 (Limbo), 64 time units to go to node 17 (Maxima Centauri) and 32 time units to node 15 (Hades). The double zero marks the end of a sequence of neighbours. Thus from this node the allowable 'operators' are three – taking a single step to node 13, 15 or 17.

We could have used a 17 × 17 matrix to hold this information, but most of its 289 entries would have been empty, wasting space. This method gives a simple and compact representation of the network.

Notice that the distances are symmetrical except for Hades which, being a black hole, is extremely difficult to leave. Note also that Maxima Centauri is connected to Helios by a hyperspace expressway, while Trogstar Beta is connected to Maxima Centauri by a conventional stellar highway, hence the former is a quicker link even though it is more distant. Of course, there is an additional toll to pay on the hyperspace expressway, but since you will be hitching a lift, why worry about that?

Below is a listing in BASIC of the DATA statements holding this information and the code which reads them and constructs the network in memory.

Listing 7.1 Node code

```
10   REM   ************************
11   REM   ** LISTING 7.1        **
12   REM   ** NODE CODE          **
13   REM   ************************
110  GOSUB 1000
999  END
1000   REM  -- ROUTINE TO SET UP MAP-NET:
1010   DIM NAME$(20),LINK%(20)
1020   DIM NODE%(96),TI%(96)
1030   NC% = 0:L% = 0
1040   REM   START LOOP
1050   READ N$,ID%
1060   IF ID% < > 0 THEN : GOSUB 1500
1070   IF ID% = 0 THEN 1080
1075   GOTO 1040
1080   PRINT NC%;" LOCATIONS READ IN."
1090   RETURN
1500   REM  -- INDIVIDUAL NODE & CONNECTIONS:
1510   NC% = NC% + 1
1520   IF ID% < > NC% THEN : PRINT "WARNING: NODE ";ID%;" OUT OF
       ORDER."
1530 NAME$(NC%) = N$
1540 LINK%(NC%) = L%
1550   REM   START LOOP
1560   READ NI%,NT%
1570 NODE%(L%) = NI%
1580 TI%(L%) = NT%
1588   REM  -- NODE AND TIME STORED.
1590 L% = L% + 1
1600   IF NI% < = 0 THEN 1610
1605   GOTO 1550
1610   RETURN
8000   REM   DATA FOR PLANETARY MAP:
8010   DATA   HELIOS,1
8020   DATA   2,4,17,30,0,0
8030   DATA   NIKE,2
8040   DATA   1,4,3,6,0,0
8050   DATA   APHRODITE,3
8060   DATA   2,6,5,7,0,0
```

```
8070   DATA   LUNA,4
8080   DATA   5,1,0,0
8090   DATA   TERRA FIRMA,5
8100   DATA   3,7,7,8,6,8,4,1,0,0
8110   DATA   DEMON KINGDOM,6
8120   DATA   5,8,7,1,9,12,8,12,0,0
8130   DATA   PHOBIA,7
8140   DATA   5,8,9,13,8,11,6,1,0,0
8150   DATA   EUREKA,8
8160   DATA   6,12,7,11,9,1,10,16,11,25,0,0
8170   DATA   GALILEO II,9
8180   DATA   10,15,8,1,6,12,7,13,0,0
8190   DATA   TITANIC CITY,10
8200   DATA   9,15,12,24,11,20,8,16,0,0
8210   DATA   UMBRIA,11
8220   DATA   8,25,10,20,12,17,13,28,0,0
8230   DATA   TRIDENT,12
8240   DATA   10,24,14,22,13,20,11,17,0,0
8250   DATA   LIMBO,13
8260   DATA   12,20,14,1,16,48,15,23,11,28,0,0
8270   DATA   SUNSET BOULEVARD,14
8280   DATA   12,22,13,1,0,0
8290   DATA   HADES,15
8300   DATA   13,223,16,232,0,0
8310   DATA   TROGSTAR BETA,16
8320   DATA   13,48,17,64,15,32,0,0
8330   DATA   MAXIMA CENTAURI,17
8340   DATA   16,64,1,30,0,0
8350   DATA   NOWHERE,0
8360   REM    -- THAT'S ALL FOLKS !
```

Having thus established the state-space, we can try various methods for searching it. We will start with some simple ones and progressively refine and improve them.

Since the search begins in a bar (and ends at a party) the Drunkard's Walk is an appropriate point of departure. It is interesting to see just how badly it fares.

7.4 The drunkard's walk

To implement this random-choice method, the routine at line 2000 of Listing 7.2 is used. This picks a successor node at random.

A couple of example runs are shown at the end of the listing. As you would expect, they are rather rambling and costly routes. The results you get depend on the random number generator, but over six runs of this program the average route took 29 steps and 910.5 time units. Clearly the drunk will arrive after the party is over, which may be just as well.

Listing 7.2 Drunkard's walk

```
10   REM   *************************
11   REM   ** LISTING 7.2       **
12   REM   ** DRUNKARD'S WALK    **
13   REM   *************************
100   REM   -- RANDOM SEARCH:
110   GOSUB 1000: REM   GET THE DATA
120  S% = 16: REM   STARTING POINT
130  D% = 5: REM   DESTINATION
140  TU% = 0: REM   TIME USED
150  NC% = 0: REM   NO. OF NODES EXAMINED
155   PRINT "START AT : ";NAME$(S%)
160   REM   START LOOP
170   GOSUB 2000: REM   SEARCH
180  NC% = NC% + 1
190   IF S% = D% OR NC% > 100 THEN 200
195   GOTO 160
200   IF S% = D% THEN : PRINT "SOLVED IN ";NC%;" STEPS."
210   IF S% < > D% THEN : PRINT "DRUNK COLLAPSES AT ";NAME$(S%); CHR$
      (7)
220   REM   -- DONE !
999   END
1000   REM   -- ROUTINE TO SET UP MAP-NET:
1010   DIM NAME$(20),LINK%(20)
1020   DIM NODE%(96),TI%(96)
1030  NC% = 0:L% = 0
1040   REM   START LOOP
1050   READ N$,ID%
1060   IF ID% < > 0 THEN : GOSUB 1500
1070   IF ID% = 0 THEN 1080
1075   GOTO 1040
1080   PRINT NC%;" LOCATIONS READ IN."
1090   RETURN
1500   REM   -- INDIVIDUAL NODE & CONNECTIONS:
1510  NC% = NC% + 1
1520   IF ID% < > NC% THEN : PRINT "WARNING: NODE ";ID%;" OUT OF
      ORDER."
1530  NAME$(NC%) = N$
1540  LINK%(NC%) = L%
1550   REM   START LOOP
1560   READ NI%,NT%
1570  NODE%(L%) = NI%
1580  TI%(L%) = NT%
1588   REM   -- NODE AND TIME STORED.
1590  L% = L% + 1
1600   IF NI% < = 0 THEN 1610
1605   GOTO 1550
1610   RETURN
2000   REM   -- RANDOM SEARCH ROUTINE:
2010  L% = LINK%(S%)
2020  N% = 0
2030   REM   START LOOP
```

```
2040  IF NODE%(L% + N%) > 0 THEN :N% = N% + 1
2050  IF NODE%(L% + N%) = 0 THEN 2060
2055  GOTO 2030
2060  REM  -- N% IS NO. OF NEIGHBOURS.
2070  R% = RND (1) * N%: REM  PICK 1 AT RANDOM
2080  N% = NODE%(L% + R%)
2090  TU% = TU% + TI%(L% + R%): REM  TIME USED
2100  REM  -- SHOW PROGRESS:
2110  PRINT NC% + 1;" ";NAME$(N%); SPC( 28 -  LEN (NAME$(N%)) -  LEN
      ( STR$ (NC% + 1)));TU%
2120  S% = N%: REM  NEW STATE
2130  RETURN
8000  REM  DATA FOR PLANETARY MAP:
8010  DATA  HELIOS,1
8020  DATA  2,4,17,30,0,0
8030  DATA  NIKE,2
8040  DATA  1,4,3,6,0,0
8050  DATA  APHRODITE,3
8060  DATA  2,6,5,7,0,0
8070  DATA  LUNA,4
8080  DATA  5,1,0,0
8090  DATA  TERRA FIRMA,5
8100  DATA  3,7,7,8,6,8,4,1,0,0
8110  DATA  DEMON KINGDOM,6
8120  DATA  5,8,7,1,9,12,8,12,0,0
8130  DATA  PHOBIA,7
8140  DATA  5,8,9,13,8,11,6,1,0,0
8150  DATA  EUREKA,8
8160  DATA  6,12,7,11,9,1,10,16,11,25,0,0
8170  DATA  GALILEO II,9
8180  DATA  10,15,8,1,6,12,7,13,0,0
8190  DATA  TITANIC CITY,10
8200  DATA  9,15,12,24,11,20,8,16,0,0
8210  DATA  UMBRIA,11
8220  DATA  8,25,10,20,12,17,13,28,0,0
8230  DATA  TRIDENT,12
8240  DATA  10,24,14,22,13,20,11,17,0,0
8250  DATA  LIMBO,13
8260  DATA  12,20,14,1,16,48,15,23,11,28,0,0
8270  DATA  SUNSET BOULEVARD,14
8280  DATA  12,22,13,1,0,0
8290  DATA  HADES,15
8300  DATA  13,223,16,232,0,0
8310  DATA  TROGSTAR BETA,16
8320  DATA  13,48,17,64,15,32,0,0
8330  DATA  MAXIMA CENTAURI,17
8340  DATA  16,64,1,30,0,0
8350  DATA  NOWHERE,0
8360  REM  -- THAT'S ALL FOLKS !

]RUN
17 LOCATIONS READ IN.
START AT : TROGSTAR BETA
1 HADES                        32
2 LIMBO                        255
```

```
3 TROGSTAR BETA          303
4 LIMBO                  351
5 TROGSTAR BETA          399
6 HADES                  431
7 TROGSTAR BETA          663
8 LIMBO                  711
9 UMBRIA                 739
10 TRIDENT               756
11 TITANIC CITY          780
12 GALILEO II            795
13 DEMON KINGDOM         807
14 EUREKA                819
15 PHOBIA                830
16 DEMON KINGDOM         831
17 GALILEO II            843
18 DEMON KINGDOM         855
19 GALILEO II            867
20 EUREKA                868
21 TITANIC CITY          884
22 GALILEO II            899
23 DEMON KINGDOM         911
24 EUREKA                923
25 GALILEO II            924
26 PHOBIA                937
27 TERRA FIRMA           945
SOLVED IN 27 STEPS.


]RUN
17 LOCATIONS READ IN.
START AT : TROGSTAR BETA
1 MAXIMA CENTAURI         64
2 HELIOS                  94
3 NIKE                    98
4 APHRODITE              104
5 NIKE                   110
6 APHRODITE              116
7 NIKE                   122
8 HELIOS                 126
9 NIKE                   130
10 APHRODITE             136
11 TERRA FIRMA           143
SOLVED IN 11 STEPS.
```

In fact, it can be shown that the number of nodes examined in such a haphazard process is proportional to the square of the number of links intervening on the optimal route which is $5 \times 5 = 25$ in this case. In addition, the drunk wastes a lot of time with this particular set-up journeying to Hades and back. There is a moral there somewhere.

But, of course, we know we can do far better merely by examining nodes in a systematic fashion. We have paused to consider a random method because there are some problems, as we shall see, where controlled randomness is useful in reaching a solution. Methods that rely on random decisions are known as Monte Carlo methods, and they have an important place in certain branches of operational research and statistics where purely analytic solutions are prohibitively hard to compute.

A genuine Monte Carlo approach to the path-finding problem would involve generating not one but several Drunkard's Walks and retaining the best so far. The more attempts made, the more likely the drunkard will 'strike it lucky' and get close to an optimal path. In AI, such an approach would be called a Monkeys-with-Typewriters method, after the roomful of monkeys who bash away for aeons failing to write *Hamlet*. In its plain form it is infeasible, but some monkeys are smarter than others.

7.5 Graph traversal methods

From now on, all our search strategies will conform to a common pattern, illustrated by the flow chart in Fig. 7.3.

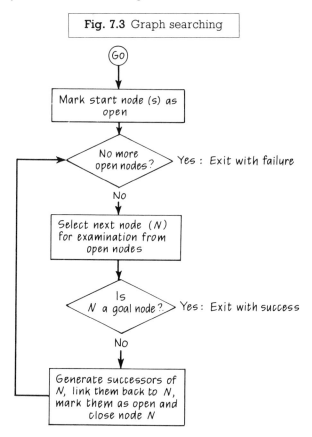

Fig. 7.3 Graph searching

The diagram shows the general outline of a family of AI search methods. A particular member of the family is selected by a particular choice of how to fill the central box, which decides which node is to be examined or investigated next (as a possible solution).

The terms 'open' and 'closed' refer to the status of any node on the solution path from starting point to goal. As the search unfolds, the program must decide which node to examine next. Open nodes are candidates for examination; closed nodes have already been dealt with. The key point is the order in which they are processed.

7.6 Breadth-first search

Breadth-first search brings us up to level 1, since it is a way of enumerating all possible nodes. It examines nodes in order of proximity to the start node. Thus it considers every sequence of N steps (arcs) before any sequence of $N+1$ steps. Though the search may be a long one, it is guaranteed to find a solution which takes the shortest number of steps.

However, if the steps are not equally costly, this may not be the optimal solution. In our case the connections are weighted, so that the arc from Eureka to Phobia takes 11 units but from Eureka to Umbria (also a single step) takes 25. For this task, as it happens, breadth-first search does not find the lowest-cost path.

The method is implemented in the program of Listing 7.3. A sample run is appended in which it discovers a route taking 121 time units. It is not optimal, but it is very much better than the random-search method.

Listing 7.3 Breadth-first search

```
10   REM    ***************************
11   REM    ** LISTING 7.3:          **
12   REM    ** BREADTH-FIRST SEARCH **
13   REM    ***************************
100  REM    -- BREADTH-1ST SEARCH:
110  GOSUB 1000: REM   GET THE DATA
115 N% = NC%
120 S% = 16: REM    STARTING POINT
130 D% = 5: REM    DESTINATION
140 TU% = 0: REM    TIME USED
150 NC% = 0: REM    NO. OF NODES EXAMINED
160 K% = 0: REM    COUNTER
170  GOSUB 2000: REM    CLEAR ALL PATHS
180 LX%(S%) = 1: REM    START NODE IS OPEN
188 PA%(S%) = 0: REM    COST SO FAR
190  REM  START LOOP
200  GOSUB 3000: REM    PICK NEXT NODE P%
210 NC% = NC% + 1:S% = P%
```

```
220   PRINT NC%;" ";NAME$(S%); SPC( 27 -  LEN (NAME$(S%)) -  LEN (
      STR$ (NC%)));PA%(S%)
230   GOSUB 4000: REM    GENERATE SUCCESSORS
240   IF S% = D% OR NC% > 100 THEN 250
245   GOTO 190
250   IF S% = D% THEN : GOSUB 5000: REM    RETRACE STEPS
255   IF S% < > D% THEN : PRINT "FAILED !"; CHR$ (7)
256   PRINT NC%;" NODES EXAMINED."
900   END
1000  REM    -- ROUTINE TO SET UP MAP-NET:
1010  DIM NAME$(20),LINK%(20)
1020  DIM NODE%(88),TI%(88)
1024  DIM PA%(20),PW%(20),LX%(20)
1030 NC% = 0:L% = 0
1040  REM   START LOOP
1050  READ N$,ID%
1060  IF ID% < > 0 THEN : GOSUB 1500
1070  IF ID% = 0 THEN 1080
1075  GOTO 1040
1080  PRINT NC%;" LOCATIONS READ IN."
1090  RETURN
1500  REM    -- INDIVIDUAL NODE & CONNECTIONS:
1510 NC% = NC% + 1
1520  IF ID% < > NC% THEN : PRINT "WARNING: NODE ";ID%;" OUT OF
      ORDER."
1530 NAME$(NC%) = N$
1540 LINK%(NC%) = L%
1550  REM   START LOOP
1560  READ NI%,NT%
1570 NODE%(L%) = NI%
1580 TI%(L%) = NT%
1588  REM    -- NODE AND TIME STORED.
1590 L% = L% + 1
1600  IF NI% < = 0 THEN 1610
1605  GOTO 1550
1610  RETURN
2000  REM    -- INITIALISATION ROUTINE:
2010  FOR I = 1 TO N%
2020 PA%(I) = 9999: REM    TIME TAKEN
2030 LX%(I) = 0: REM    OPENING ORDER
2040 PW%(I) = 0: REM    LINK BACK FOR RETRACE
2050  NEXT
2060  RETURN
3000  REM    -- PICK THE NEXT NODE :
3010  B% = 9999: REM   BEST COST
3020  P% = 0: REM   NEW NODE TO LOOK AT
3030  FOR I = 1 TO N%
3040  IF LX%(I) > 0 AND LX%(I) < B% THEN :B% = LX%(I):P% = I
3050  NEXT
3060  IF P% = 0 THEN : PRINT "WARNING: FAILURE!":NC% = 101
3070  RETURN
4000  REM    -- OPEN-SUCCESSORS ROUTINE:
4010  IF S% = D% THEN : RETURN
4020  REM    -- QUIT IF ALREADY THERE.
4030 L% = LINK%(S%)
```

```
4040    REM    START LOOP
4050    GOSUB 4400
4060    L% = L% + 1
4070    IF NODE%(L%) < = 0 THEN 4080
4075    GOTO 4040
4080    LX%(S%) = - 1: REM    CLOSED
4090    RETURN
4400    REM    -- OPEN ONE SUCCESSOR:
4410    IF NODE%(L%) = 0 THEN : RETURN
4420    R% = NODE%(L%)
4430    TU% = TI%(L%) + PA%(S%)
4440    REM    -- TIME USED SO FAR.
4450    IF LX%(R%) = 0 THEN : GOSUB 4800
4460    RETURN
4800    REM    -- LINK R% BACK TO ITS SOURCE:
4810    K% = K% + 1: REM    ORDER OF EXAMINATION.
4820    PA%(R%) = TU%
4830    LX%(R%) = K%
4840    PW%(R%) = S%: REM    WHERE IT CAME FROM
4850    RETURN
5000    REM    SHOW THE ROUTE BACKWARDS:
5010    P% = D%
5020    PRINT ".... THE PATH-WAY ...."
5030    REM    START LOOP
5040    PRINT P%;" ";NAME$(P%); SPC( 27 -  LEN (NAME$(P%)) -  LEN (
        STR$ (P%)));PA%(P%)
5050    P% = PW%(P%)
5060    IF P% < = 0 THEN 5070
5065    GOTO 5030
5070    PRINT
5080    RETURN
8000    REM    DATA FOR PLANETARY MAP:
8010    DATA    HELIOS,1
8020    DATA    2,4,17,30,0,0
8030    DATA    NIKE,2
8040    DATA    1,4,3,6,0,0
8050    DATA    APHRODITE,3
8060    DATA    2,6,5,7,0,0
8070    DATA    LUNA,4
8080    DATA    5,1,0,0
8090    DATA    TERRA FIRMA,5
8100    DATA    3,7,7,8,6,8,4,1,0,0
8110    DATA    DEMON KINGDOM,6
8120    DATA    5,8,7,1,9,12,8,12,0,0
8130    DATA    PHOBIA,7
8140    DATA    5,8,9,13,8,11,6,1,0,0
8150    DATA    EUREKA,8
8160    DATA    6,12,7,11,9,1,10,16,11,25,0,0
8170    DATA    GALILEO II,9
8180    DATA    10,15,8,1,6,12,7,13,0,0
8190    DATA    TITANIC CITY,10
8200    DATA    9,15,12,24,11,20,8,16,0,0
8210    DATA    UMBRIA,11
8220    DATA    8,25,10,20,12,17,13,28,0,0
8230    DATA    TRIDENT,12
```

```
8240  DATA   10,24,14,22,13,20,11,17,0,0
8250  DATA   LIMBO,13
8260  DATA   12,20,14,1,16,48,15,23,11,28,0,0
8270  DATA   SUNSET BOULEVARD,14
8280  DATA   12,22,13,1,0,0
8290  DATA   HADES,15
8300  DATA   13,223,16,232,0,0
8310  DATA   TROGSTAR BETA,16
8320  DATA   13,48,17,64,15,32,0,0
8330  DATA   MAXIMA CENTAURI,17
8340  DATA   16,64,1,30,0,0
8350  DATA   NOWHERE,0
8360  REM    -- THAT'S ALL FOLKS !

]RUN
17 LOCATIONS READ IN.
1 TROGSTAR BETA            0
2 LIMBO                    48
3 MAXIMA CENTAURI          64
4 HADES                    32
5 TRIDENT                  68
6 SUNSET BOULEVARD         49
7 UMBRIA                   76
8 HELIOS                   94
9 TITANIC CITY             92
10 EUREKA                  101
11 NIKE                    98
12 GALILEO II              107
13 DEMON KINGDOM           113
14 PHOBIA                  112
15 APHRODITE               104
16 TERRA FIRMA             121
.... THE PATH-WAY ....
5 TERRA FIRMA              121
6 DEMON KINGDOM            113
8 EUREKA                   101
11 UMBRIA                  76
13 LIMBO                   48
16 TROGSTAR BETA           0

16 NODES EXAMINED.
```

The important routines are as follows:

3000   Pick the next node to examine.
4000   Open the successors of the current node.
4400   Open a single successor node.

The program displays each node as it considers it, and shows the final route (in reverse order) when it has been found. The routine at line 3000 is the one that makes this a breadth-first process. In order to do so, it employs three extra arrays, defined in the DIM statement at line 1024,

$PA\%(I)$ Cost so far from start to node I.
$PW\%(I)$ Pointer to the predecessor of node I, for retracing the route.
$LX\%(I)$ Whether I is open or shut.

The $LX\%$ array contains 0 for unexamined nodes, -1 for closed nodes, and a positive number for open nodes. This number gives the order in which the node was placed on the open list, calculated with the help of a counter $K\%$. In this program a node is never re-opened once it has been closed (although there are circumstances when re-opening on a newly found shorter route may become necessary).

By drawing a diagram of the search tree as it is created, we can see how the process works.

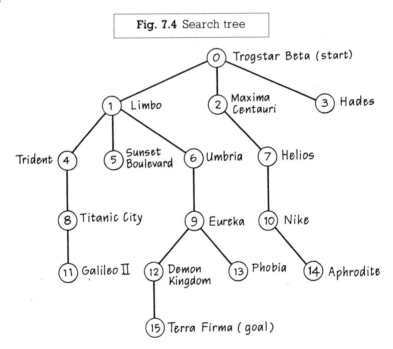

Fig. 7.4 Search tree

The numbering of the nodes in Fig. 7.4 shows the order in which they were opened, and governs the search process. When each successor node is generated it is, in effect, placed on a queue to wait its turn before its successors are generated. All the nodes at one level of the tree are dealt with before proceeding to the next level down – hence the name. No nodes are examined more than once by this program, so many potential branches are pruned off the tree. For instance, the link from Umbria to Titanic City is never developed because Titanic City has been reached from Trident (step 8) before Umbria's successors are opened. This cures the drunkard's main problem of backtracking to a previously visited node.

7.6.1 Improving on breadth-first search

This is a blind-search process in the sense that it uses no knowledge about the problem. We can improve it by altering subroutine 3000 to pick the node which is the shortest distance from the start, rather than the fewest steps from the start. This minor modification has been made for Listing 7.4, to take account of the weights on the arcs of our graph. (Only the changed portions are shown. The rest is as in Listing 7.3.)

Listing 7.4 Least-cost-first search

```
10   REM      ****************************
11   REM      ** LISTING 7.4:          **
12   REM      ** LEAST-COST-1ST SEARCH **
13   REM      ****************************


]LIST 3000,3070

3000  REM  -- PICK THE NEXT NODE:
3010  B% = 9999: REM  BEST COST
3020  P% = 0: REM  NEW NODE TO LOOK AT
3030   FOR I = 1 TO N%
3040   IF PA%(I) < B% AND LX%(I) > 0 THEN :B% = PA%(I):P% = I
3050   NEXT
3060   IF P% = 0 THEN : PRINT "WARNING: FAILURE!":NC% = 101
3070   RETURN


]RUN
17 LOCATIONS READ IN.
1 TROGSTAR BETA          0
2 HADES                  32
3 LIMBO                  48
4 SUNSET BOULEVARD       49
5 MAXIMA CENTAURI        64
6 TRIDENT                68
7 UMBRIA                 76
8 TITANIC CITY           92
9 HELIOS                 94
10 NIKE                  98
11 EUREKA                101
12 APHRODITE             104
```

```
13 GALILEO II              107
14 TERRA FIRMA             111
.... THE PATH-WAY ....
5 TERRA FIRMA              111
3 APHRODITE                104
2 NIKE                      98
1 HELIOS                    94
17 MAXIMA CENTAURI          64
16 TROGSTAR BETA             0

14 NODES EXAMINED.
```

As you can see the program now finds a better route (the quickest in fact) and examines slightly fewer nodes, though it still looks at 14 out of the 17 before finding the solution.

To make it better still, we must take account of additional heuristic information (the 'warm' versus 'cold' of Hunt the Thimble). It would appear that we do not have any in this instance, but in fact we do.

What we want is an estimate of how near the search is to its goal. If you look back at the original map (Fig. 7.1) you will see that the nodes are numbered in an orderly manner from the top downwards. On the whole, therefore, the smaller the numeric difference between two node numbers, the closer they are on the map. Thus node 12 is closer to node 13 than, say, node 4.

When you look at the map you see at a glance that nodes 2 and 3, for example, are close together. The numbering scheme enables the computer to do something similar. The main snag is that Helios (node 1) and Maxima Centauri (node 17) are linked so their map-distance does not correspond very well to the time needed to pass from one to the other.

Nevertheless, by altering subroutine 3000 to pick the open node which is closest to the destination, as estimated from the node numbers, we can implement the nearest-first search method. See Listing 7.5, line 3033.

Listing 7.5 Best-first search

```
10   REM   **************************
11   REM   ** LISTING 7.5:        **
12   REM   ** BEST-FIRST SEARCH   **
13   REM   **************************

]LIST 3000,3070

3000  REM  -- PICK THE NEXT NODE:
3010  B% = 9999: REM  BEST COST
3020  P% = 0: REM  NEW NODE TO LOOK AT
3030  FOR I = 1 TO N%
```

```
3033 HD% =  ABS (I - D%): REM  HEURISTIC DISTANCE
3040   IF HD% < B% AND LX%(I) > 0 THEN :B% = HD%:P% = I
3050   NEXT
3060   IF P% = 0 THEN : PRINT "WARNING: FAILURE!":NC% = 101
3070   RETURN


]RUN
17 LOCATIONS READ IN.
1 TROGSTAR BETA             0
2 LIMBO                     48
3 UMBRIA                    76
4 EUREKA                    101
5 DEMON KINGDOM             113
6 TERRA FIRMA               121
.... THE PATH-WAY ....
5 TERRA FIRMA               121
6 DEMON KINGDOM             113
8 EUREKA                    101
11 UMBRIA                   76
13 LIMBO                    48
16 TROGSTAR BETA            0

6 NODES EXAMINED.
```

Now it homes in straight on the target, looking at only six nodes; and there are only six nodes on the route. The problem is that the route itself is no longer optimal (121 versus 111 time units). The computer has taken the obvious rather than the optimal route.

This method is also known as 'hill climbing' by analogy with attempting to find the top of a hill in thick fog. A sensible plan is to keep ascending – though this plan may lead you up a lesser peak rather than the summit itself.

For some purposes hill climbing might be satisfactory, but what we require is a way of finding the quickest route which does no more work than necessary.

7.7 The A* algorithm

The method is called the A* (A-star) algorithm, and it involves a compromise between nearest-first (Listing 7.5) and least-first (Listing 7.4) search.

The A* search fits into the framework we have developed. It differs from the methods so far described in the way it selects which node to examine next (subroutine 3000). This is based on two quantities

(1) the cost so far from the start and

(2) the estimated future cost to the destination

which are added together. The node with the lowest total cost-so-far + estimated-cost is the one to look at next. The idea behind this algorithm is to stay on what appears to be the best path at all times. In our version (Listing 7.6) we use $PA\%(I)$ to find the cost already incurred to reach node I and $HD\%$ as a heuristic estimate of the future cost of getting from I to the destination. $HD\%$ is based on the difference between the node numbers, as described earlier. See line 3033. A listing and run is shown below.

Listing 7.6 A-star algorithm

```
10  REM    ***************************
11  REM    ** LISTING 7.6:         **
12  REM    ** A-STAR ALGORITHM     **
13  REM    ***************************


]LIST 3000,3070

3000  REM  -- PICK THE NEXT NODE:
3010  B% = 9999: REM  BEST COST
3020  P% = 0: REM  NEW NODE TO LOOK AT
3030  FOR I = 1 TO N%
3033  HD% =  ABS (I - D%): REM  HEURISTIC DISTANCE
3035  V% = HD% + PA%(I)
3040  IF V% < B% AND LX%(I) > 0 THEN :B% = V%:P% = I
3050  NEXT
3060  IF P% = 0 THEN : PRINT "WARNING: FAILURE!":NC% = 101
3070  RETURN


]RUN
17 LOCATIONS READ IN.
1 TROGSTAR BETA              0
2 HADES                     32
3 LIMBO                     48
4 SUNSET BOULEVARD          49
5 TRIDENT                   68
6 MAXIMA CENTAURI           64
7 UMBRIA                    76
8 TITANIC CITY              92
9 HELIOS                    94
10 NIKE                     98
11 EUREKA                  101
12 APHRODITE               104
13 TERRA FIRMA             111
.... THE PATH-WAY ....
5 TERRA FIRMA              111
3 APHRODITE                104
2 NIKE                      98
```

```
1 HELIOS                    94
17 MAXIMA CENTAURI          64
16 TROGSTAR BETA            0

13 NODES EXAMINED.
```

Now the program finds the optimal route after examining 13 nodes. If we tabulate the results so far we can see how the methods compare.

Method	Nodes	Cost
7.2 Drunkard's Walk	29	910.5 (ave)
7.3 Breadth-first search	16	121
7.4 Least-cost-first search	14	111
7.5 Hill climbing	6	121
7.6 A* (best-first search)	13	111

Only two of the methods find the quickest route, and of those the A* algorithm finds it marginally sooner.

By altering $S\%$ (start) and $D\%$ (destination) on lines 120 and 130 you can experiment with the A* program and make it seek a path from any node to any other. It is not always equally quick to find the solution in both directions; but it will always find the minimum-cost path, provided that the heuristic estimate of closeness to the goal ($HD\%$) never overestimates the true cost. If the heuristic errs, as it must, it should err by underestimating the true cost remaining.

It has been proved that, as long as the heuristic never overestimates the true future cost, this method is optimal in the sense that it does not examine more nodes than any other method of using the same information when finding the quickest route. Whether it is genuinely optimal for a given application depends on the trade-offs you are willing to make. For example, you may be prepared to accept a slightly less than optimal path if the time taken to find it is substantially reduced. If this is so, you can weight the heuristic estimate as more important than the cost incurred so far when deciding which node to examine next. For example, on line 3035,

V% = 2*HD% + PA%(I)

thus tending more towards hill-climbing than least-cost-first search.

In fact most real-life problems are not concerned with optimizing a single measure, but with satisfying a number of constraints. The constraints may interlock so that improvements in one direction cause deterioration in another. The problem is then to find a satisfactory balance rather than an optimal solution.

7.8 The grand tour

One well-known problem where an optimal solution is, in general, out of the question is the grand tour, also known as the travelling-salesman problem (TSP).

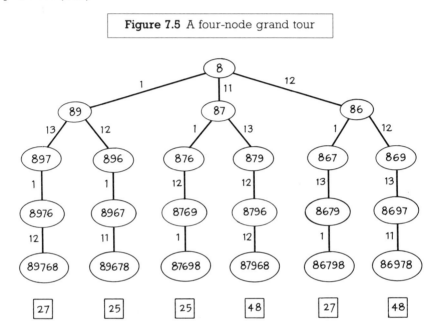

Figure 7.5 A four-node grand tour

Figure 7.5 shows a table of inter-node distances for four of the space-ports extracted from the map of Fig. 7.1. Below it is the complete search tree for a grand tour starting and ending at node number 8 (Eureka) and visiting the other three locations once each. The first level of the tree has three branches, corresponding to the three choices of which node to visit first. The second level has two and the third and fourth levels have one, since there are by then no alternatives.

Because the inter-node distances are in this particular case symmetrical, the round-trip costs are paired. For example, trips 89768 and 86798 are inverses of one another and have the same total, 27 time units. The shortest route turns out to be 89678 or its inverse 87698 (Eureka–Phobia–Demon Kingdom–Galileo–Eureka).

This might seem trivial, but the TSP is usually posed in connection with touring the 48 state capitals of the continental USA, excluding Alaska. The travelling salesman is given a 48 × 48 table of inter-city distances, and his problem is to visit each city once and return to his starting point by the shortest possible route. It turns out that there are more potential routes to consider than atoms in the known universe! At the first choice point there are 47 possibilities, each of these 47 leads to 46 successors, each of them gives rise to a further 45, and so on.

It can be shown that for N cities the number of routes is factorial $(N-1)$ or $(N-1)!$ where $M!$ denotes $M \times (M-1) \times (M-2) \ldots \times 3 \times 2 \times 1$. Thus 4! is

$$4 \times 3 \times 2 \times 1 = 24$$

and 6! is

$$6 \times 5 \times 4 \times 3 \times 2 \times 1 = 720$$

Even with the 17 locations of our hypothetical spacemap the number of potential routes confronting the would-be grand tourist is 16! which is more than

20 000 000 000 000 (twenty million million)

In our example most of those routes would be debarred since some pairs of nodes are not connected at all. (Actually the map as it stands does not permit a proper grand tour since it is impossible to visit Luna without passing Terra Firma twice, and would therefore need additional links for this problem.)

The point is that the grand tour or TSP is, in general, a much more complex problem than that of finding the shortest point-to-point route. It is, in fact, our first encounter with the so-called 'combinatorial explosion' – the exponential growth in the complexity of a multi-step task as the number of options at each decision point increases. The unmodified A* algorithm cannot cope with such complexity; and an exhaustive search would exhaust time itself.

In such situations it becomes necessary to 'prune' branches from the search tree. That may entail discarding some partially explored pathways without knowing for sure whether they lead to a solution.

An intelligent method of pruning is one that can tell a 'hopeless' potential solution from a 'promising' one. Once again we need a source of heuristic information: often it will be possible to make use of the same heuristic as used to guide the A* search, or one that has been only slightly modified.

When the A* algorithm is modified to discard unpromising paths it is called the beam search, because it is like a beam of light moving through the search space but only illuminating a small patch at any one time.

7.9 The tile puzzle

Let us give our interplanetary traveller a well-deserved rest and look at a non-spatial problem to see how the beam search deals with the combinatorial explosion. We will try it out on the 15-tile puzzle, which provides an opportunity to extend the search metaphor to a search space defined not by any kind of map but by the rules of a game.

Fig. 7.6 Fifteen-tile puzzle

1	6	5	12
4	2	10	13
15	11	8	9
3		14	7

The tile puzzle is played on a grid of 4 squares × 4 squares, as in Fig. 7.6 (You may also have seen the 3 × 3 version which is considerably less challenging.) Each tile is numbered and one square is left vacant. A move consists of sliding one of the tiles that is adjacent to the empty square into that space, e.g in Fig. 7.6 the 11, 14 or 3 could be moved into the empty square. The objective is to arrange the tiles in some desired configuration, typically in ascending numerical order, as in Fig. 7.7.

Fig. 7.7 Goal state

1	2	3	4
5	6	7	8
9	10	11	12
13	14	15	

The fewer moves it takes to reach the desired arrangement, the better.

The search tree is grown from the root (the starting configuration) by applying the legal moves (operators) to generate the resulting configurations at the first level, then doing so again at the next level down, as illustrated in Fig. 7.8

In the diagram the moves are labelled N, E, W, S since the simplest way to think about a move is as a shift of the blank space (north, east, west or south). Notice that the sequence of moves N–S brings the grid back, as you would expect, to its initial state – which is something to avoid. Each node

Fig. 7.8 Partial tile puzzle search tree

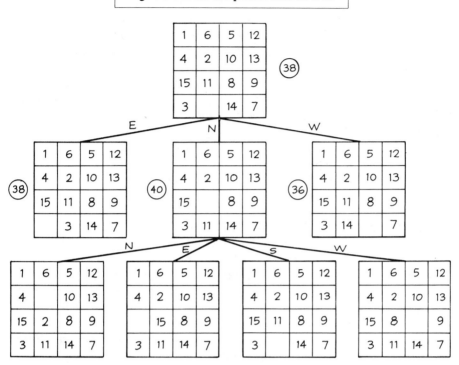

in the tree corresponds to a particular board state, and the path down from the route defines a sequence of operators (moves) to arrive at that state. The tree is grown until a solution is reached, or, more likely, till memory is filled with nodes waiting to be examined.

Overflow occurs, even with this simple game, because each node has on average approximately three successors. This implies that a 20-move solution would require at least 3^{20} (about 3.5 billion) nodes in the search tree – far too many to hold at one time.

When memory is full up, it will be necessary to call a 'garbage collection' routine. For this to work we need a heuristic that can discriminate nodes that are unlikely to lie on the solution path from those that are likely to do so. For simplicity, we will use the same heuristic that guides the search in the first place (though sometimes this is not advisable).

A suitable measure is the 'Manhattan Distance'. On Manhattan Island most streets and avenues intersect at right angles, so the natives reckon distance as, for example, four blocks north and three blocks east. To apply Manhattan Distance (*MD*) to the tile puzzle we simply add up the horizontal and vertical distance of every tile from its destination.

In the root node of Fig. 7.8, tile 1 is no distance from its desired location, tile 2 is one place vertically, tile 3 is five places (three vertical plus two horizontal) and so on. The total displacement of all 16 pieces, including the empty square, is 38. This heuristic value is obviously related to the distance from the goal state; and it reduces to zero when all tiles are in position, i.e. when the puzzle is solved.

Of the three immediate successor nodes in Fig. 7.8, the leftmost branch (E) leads to a score of 38, the same as its parent; the middle one (N) scores 40, worse than the root; and the rightmost (W) scores 36, which is an improvement. (A move south is not possible.) The third, therefore, appears to be the most promising, and should have been expanded before the middle one.

Our evaluation function will be based on the sum

$$MD + SF$$

where *MD* is the total Manhattan Distance of the 16 tiles, as explained above, and *SF* is the number of steps taken to reach that state. The program will try to minimize this quantity. *SF* is necessary as well as *MD* to avoid deep search of a superficially promising blind alley. *MD* approximates quite well to the number of moves actually needed to reach the solution (though it does tend to overestimate).

This sum will serve to guide the decision of what node to expand next, as in the A* search: we simply pick the node with the lowest score. When it comes to garbage collection, things get a litle more complicated. One attractive possibility would be to go through all the nodes of the search tree, compute the average score, and drop all those that are greater than average, freeing the storage they occupied. The problem is that this would inevitably prune away the deeper nodes in the tree (including some which may be on the solution path) only to re-grow them later. A secondary problem is that this could have the effect of severing the link back from child to parent node if the child was more promising than its parent, leaving dangling branches in the tree.

Both these difficulties are resolved by confining our attention to leaf nodes only – considering for deletion only those nodes at the tip of the tree which are worse than average. The parent nodes are closed anyway and will never be re-opened. The leaf nodes represent the growing edge of the search process and some of them, those that are better than average, are bound to survive the pruning.

Even with this system, available storage may become exhausted if the solution path is long compared with the number of nodes which can be accommodated in memory. It could be that the number of nodes released by pruning is less than the number of successors to be generated by expanding from the currently most-promising node. In such a case a more drastic form of purge would be necessary. The program would have to print out the path to the best node found so far, retain only that node as the root of a new search tree, and continue from there. This does not, however, guarantee that an optimal solution will be found; and we will not require this more drastic form of pruning in our example program.

7.9.1 The tile-puzzle program

Our implementation of the beam search is given as Listing 7.7. Before presenting the BASIC code, however, we show here a skeleton of the main program in a pseudo-code form.

```
select level of difficulty
jumble up the board                          [1000]
initialize the search tree                   [2000]
REPEAT
        pick next open node to examine    [3000]
        display it                        [3500]
        open its successors               [4000]
        prune tree if full up             [5000]
UNTIL solved OR exhausted
retrace solution path                        [6000]
END
```

The number in square brackets on the right refer to subroutines in the BASIC listing.

The search cannot be accomplished without supporting data structures for the search tree. These are held in four arrays, described below.

$ST\$(N\%)$ Board state of node $N\%$, as a string.

$PW\%(N\%)$ Path back from $N\%$ to its predecessor, plus code for direction taken $0=N$, $1=E$, $2=S$, $3=W$.

$SF\%(N\%)$ Steps so far taken to reach node $N\%$ (9999 indicating a dead node).

$MD\%(N\%)$ Manhattan Distance of node $N\%$ from the goal (negative to mark $N\%$ as closed).

Thus each node in the tree has four items of information associated with it. A string representation of the board state, with letters A–O standing for tiles 1–15, was chosen to keep things simple yet reasonably compact. There are better ways of doing it, but not without stooping to tricky code involving PEEKs and POKEs or worse.

With this string representation the target configuration becomes the 16-character string 'ABCDEFGHIJKLMNOP' and a move consists of swapping the P (representing the blank space) with another character. The move routine begins at line 1200 in the listing.

The other main data structure is the array

MT%(16,3)

which is created in subroutine 1500 and used at line 4070

PP% = MT%(P%,D)

in the generation of the next move. This line sets *PP%* to the position in the string obtained by moving the blank square from position *P%* in direction *D*, where *D* is $0 = N$, $1 = E$, $2 = S$, $3 = W$. Note that the expression $ABS(D - DD\%)$ on line 4090 is included to prevent immediate backtracking (i.e. north–south or east–west or vice versa) which would be futile.

The program proved capable of solving the puzzle from positions up to 23 steps removed from the solution. A few reasonably easy solutions are shown. Above 20 or so steps the present pruning system proved inadequate; but the number of possible paths of that length, even excluding immediate back-steps, is well over a million, so the program was hardly disgraced.

Listing 7.7 15-puzzle program

```
10   REM    **************************
11   REM    ** LISTING 7.7  '      **
12   REM    ** 15-PUZZLE PROGRAM   **
13   REM    **************************
100  REM     -- THE TILE GAME BY BEAM SEARCH:
105  DEF  FN MOD(I) =  INT ((I / 4 -  INT (I / 4)) * 4 + .05) *  SGN
     (I / 4)
110  SIZE% = 200
120   DIM ST$(SIZE%),PW%(SIZE%)
130   DIM SF%(SIZE%),MD%(SIZE%)
140   GOSUB 1500: REM   MAKE MOVE TABLE
150   HOME : INPUT "LEVEL OF DIFFICULTY (1-100) ";LD%
160  NN% = 0:DEAD% = 9999
170  NC% = 0
175  S% = 0
180  NX% = 0
200   GOSUB 1000: REM   JUMBLE THE BOARD
220   GOSUB 2000: REM   INITIALIZE SEARCH TREE
230  OK% = 0
240   REM    -- MAIN LOOP
250   REM    START LOOP
260   GOSUB 3000: REM   PICK NEXT NODE S%
270  NC% = NC% + 1
280   GOSUB 3500: REM    DISPLAY BOARD
```

```
290   PRINT "STEP ";NC%
300   IF G$ = S$ THEN :OK% = 1
310   IF OK% = 0 THEN : GOSUB 4000
320   REM    -- OPENS SUCCESSORS.
350   IF OK% = 1 OR NC% > 256 THEN 360
355   GOTO 250
360   IF OK% = 1 THEN : GOSUB 6000
370   REM    -- RETRACES PATH TO SOLUTION.
400   END
1000   REM    -- BOARD JUMBLING ROUTINE:
1010   B$ = "P": REM   CHAR FOR BLANK SQUARE.
1020   G$ = "ABCDEFGHIJKLMNOP"
1022   S$ = G$
1030   FOR I = 0 TO LD%
1039   P% = 0
1040   FOR J = 1 TO  LEN (G$) -  LEN (B$) + 1
1041   IF B$ =  MID$ (G$,J, LEN (B$)) THEN :P% = J:J =  LEN (G$)
1042   NEXT J
1050   D% =  RND (1) * 4: REM    RANDOM DIRECTION
1060   PP% = MT%(P%,D%)
1070   IF PP% > 0 THEN : GOSUB 1200
1080   NEXT I
1090   REM    -- G$ IS JUMBLED BOARD STATE.
1100   RETURN
1200   REM    -- MAKE MOVE P% TO PP% ON G$:
1205   X$ =  MID$ (G$,PP%,1)
1206   A$ = "": IF PP% > 1 THEN :A$ =  LEFT$ (G$,PP% - 1)
1210   G$ = A$ + B$ +  MID$ (G$,PP% + 1)
1215   A$ = "": IF P% > 1 THEN :A$ =  LEFT$ (G$,P% - 1)
1220   G$ = A$ + X$ +  MID$ (G$,P% + 1)
1230   RETURN
1240   REM    -- EASIER IF MID$ CAN BE ASSIGNED TO.
1500   REM    -- CREATE LEGAL MOVE TABLE:
1510   DIM MT%(16,3)
1520   REM   DIRECTIONS: ON, 1E, 2S, 3W
1530   FOR I = 1 TO 16
1540   REM    N=0
1550   IF I < 5 THEN :MT%(I,0) = 0
1555   IF I > = 5 THEN :MT%(I,0) = I - 4
1560   REM    E=1
1570   IF  FN MOD(I) = 0 THEN :MT%(I,1) = 0
1575   IF  FN MOD(I) < > 0 THEN :MT%(I,1) = I + 1
1580   REM    S=2
1590   IF I > 12 THEN :MT%(I,2) = 0
1595   IF I < = 12 THEN :MT%(I,2) = I + 4
1600   REM    W=3
1610   IF  FN MOD(I) = 1 THEN :MT%(I,3) = 0
1615   IF  FN MOD(I) < > 1 THEN :MT%(I,3) = I - 1
1620   NEXT I
1630   REM    0 SIGNIFIES ILLEGAL MOVE.
1640   RETURN
2000   REM    -- CLEAR THE SEARCH TREE:
2010   NULL$ = " "
2020   FOR I = 1 TO SIZE%
2030   ST$(I) = NULL$
```

```
2040  PW%(I) = 0
2050  SF%(I) = DEAD%
2060  MD%(I) = DEAD%
2070  NEXT
2080  REM    -- OPEN WITH GOAL AS ROOT:
2090  ST$(0) = G$
2100  PW%(0) = 9
2110  SF%(0) = 0
2120  GOSUB 2200: REM   MANHATTAN DISTANCE.
2130  MD%(0) = MH%
2140  RETURN
2200  REM    -- COMPUTE M.D. OF G$ IN MH%:
2210  MH% = 0
2220  FOR I = 1 TO 16
2230  IX% = ASC ( MID$ (G$,I,1)) - 65
2240  RD% = INT (IX% / 4) - INT ((I - 1) / 4)
2244  RD% = ABS (RD%)
2250  CD% = FN MOD(IX%) - FN MOD(I - 1)
2252  CD% = ABS (CD%)
2255  IF IX% = 15 THEN :RD% = 0:CD% = 0
2256  IF IX% < 8 AND RD% > 0 THEN :RD% = RD% + 1
2257  IF IX% < 7 AND CD% > 0 THEN :CD% = CD% + 1
2260  MH% = MH% + RD% + CD%
2270  NEXT
2275  MH% = MH% * 2
2280  RETURN
2290  REM    -- SUMS ROW AND COLUMN DISTANCE
3000  REM    -- PICK NEXT NODE S%:
3010  S% = 0:B% = DEAD%
3020  FOR I = 1 TO SIZE%
3030  V% = SF%(I) + ABS (MD%(I))
3040  IF V% < B% AND MD%(I) > = 0 THEN :S% = I:B% = V%
3050  NEXT
3060  IF S% = 0 THEN : PRINT "HELP!"
3070  G$ = ST$(S%): REM   CURRENT NODE
3080  RETURN
3500  REM    -- DISPLAY BOARD STATE S%/G$ :
3501  VTAB 10: HTAB 1
3505  PRINT  SPC( 15);S%;" <- "; INT (PW%(S%) / 10); SPC( 10): PRINT
      : PRINT
3510  FOR I = 1 TO 16
3520  X% = ASC ( MID$ (G$,I,1)) - 64
3530  IF X% = 16 THEN : PRINT "   *";
3535  IF X% < > 16 THEN : PRINT  SPC( 4 - LEN ( STR$ (X%)));X%;

3540  IF  FN MOD(I) = 0 THEN : PRINT
3550  NEXT
3555  PRINT : PRINT  SPC( 15);SF%(S%);" "; ABS (MD%(S%)); SPC( 10
      )
3560  PRINT
3570  RETURN
4000  REM    -- OPEN SUCCESSORS OF NODE S%
4020  IF OK% THEN : RETURN
4030  DD% = INT ((PW%(S%) / 10 - INT (PW%(S%) / 10)) * 10 + .05)
      * SGN (PW%(S%) / 10): REM    PRIOR DIRECTION
```

```
4040 P% = 0
4041  FOR J = 1 TO  LEN (ST$(S%)) -  LEN (B$) + 1
4042  IF  MID$ (ST$(S%),J, LEN (B$)) = B$ THEN :P% = J:J =  LEN (
     ST$(S%))
4043  NEXT J
4050 C% = SF%(S%)
4060  FOR D = 0 TO 3
4070 PP% = MT%(P%,D)
4080 G$ = ST$(S%)
4090  IF PP% = 0 OR  ABS (D - DD%) = 2 THEN 4200
4100  GOSUB 1200: REM   REVISE G$
4110  GOSUB 4400: REM   FIND FREE LOC.
4120 ST$(NN%) = G$
4130 PW%(NN%) = S% * 10 + D
4140 SF%(NN%) = C% + 1
4150  GOSUB 2200
4160 MD%(NN%) = MH%
4200  NEXT D
4210  REM   -- ALSO CLOSE NODE S% :
4220 MD%(S%) =  - MD%(S%)
4222  IF MD%(S%) > 0 THEN : PRINT "UGH!"
4230  RETURN
4400  REM    -- FIND NEXT FREE LOCATION :
4410 NX% = 0
4420  REM   START LOOP
4430  IF SF%(NN%) < > DEAD% THEN :NX% = NX% + 1:NN% = NN% + 1
4435  IF NN% > SIZE% THEN :NN% = 0
4436  IF NX% > SIZE% THEN :NX% = 0: GOSUB 5000
4440  IF SF%(NN%) = DEAD% THEN 4460
4450  GOTO 4420
4460  RETURN
5000  REM   -- GARBAGE COLLECTION ROUTINE:
5010 GV = 0:GC = 0
5020  FOR G = 1 TO SIZE%
5030 V = SF%(G) +  ABS (MD%(G))
5040  IF MD%(G) > 0 THEN :GC = GC + 1:GV = GV + V
5050  NEXT
5060 GV = GV / GC
5070  REM   AVERAGE.
5080 GK% = 0
5090  FOR G = 1 TO SIZE%
5100 V = SF%(G) +  ABS (MD%(G))
5110  IF MD%(G) > 0 AND  V > GV THEN :SF%(G) = DEAD%:GK% = GK% + 1

5120  NEXT
5130  PRINT : PRINT "GARBAGE COLLECTION:"
5133  PRINT "PRESS A KEY TO GO ON:"
5135  GET X$
5140  PRINT GC;" OPEN NODES, MEAN VAL. ";GV
5150  PRINT GK%;" NODES FREED."
5155  IF GK% < 2 THEN : PRINT "I GIVE UP !": STOP
5160  RETURN
6000  REM   -- RETRACE SOLUTION PATH:
6010  PRINT "PRESS ANY KEY TO SEE SOLUTION"
```

```
6015   DIM PA%(LD%)
6020   GET K$
6030 K% = 0
6040   REM    START LOOP
6060 K% = K% + 1
6070   PRINT K%,S%
6080 PA%(K%) = S%
6090 Q% =  INT ((PW%(S%) / 10 -  INT (PW%(S%) / 10)) * 10 + .05) *
       SGN (PW%(S%) / 10)
6100 S% = PW%(S%) / 10
6110   IF Q% = 9 OR S% = 0 THEN 6120
6115   GOTO 6040
6120   PRINT "FOUND IN ";K%;" STEPS."
6122   PRINT NC%;" NODES CLOSED."
6123   PRINT :S% = 0:G$ = ST$(S%): PRINT "PRESS ANY KEY TO CONTINU
       E ";: GET A$: PRINT : HOME
6124   GOSUB 3500
6125   REM    START LOOP
6130 S% = PA%(K%)
6140 G$ = ST$(S%)
6150   PRINT : GOSUB 3500
6160 K% = K% - 1: IF K% < = 0 THEN 6190
6170   GOTO 6125
6190   RETURN
```

```
]RUN
LEVEL OF DIFFICULTY (1-100) 17
HELP!
                0 <- 0

    1    2   3    4
    5   10   6    8
    9   14   7   12
   13    *  11   15

                0 16
STEP 1
                1 <- 0

    1    2   3    4
    5   10   6    8
    9    *   7   12
   13   14  11   15

                1 14
STEP 2
                4 <- 1

    1    2   3    4
    5    *   6    8
    9   10   7   12
   13   14  11   15
```

```
                    2 12
STEP 3
                    8 <- 4

    1    2    3    4
    5    6    *    8
    9   10    7   12
   13   14   11   15

                    3 8
STEP 4
                   12 <- 8

    1    2    3    4
    5    6    7    8
    9   10    *   12
   13   14   11   15

                    4 4
STEP 5
                   14 <- 12

    1    2    3    4
    5    6    7    8
    9   10   11   12
   13   14    *   15

                    5 2
STEP 6
                   16 <- 14

    1    2    3    4
    5    6    7    8
    9   10   11   12
   13   14   15    *

                    6 0
STEP 7
PRESS ANY KEY TO SEE SOLUTION
1                  16
2                  14
3                  12
4                   8
5                   4
6                   1
FOUND IN 6 STEPS.
7 NODES CLOSED.

PRESS ANY KEY TO CONTINUE
                    0 <- 0

    1    2    3    4
    5   10    6    8
    9   14    7   12
   13    *   11   15
```

```
                    0 16

                    1 <- 0

  1   2   3   4
  5  10   6   8
  9   *   7  12
 13  14  11  15

                    1 14

                    4 <- 1

  1   2   3   4
  5   *   6   8
  9  10   7  12
 13  14  11  15

                    2 12

                    8 <- 4

  1   2   3   4
  5   6   *   8
  9  10   7  12
 13  14  11  15

                    3 8

                   12 <- 8

  1   2   3   4
  5   6   7   8
  9  10   *  12
 13  14  11  15

                    4 4

                   14 <- 12

  1   2   3   4
  5   6   7   8
  9  10  11  12
 13  14   *  15

                    5 2

                   16 <- 14

  1   2   3   4
  5   6   7   8
  9  10  11  12
 13  14  15   *

                    6 0
```

```
]RUN
LEVEL OF DIFFICULTY (1-100) 19
HELP!
                    0 <- 0

    5   1   3   4
    2  10   6   8
    *   9   7  11
   13  14  15  12

                    0 32
STEP 1
                    2 <- 0

    5   1   3   4
    2  10   6   8
    9   *   7  11
   13  14  15  12

                    1 30
STEP 2
                    4 <- 2

    5   1   3   4
    2   *   6   8
    9  10   7  11
   13  14  15  12

                    2 28
STEP 3
                    8 <- 4

    5   1   3   4
    2   6   *   8
    9  10   7  11
   13  14  15  12

                    3 24
STEP 4
                   12 <- 8

    5   1   3   4
    2   6   7   8
    9  10   *  11
   13  14  15  12

                    4 20
STEP 5
                   13 <- 12

    5   1   3   4
    2   6   7   8
    9  10  11   *
   13  14  15  12
```

```
                        5 18
STEP 6
                      17 <- 13

    5    1    3    4
    2    6    7    8
    9   10   11   12
   13   14   15    *

                        6 16
STEP 7
                      18 <- 17

    5    1    3    4
    2    6    7    8
    9   10   11   12
   13   14    *   15

                        7 18
STEP 8
                       9 <- 4

    5    1    3    4
    *    2    6    8
    9   10    7   11
   13   14   15   12

                        3 24
STEP 9
                      21 <- 9

    *    1    3    4
    5    2    6    8
    9   10    7   11
   13   14   15   12

                        4 20
STEP 10
                      23 <- 21

    1    *    3    4
    5    2    6    8
    9   10    7   11
   13   14   15   12

                        5 16
STEP 11
                      25 <- 23

    1    2    3    4
    5    *    6    8
    9   10    7   11
   13   14   15   12

                        6 12
```

STEP 12

```
                26 <- 25

   1    2    3    4
   5    6    *    8
   9   10    7   11
  13   14   15   12
```

```
                7 8
```

STEP 13

```
                31 <- 26

   1    2    3    4
   5    6    7    8
   9   10    *   11
  13   14   15   12
```

```
                8 4
```

STEP 14

```
                32 <- 31

   1    2    3    4
   5    6    7    8
   9   10   11    *
  13   14   15   12
```

```
                9 2
```

STEP 15

```
                36 <- 32

   1    2    3    4
   5    6    7    8
   9   10   11   12
  13   14   15    *
```

```
               10 0
```

STEP 16

PRESS ANY KEY TO SEE SOLUTION

```
1              36
2              32
3              31
4              26
5              25
6              23
7              21
8               9
9               4
10              2
```

FOUND IN 10 STEPS.
16 NODES CLOSED.

PRESS ANY KEY TO CONTINUE

```
                0 <- 0
```

```
 5   1   3   4
 2  10   6   8
 *   9   7  11
13  14  15  12
```

```
              0 32
```

```
              2 <- 0
```

```
 5   1   3   4
 2  10   6   8
 9   *   7  11
13  14  15  12
```

```
              1 30
```

```
              4 <- 2
```

```
 5   1   3   4
 2   *   6   8
 9  10   7  11
13  14  15  12
```

```
              2 28
```

```
              9 <- 4
```

```
 5   1   3   4
 *   2   6   8
 9  10   7  11
13  14  15  12
```

```
              3 24
```

```
             21 <- 9
```

```
 *   1   3   4
 5   2   6   8
 9  10   7  11
13  14  15  12
```

```
              4 20
```

```
             23 <- 21
```

```
 1    *    3    4
 5    2    6    8
 9   10    7   11
13   14   15   12
```

                    5 16

                    25 <- 23

```
 1    2    3    4
 5    *    6    8
 9   10    7   11
13   14   15   12
```

                    6 12

                    26 <- 25

```
 1    2    3    4
 5    6    *    8
 9   10    7   11
13   14   15   12
```

                    7 8

                    31 <- 26

```
 1    2    3    4
 5    6    7    8
 9   10    *   11
13   14   15   12
```

                    8 4

                    32 <- 31

```
 1    2    3    4
 5    6    7    8
 9   10   11    *
13   14   15   12
```

                    9 2

                    36 <- 32

```
 1    2    3    4
 5    6    7    8
 9   10   11   12
13   14   15    *

               10  0
```

]

The keen reader may care to improve on the program as written. One improvement would be to adopt the more drastic pruning method mentioned in the previous section – printing the best route so far, then lopping off all nodes except the current best and continuing the search from there. The root node is always at position 0 in the tree, so this would involve re-setting

ST$(0) = ST$(S%)
PW%(0) = PW%(S%)
SF%(0) = SF%(S%)
MD%(0) = MD%(S%)

and clearing the other nodes 1 to SIZE% before continuing. A routine to carry out these tasks could then be called at line 5155 instead of the STOP statement, which just gives up.

The other line of improvement would be to tinker with the heuristic estimate $MD\%$. This is computed in subroutine 2200. In the end we settled for double the raw Manhattan Distance (see line 2275). This generally led to a quicker solution by biasing the system towards hill-climbing and away from breadth-first search. However, there were cases where the program needed to increase $MD\%$ to get to a solution, and such situations demonstrate that the measure used for $MD\%$ is far from perfect.

Other measures might perform better. For example, simply counting the number of tiles out of position (not their distance away) might be just as effective. It might also be a good idea to bias the program to prefer solving the upper two lines

```
1  2  3  4
5  6  7  8
```

before turning its attention to the lower half of the grid. You can have some fun trying to devise your own measure of remoteness from the goal.

As explained already, the key to intelligence in a search process is the heuristic evaluation (the 'warm/cold' of Hunt the Thimble), and Manhattan Distance is a rather crude measure. It would pay the enterprising reader to experiment with the routine at line 2200 onwards until a really good one is found.

7.10 Summary and conclusions

The theme of this chapter has been that problem solving can profitably be viewed as a search through a space of possible solutions. This search-space may correspond to physical space (as in the route-finding examples) or it may not (as in the 15-tile puzzle). In the latter case an abstract space is defined by the rules of a one-person game.

The search can be made 'intelligent' by:

(1) Ordering potential or partial solutions and examining them in order of apparent merit.
(2) Pruning unpromising lines of investigation entirely.

The more effective the means of ordering and pruning, the less work the search program has to do and the more intelligent the procedure is considered to be.

A large variety of interesting problems can be cast in the searching mould. To name only a few:

Finding your way out of a maze.
The grand tour or Travelling-Salesman Problem.
The 15-tile puzzle.
Finding the shortest route between two points.
Cabling up a building using as little wire as possible.
Solving cryptarithmetic puzzles.
Proving theorems in propositional calculus.

You are invited to think of ways of tackling your own problems within this heuristic-search framework.

8

Computer game-playing strategies

Heuristic problem solving, as we saw in the last chapter, is a tricky business even without an opponent. Introduce an adversary whose chief aim is to thwart your plans, and a whole new dimension of complexity opens up. This is one reason why games of mental skill, and chess in particular, have always exerted a special fascination for the AI community. Game playing provides the ideal arena for testing various methods of strategic reasoning – open competition.

In August 1968 David Levy, then Scottish chess champion, issued a challenge to Professor Donald Michie of the Machine Intelligence Department at Edinburgh University. He wagered £250 that no computer program would beat him across the board at chess within 10 years. Michie accepted, indeed he doubled the stakes, and the bet was on. The final match of the challenge was arranged, with considerable fanfare, at the 1978 IFIP autumn conference in Toronto. By that time several other AI professors had joined in the wager. Levy, by now an international master and a specialist in computer gamesmanship, duly won his bets by beating Chess 4.7 – the world computer chess champion – three games to one with one drawn. He had improved more than the programs he faced.

But Levy could not rest on his laurels. His exploits had made him a recognized 'benchmark' for ambitious chess programmers, and in April 1984 he met the new world computer chess champion, the Cray Blitz, with $4000 offered by Omni magazine to play for plus a $1000 side bet of his own. This best-of-four match was held at Brunel University, near London, during a computer chess conference. Blitz's handler was connected by telephone to the world's most powerful computer, the experimental Cray XMP in Minneapolis, a 9-nanosecond dual-processor brute which Bob Hyatt, Blitz's co-author, disarmingly described as 'relatively quick'. Levy won convincingly 4–0, assisted in one game by a transatlantic telephone break and in another by a computer failure.

Most people find the tale of Levy's David-versus-Goliath victories reassuring. In the battle of wits between man and machine, we take vicarious comfort from the triumph of one of our own kind (even though most of us would surely have lost).

Yet while you and I may sleep easier knowing that there are still people capable of putting the computer in its place, it makes some AI researchers restless. For the dedicated computer gamester, Levy is merely a stepping stone on the road to Karpov, Kasparov and glory. The challenge is to devise a program that can match the very best human brains in a contest of wits.

With some games that objective has already been achieved. In 1980 Hans Berliner's backgammon program defeated the reigning world champion, Luigi Villa, in an exhibition match, although Berliner admitted that the dice fell in its favour at a critical moment; and in checkers (draughts), Kalah (Owari) and Othello (Reversi), programs exist that can take on the world's best human players. In the rest of this chapter we look at some of the techniques they use.

8.1 Look-ahead and minimaxing

Most programs that play games of intellectual skill rely on tree-search procedures rather like the heuristic-search techniques we encountered in Chapter 7, but modified to take account of the opposing player. The central idea is that of *look-ahead*. The program builds a game tree by considering its own moves, looking ahead to the counter-moves available to the opponent, then for each of them looking at its own responses and so on. It uses the tree thus built to guide its own play.

Noughts and crosses (tic tac toe) is a trivial game, but it serves to introduce the basic ideas behind game-tree searching. Figure 8.1 shows a position reached after six moves in a game of noughts and crosses. The current position is the root of the tree which fans out downwards. The program has to select which path to pursue.

The nodes of this tree are board states, and its branches are legal moves. The root node is said to be at ply 0 (zero); and in this case it is $\bigcirc$'s turn to move at ply 0. $\bigcirc$ has three choices left, leading to the three nodes at ply 1, where it is $\times$'s turn to move. $\times$ has only two moves at each node, leading to the six nodes at ply 2, by which time $\bigcirc$'s replies are all predetermined, so there are six terminal positions at the bottom level (ply 3). Note that at even plies it is $\bigcirc$'s turn, while at odd plies it is $\times$'s turn to play.

This tree can be used in evaluating the root position, and thereby in selecting which move to make, by a process called minimaxing. The minimax principle was first clearly enunciated by Claude Shannon in 1949. It works by first assigning numeric values to the terminal nodes. In our

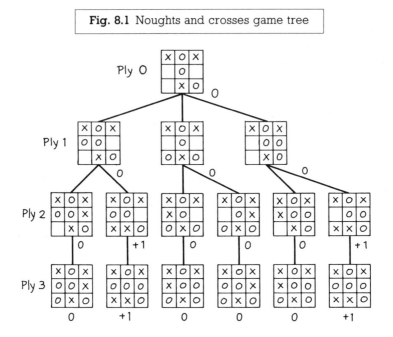

Fig. 8.1 Noughts and crosses game tree

example we give +1 to a win for ○, 0 to a draw and −1 to a win for ×
(which cannot in fact be achieved from the given starting position). These
values are then backed up the tree on the assumption that the player always
chooses the largest value while the opponent always chooses the smallest.

In the present case the backed-up value of the root node is 0, meaning
that the game is drawn (so long as neither side makes a mistake). Note that
in general minimaxing assumes error-free play on both sides. In practice
this assumption may have to be modified. For example, all three top-level
branches in Fig. 8.1 lead to a drawn game; but the left and right branches
allow the possibility of a win, whereas in the middle branch a win is not
possible at all. The minimax principle does not differentiate between the
three alternatives; but an intelligent game-playing program should, when
faced with objectively equal moves, make the choice that maximizes the
opponent's chances of error.

8.2 The evaluation function

In noughts and crosses it is feasible to grow a complete game tree, right
to the bitter end. In general, however, it will not be possible to see the
process right through to the conclusion of the game. Chess, for instance,
has a 'branching factor' of about 30. This means that there are

approximately 30 legal moves in a typical chess position. To look ahead 4-ply (which is only two moves by each player) would generate

$$30 \times 30 \times 30 \times 30 = 810\,000$$

tip nodes. To look ahead from the opening to the end of the game (averaging around 40 moves) would require examination of over 10^{120} nodes. Even if the entire universe was a computer it would be cold and dead long before deciding its first move; and hence the referee would declare the game forfeit, if he could find somewhere to stand! This is our second encounter with the combinatorial explosion.

So most game-playing progams do not look to the end of the game, except when it is almost finished. Instead they look as far ahead as they can – subject to the space and time limits in operation – and evaluate the positions at the tip of the tree. To do so requires some means of computing how favourable or unfavourable the leaf nodes are without knowing the result of the game. This is known as the static evaluation function.

It is important to realize that the evaluation function inevitably introduces a degree of imprecision because the terminal nodes are no longer known to be won, drawn or lost. The static evaluation is merely an estimate. If the program could look forward to the very end, there would be no need for this estimate. On the other hand, if the estimate were always accurate, there would be no need to look ahead.

The rationale for the compromise of looking some way ahead and using an imperfect evaluation function is that it will be applied closer to the end of the game than it would be without any search. Usually this gives a reasonable assessment of how the game will develop.

To take checkers (draughts) as an example, a very simple evaluation function could be constructed with only four terms.

k King advantage = number of own kings – number of opposing kings

p Piece score = number of own pieces (other than kings) – number of opponent's pieces (other than kings)

m Mobility difference = number of own legal moves – number of opponent's legal moves

c Centre control = number of own pieces on central squares – number of opponent's pieces likewise

Each term is a quantity which can be measured from the state of the game-board.

In checkers kings are dominant since they can move backwards as well as forwards, so the king advantage will be an important feature. It is also advantageous to have more ordinary pieces than the other player (after all the loser is the one left without any pieces), so the p term will reflect whether the computer is ahead or behind on material. In many games, including checkers, it is better to have a wide choice of moves than to be restricted to a few choices only: the mobility term is intended to capture this feature and can be calculated simply by counting one side's legal moves and subtracting the other's. The fourth term (c) can be computed by examining the central squares and seeing which side occupies (or threatens) them. In checkers as in chess the central squares are more strategically important than those at the edge of the board.

Having quantified such features, the program must somehow combine them to give an overall assessment of the game. This usually means that they must be weighted to reflect their different levels of importance, then added up. Suppose we decide that a king (k) is twice as valuable as a normal piece (p); that having an extra piece (p) is worth three additional moves (m); and that an additional move (m) is twice as good as controlling an extra central square (c). Then our evaluation function would look like this:

$$v = 12k + 6p + 2m + c$$

(Integer values and weightings are commonly used to speed the computation, with non-integer values scaled accordingly, as here.)

It should be emphasized that this is a very crude evaluation function. By contrast, Arthur Samuel's classic checker-playing program, developed during the period 1959–1967, had an evaluation function comprising up to 25 parameters. Here we are merely pointing out the form of a typical evaluation polynomial.

Nor is this meant to yield a very accurate value. The weighting coefficients of 12, 6, 2 and 1 are somewhat arbitrary. Part of the fun of computer gamesmanship lies in 'tuning' the evaluation function by adjusting the weights until a good balance is achieved. One of the strong points of Samuel's program, which eventually reached master-level performance, was that it adjusted these weightings automatically by playing one version of the program against another (and by other means) – thus 'learning' in a rather simple-minded fashion.

Another point we will skate over is that a serious program will be likely to have several evaluation functions, not just one. Some features which are beneficial in the opening phase are relatively unimportant in the middle game and may even be disadvantageous in the endgame. The more sophisticated game programs vary the weighting coefficients smoothly as the game progresses to take account of such changes.

Overall, however, the idea of giving numerical values to features of the game state and combining them in a weighted sum to quantify the estimated value of any position has proved its worth in computer game-playing programs over the past 35 years. The evaluation function plays a similar role in game playing to that of the heuristic distance measure in the search procedures described in Chapter 7. It is the place where game-specific knowledge is embedded.

8.3 Quiescent positions and the horizon effect

A program that simply looks ahead a fixed number of ply and evaluates the terminal positions found at a uniform depth will run into serious problems. These problems arise because some game positions are 'quiet' while others are highly dynamic. In chess, for example, the state of play after a queen capture or a pawn promotion is likely to be unstable: the queen may be re-captured or the promoted pawn may be taken on the very next move. If the re-capture takes place one ply beyond the program's 'horizon' its evaluation will be seriously biased.

To combat this effect, most game programs do not have a fixed depth of look-ahead. Instead they have some measure of 'quiescence' which tells them, in effect, whether it is safe to evaluate a position as it stands or whether the look-ahead must be pushed further to check for dramatic changes in evaluation. In a chess-playing system, for instance, one might ensure that the program always looked at least 5-ply and that it never went further than 9-ply. In between those limits it would stop if the position appeared stable and look deeper if it was particularly active.

8.4 The alpha–beta algorithm

The alpha–beta algorithm was first used in Greenblatt's chess-playing program MacHack which appeared in 1967 and was the first computer system to play at a respectable level of skill. It is a significant refinement of the basic minimax method: it is guaranteed to give the same result as full minimaxing while examining only a fraction of the tree. In ideal conditions the alpha–beta algorithm considers only twice the square-root of the number of nodes examined by full-width minimaxing, for the same result.

The diagram of Fig. 8.2 shows the look-ahead tree of a hypothetical game between two players called Max and Mini. The search has been carried out to a depth of 3-ply and the resultant 21 terminal nodes have been assigned values as they would be by a static evaluation function. (In fact these values were produced by a random-number generator.)

The backed-up values from a full minimax evaluation are shown. At even plies Max chooses the larger values, and at odd plies Mini chooses the smaller ones. As a result the value of the root is 56, indicating that the leftmost move should be chosen.

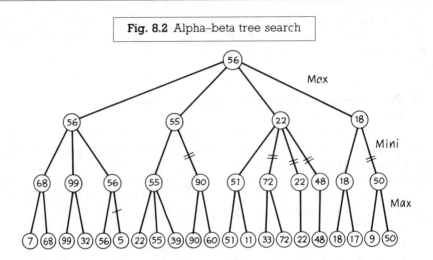

Fig. 8.2 Alpha–beta tree search

However, of the 37 nodes in the tree, 14 can safely be ignored. They cannot have any effect on the move chosen at the top level. We have struck lines through the branches leading to such nodes, to show that they could be pruned off the tree.

Consider the left half of the tree, which has been re-drawn as Fig. 8.3 with the nodes labelled by letters of the alphabet. If the nodes are visited in a depth-first order, as shown by the letters A–S beside the circles in the figure, nodes O, P and Q are completely irrelevant. So is node H.

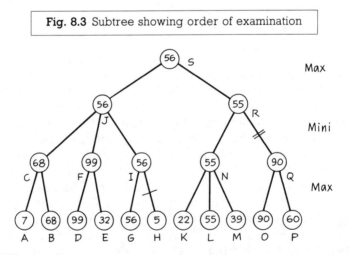

Fig. 8.3 Subtree showing order of examination

By the time we reach node O, we know that node N has a value of 55. This means that the opponent who is minimizing, will restrict us to 55 at best if we take the move leading to node Q, O's parent. But we already know that node J is worth 56. So there is no point in considering any other descendants of node R: they can only make matters worse, and we have already decided that R is not good enough. The 90 at node O cannot be attained because the opponent will not let us (unless he blunders).

You should be able to convince yourself that node Q could have 1000 or more descendants and any value from $-\infty$ to $+\infty$ without affecting the argument. Whatever the outcome, node J is preferable to node R.

The single strikes in the diagram mark what are known as alpha cutoffs, and the double strikes mark beta cutoffs. To make sure you have grasped these concepts, Fig. 8.4 illustrates a different game tree showing one alpha cutoff and one beta cutoff. The alpha cutoff occurs at node E, which need never be evaluated. Nor need its descendants, if it has any. We know by then that node C obtains a score of 15; but at node D the opponent can force us down to 10. There is no point in finding out if he can force us even lower: node F's other descendants can be eliminated from further consideration.

Fig. 8.4 Alpha–beta cutoffs

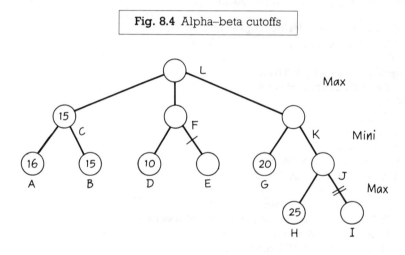

The same argument applies in reverse at node J. By the time we get there we know that node G yields a score of 20. Node H looks better, with an evaluation of 25, but the opponent will never let us get there because it is Mini not Max who chooses between nodes G and J. Clearly Mini will prefer G. There is thus no need to see whether I is even more inviting because we will never be allowed to get there.

If we borrow family-tree terminology, we can say that from Max's viewpoint node C is the uncle of nodes D and E, which are both sons of the same father; and that as far as Mini is concerned G is the aunt of the two sisters H and I, who are both daughters of mother J. This allows us to state the two aspects of the alpha–beta rule quite concisely:

(1) As soon as Max finds a son who is *worse* than any of his uncles, he ignores all that son's other brothers.

(2) As soon as Mini finds a daughter who is *better* than any of her aunts, she ignores that daughter's remaining sisters.

We have laboured these points because the alpha–beta algorithm is at the heart of almost all successful computer chess programs, including those which approach grandmaster performance such as Cray Blitz. It has also been successfully employed in many other games of skill, notably checkers. It derives its name from two parameters (alpha and beta) which indicate the value of the best and worst moves so far at any given level of the tree. These parameters are initialized with $-\infty$ and $+\infty$, respectively.

The clearest specification of the alpha–beta algorithm relies heavily on recursion, and since many forms of BASIC do not provide recursive procedures, we show it here in a PASCAL-like pseudocode. Later we will discuss its implementation in BASIC.

```
FUNCTION evaluate (Position,alpha,beta,depth)
LOCAL VARS v,e,p,done
BEGIN
IF depth > = Maxdepth THEN
   v = Static Evaluation of Position
ELSE BEGIN
   v = alpha
   REPEAT
     done = Null
     p = Generate Next Move
     IF p < > Null THEN BEGIN
       Play Move p
       e = - evaluate(p, - beta, - v,depth + 1)
       REM call self on new pos. with result inverted
       IF e > v THEN v = e
       IF v > = beta THEN done = p
       Retract Move p
       END
   UNTIL (p = Null) OR (done < > Null)
   END
IF v is best so far at top level THEN
   Remember Move p
Return v
END of alpha–beta evaluation routine
```

Readers should be able to see how to translate this into C, PASCAL or one of the modern versions of BASIC (e.g. BBC BASIC, QL SUPERBASIC or COMAL).

The outer IF decides whether to use the static evaluation or whether to search deeper in the game tree. (In reality this would also depend on some measure of quiescence, as discussed previously.) If it goes deeper the REPEAT/UNTIL loop proposes and examines all possible moves from the current position. They are evaluated by calling the function evaluate itself – recursively – with alpha and beta *swapped* and *negated* and the result *negated* too. This assumes an evaluation function that scores favourable positions as positive, neutral ones as zero and unfavourable ones as negative.

The lines

Play Move p

and

Retract Move p

are intended to put a proposed move into effect (e.g. on a chess board) and then undo its effect after the evaluation. As long as this can be done, only one board will be needed. The descendants will be evaluated as if their parent move had been made, and it will be cleaned off afterwards when alternative moves are being considered. This saves storing many copies of the board state as the search tree grows; though obviously it can only be done in games where the moves are reversible (e.g. placing a piece on a board which can later be removed).

The final IF

IF v is best so far at top level THEN
  Remember Move p

is a reminder that the object of the exercise is to pick a move rather than merely to evaluate the present game state. So when a new best move is found at the top level, it should be kept.

The alpha–beta procedure is an elegant enhancement of pure minimaxing, and in the best case only examines

2 × SQRT(N)

nodes, where N is the number of nodes in the minimax tree of the same depth. The proportional improvement increases with increasing tree size. Thus in a 100-node tree alpha–beta minimaxing would require about 20 nodes (20%) but in a 1000-node tree it would scan about 64 (6%). Nevertheless, in the worst case, alpha–beta looks at just as many nodes as full minimax and takes slightly longer to do so.

In order to avoid this worst-case behaviour, it is important to generate the moves at each level in a sensible order. The optimum ordering is best first at the maximizing levels and worst first (i.e. best for the other side) at minimizing levels.

Now if the computer knew which moves were best and worst at each level, it would not need to search, so this desirable ordering can only be approximated. The better programs use a simple plausibility rating to rank the moves for this purpose. The plausibility function can be based on the static evaluation function, but in general the static evaluation function will be too slow, so a simplified version is used. After all, it is important not to waste more time re-arranging the moves than can be saved by the alpha–beta procedure considering them in the optimal order. For microcomputer programs the best advice is to have a fixed-order move generator which – on the whole – comes up with sensible moves for the side to play before silly ones. Even something as simple as spiralling outwards from the centre of the board looking for pieces to move (rather than working mechanically from bottom left to top right) can prove helpful – at no extra cost.

8.5 Terminology review

At this point let us pause to digest some of the jargon that has been introduced so far.

Game tree
Tree structure formed by considering possible moves, followed by opponent's possible replies, and so on.

Ply
One level in the game tree.

Look-ahead
The process of creating a game tree of the type described.

Backed-up value
The value assigned to a node in the game tree by looking at the value(s) beneath it, working from the bottom.

Minimaxing
Choosing which value to back up the tree by minimizing at odd plies (opponent to move) and maximizing at even plies (self to move).

Alpha–beta algorithm
A refinement of minimaxing which eliminates sections of the game tree that cannot possibly affect the outcome at the top level.

Branching factor
The average number of branches or moves at each level of the game tree. Chess has a branching factor of around 32 in the middle game. The oriental game of Go has a branching factor of over 200 and hence a potentially enormous game tree.

8.6 Beyond the alpha–beta algorithm

The alpha–beta procedure is a simple yet effective technique which has proved its worth in numerous chess programs and in many other games of skill. It is a great improvement on straightforward minimaxing, but it is not the last word on the subject.

In this section we briefly consider two alternative search strategies which have been proposed by AI researchers in recent years. The first is the B* (B-star) algorithm devised by Hans Berliner. The second is the Scout algorithm of Judea Pearl.

Berliner is a chess master who is also a professor of computer science at Carnegie-Mellon University in Pittsburgh. His backgammon program won a winner-takes-all contest against the human world champion in 1980, as mentioned earlier, but B* derives from his observations of how chess masters analyse the game.

The essence of the method is to look at the moves at the top level of the game tree and try (as quickly as possible) to do one of two things:

(1) Prove that the apparently best move really is the best available.
(2) Prove that none of the alternatives to the apparent best move is in fact better than it is.

These two strategies are implemented by a pair of routines named ProveBest and RefuteRest which rely on assigning *two* values to each node in the tree – an 'optimistic' and a 'pessimistic' evaluation. Thus the B* method deals with ranges rather than point values. The idea is to force the search algorithm to concentrate on areas in the game tree where (1) there is uncertainty and (2) this uncertainty could affect the final decision.

As soon as the pessimistic value of the most promising move equals or exceeds the optimistic value of the next most promising, the search terminates and selects that move. The two scores are updated as the search progresses and used to decide which node needs expansion next. This requires an evaluation function geared to producing an upper and lower bound, not a single number. One way of doing this is to allow self, or opponent, two moves in a row (or to waive a turn if moving is a disadvantage). With a little ingenuity these two values can be calculated almost as easily as a single-evaluation score.

In the partial game tree of Fig. 8.5 there are four branches at the top level. Each has been given two numbers, the optimistic and pessimistic evaluation. The nodes are ranked left to right in decreasing order of optimistic evaluation. (Note that the optimistic and pessimistic values will change places at each ply, as the search deepens.)

The program must decide whether to confirm that the leftmost node (20:10) is really the best available by raising the pessimistic value to 16

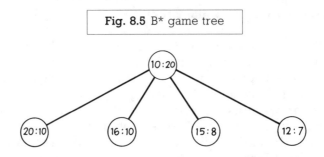

Fig. 8.5 B* game tree

at least (the next highest optimistic value) or to refute the remaining moves by reducing their optimistic values to 10 at most. The choice of which strategy to adopt – ProveBest or RefuteRest – can have dramatic consequences for the length of search. Andrew Palay, one of Berliner's associates at Carnegie-Mellon University, analysed this decision and came up with four recommendations.

1. If there are two or more positions with the same highest optimistic score, the RefuteRest method should be applied. The position chosen as benchmark should be the one with the lowest pessimistic value.

2. If the range of scores of a position lies entirely within the range of the best optimistic position, ProveBest should be chosen.

3. If both the above conditions hold, either strategy may be used.

4. In all other cases two values have to be calculated, *PB* which is the probability that ProveBest will fail and *PR* which is the probability that RefuteRest will fail. If *PB* < *PR* then ProveBest should be attempted, otherwise RefuteRest should be tried. They are computed as follows

$$PB = (O_2 - P_1)/(O_1 - P_1)$$
$$PR = \Sigma((O_x - P_n)/(O_x - P_x)) \quad \text{for } x = 2 \dots n$$

where O_1 is the top optimistic value, O_2 the next best optimistic value, P_1 is the highest optimistic node's pessimistic value, and O_x cycles from the second most-promising to the least most-promising optimistic value (similarly P_x for the corresponding pessimistic values). P_n is the pessimistic value of the node with the lowest optimistic score.

A flow chart for the B* algorithm is given in Fig. 8.6.

It is most important in the B* algorithm not to underestimate the optimistic values or overestimate the pessimistic values. Thus if the 16:10 node turned out to have a value of 22 the tree would have to be re-ordered and much of the work repeated. At the same time it is important to keep the difference between optimistic and pessimistic values relatively small,

Fig. 8.6 B* flow chart

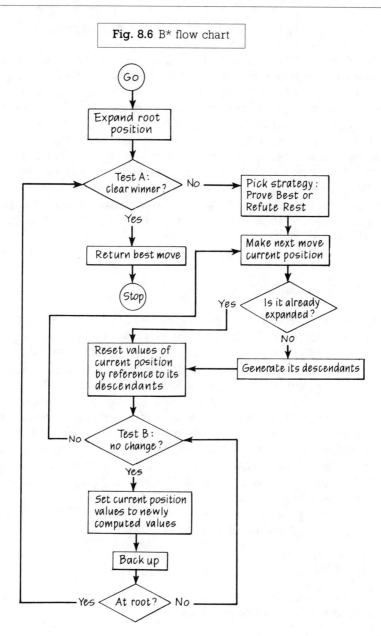

or the wide margin of uncertainty will mean that the program has to work very hard to reach a conclusion.

In practice it may sometimes be advisable to accept a small overlap to reach a quick decision. That is to say: if the best node has a range $17:12$ and its nearest competitor has $13:11$ it may save time to accept the $17:12$ move even though it might turn out to be slightly inferior in the end. One of the benefits of the B* method is that it can be terminated when time runs out and the best move so far can be selected. Because it examines the tree stepwise in an intelligent fashion it will have made good use of the time allotted, whereas the alpha–beta algorithm may get half way through without discovering a halfway decent move.

(For further details the reader is referred to the article 'B* Tree Search: A Best-1st Proof Procedure' by H. J. Berliner (1979) in Volume 12 of *Artificial Intelligence*.)

8.7 The Scout algorithm

Scout is an algorithm for searching two-person game trees due to Judea Pearl of the University of California in Los Angeles. In evaluating the worth of a position S for one of the players, Max say, the algorithm first computes EVAL (S_1), the minimax value of the leftmost child of S, then scouts the remaining children $S_2 \ldots S_n$ to determine if any have a higher value. If S_i, for instance, has a higher static evaluation than the value of S_1, the exact minimax value of S_i is computed and used in subsequent tests. Otherwise S_i is discarded from further consideration. When all descendants of S have been either evaluated or discarded, the most recently calculated minimax value is returned as EVAL(S). In a Mini position a similar idea is employed.

Scout uses two procedures EVAL and TEST together to evaluate a position and perform the scouting checks. These are listed below in a PASCAL-like pseudocode again because many BASICs lack recursion with local variables which is necessary here.

```
FUNCTION Eval (s)
LOCAL VARS v,i,n
BEGIN
IF s is terminal THEN
    v = statval (s):REM static evaluation
ELSE BEGIN
  Generate n Children of s  − > s1 .... sn
    v = Eval (s1)
    FOR i = 2 TO n DO
      IF maximizing THEN BEGIN
        IF Test(si,v,GT) THEN v = Eval (si) END
```

```
      ELSE IF test(si,v,LT) THEN V = Eval (si)
   NEXT i
Return v
END of Eval

FUNCTION Test(s,v,op)
LOCAL VARS i,n
REM Returns TRUE if statval (s) op v is TRUE, otherwise FALSE.
IF s is terminal THEN
   Return ((v > statval (s)) = GT)
ELSE BEGIN REM generate successors s1 to sn:
   FOR i = 1 TO n DO
     IF Test(si,v,op) THEN
        IF maximizing AND (op = GT) THEN Return TRUE
        ELSE IF minimizing AND (op = LT) THEN Return TRUE
      ELSE IF maximizing AND (op = LT) THEN Return FALSE
        ELSE IF minimizing AND (op = GT) THEN Return FALSE
   NEXT i
   REM goes through the descendants s1 to sn .
   END
IF maximizing THEN
   IF op = GT THEN Return FALSE ELSE Return TRUE
ELSE IF op = GT THEN Return TRUE ELSE Return FALSE
END of Test function
```

Here statval ( ) is the static evaluation function and GT and LT tell the test function the direction of comparison.

The advantage of Scout is that it rejects hopeless moves very quickly, on the basis of a superficial evaluation. This implies that the evaluation function must be a good one, and means that Scout is suitable for the knowledge-based approach to game playing, where expert knowledge is embodied in the evaluation process.

First it looks at the leftmost node in detail (which ought to be the most promising, as in alpha–beta search). Then it scans quickly through the alternatives at that level. If it finds a move that is clearly inferior, it rejects that move at once. If it finds one that appears better, it examines it more thoroughly and retains the new backed-up value to use in the subsequent tests. When all the positions have been either analysed or exempted, the latest evaluation is returned as the value of the parent node. Scout's virtue is in discarding a large proportion of obviously disastrous moves on the basis of a rapid evaluation, saving its time to examine promising moves in depth. In other words it uses its resources of time and space intelligently. This is roughly how human masters operate.

Of course, a lot depends on the accuracy of the static evaluation function. If this is far out, Scout will pass over nodes it ought to have analysed more thoroughly. The ordering of moves by apparent plausibility is also crucial; but this applies to the alpha–beta and B* algorithms too.

Scout is likely to perform a little more efficiently if the test comparisons are made against

$v + \text{delta}$

and

$v - \text{delta}$

respectively, where delta is a relatively small 'fudge factor'. This saves time examining moves that are only marginally better or worse than the current threshold, thereby allowing tolerance of a small margin of error in the evaluation function.

8.8 Seeing the wood for the trees

So far all our discussion has been couched within the tree-search framework. Even so we have not had time to describe several cunning wrinkles for improved tree-searching by more drastic pruning to combat the combinatorial explosion. For example, the number of alternative moves considered at each level of the tree can be made to depend on the depth. At lower levels only the most plausible moves (as assessed by the static evaluation function or something like it) need be generated – thus permitting a longer range, albeit narrower, search.

There are some interesting games, however, where the entire search philosophy seems to break down, no matter how ingenious the tricks adopted to streamline the process. These include some of the most popular card games (bridge and poker among them) as well as several board games (e.g. Go and Go-Moku). People are able to play these games with varying degrees of skill, and the best human players deserve to be called intelligent. Yet all efforts to program them by tree-search methods have foundered. Why?

One answer is that the branching factor is simply too great. Another answer is that even in chess – where the game-tree idea was born – tree search is only a crude metaphor for the way people approach the problem: human players only search game trees in special circumstances, and then not very effectively. Normally they rely instead on pattern-based planning.

Let us briefly consider two games where tree searching is inadequate – backgammon and Go.

Backgammon is essentially a race, with a strong chance element. In addition players can deliberately or accidentally impede each other's progress. Each side has 15 counters and the object is to move them round the 24 points of the table in opposite directions and 'bear off' the pieces from the board. The winner is the first player to bear off all 15.

Players throw a pair of dice on each turn and can move one or two pieces the number of points shown by the dice (with double moves when both dice show the same score). Thus if I throw a 5 and a 3 I can move one piece three then five steps or five then three steps; or I can move two separate pieces three and five steps onwards. By landing on a 'blot' – an isolated piece of the enemy's – I send it back to the beginning to re-start its journey.

If you think about the game-tree approach you will see that the problem is intractable. The tree is probabilistic. At the top level the player knows the dice rolls and can make the moves in 20 or so different ways, depending on the layout of the pieces. But there are 21 distinct ways that a pair of dice faces can come up. So there are 21 distinguishable outcomes even before we start to consider the opposing side's moves, and none of them can be pruned off the tree because no one can predict which will come up. In theory every one must be examined and the score divided by 21 to give an average value. In practice computer backgammon programs rely on sampling less than 21 of the possibilities (10, say) and hoping that there are no dramatic discontinuities, i.e. that most throws give similar results.

Hans Berliner's backgammon program – the one that beat the world champion in 1980 – gets round these difficulties by doing no search at all. It simply considers all its potential moves, evaluates them, and picks the one with the highest value. This naturally requires a very reliable evaluation function. What Berliner found was that the evaluation function had to vary with the state of the game.

Backgammon games can be divided into categories (e.g. running games and blockading games). The weighting coefficients of the evaluation function are varied smoothly as the transition is made from one type of game to another. In addition, the program plays to the computer's strength: it can calculate exactly how many ways a blot can be hit or what the chances are of bearing off a given configuration in a given number of moves. (In fact, such features are a kind of look-ahead in disguise.)

One thing that computers excell at compared with brains is calculating the odds, and it is here that the Carnegie-Mellon backgammon program shines. Games programmers have always known that you can trade depth of search for quality of evaluation to some extent: a shallow search demands a more careful evaluation and a deeper search can get by on a simpler evaluation. Berliner has taken this to its extreme and cut out search altogether.

Working out the odds very precisely can also be put to good effect in card games such as poker, where search in the traditional sense is problematical. After all, that is how people avoid the combinatorial explosion.

Another area in which the backgammon program plays 'humanistically' is in exploiting patterns. A student of Berliner's has tabulated all the 54 000 bearing-off positions in the endgame, when the two sides are no longer blocking one another. By looking at all the positions reachable from the present one given the current dice-roll, the program can select the one which minimizes the expected future number of plays. The next step will be to analyse those 54 000 positions down to a small set of rules that can be used to direct the program's endgame play without the need for a huge look-up table.

Go, in contrast, lacks a chance element. The players place black and white stones alternately on the intersections of a 19×19 grid. The objective is to surround and capture opposing stones. Go is extremely popular in Japan and is regarded by many experts as more intellectually demanding than chess. Since the branching factor is 361 initially and remains above 200 for the most critical part of the game, it has stubbornly resisted all attempts to computerize it by tree-searching methods.

The most successful (or rather least disgraceful) Go programs use pattern recognition in the sense that moves are classified according to the kinds of plan(s) they serve and the kinds of arrangements that exist on the board. This has the effect of creating equivalence classes so that many of the 200-odd moves available can be treated as functionally equivalent. The program can then conduct its search using broader concepts. It is necessary for such programs to 'perceive' the board in terms of higher-level units than single stones, such as 'strings', 'groups', 'eyes' and 'armies'. These are meaningful groupings to the human eye and to find them the program has to draw on results from the study of human perception – like the methods used by the nervous system to organize the information falling on the retina. (See Chapter 4.)

Progress in this field has been slow, however, partly due to our lack of understanding of human and animal perception. People, unlike computers, have evolved as highly tuned perceiving engines, which is one reason why the best players still trounce the best programs at Go. For the ambitious games programmer, Go represents the pinnacle of achievement. Perhaps the Japanese, with their fifth-generation plans and their respect for the game, should press ahead with the demanding task of building a really good Go program. There is little doubt that it will need to draw on all the arts of AI.

8.9 The game of Four-Site

We have touched on a number of different games – backgammon, checkers, chess, Go – to illustrate general techniques without confining ourselves to the peculiarities on any particular game. We do not want to alienate readers by dwelling on a game that only interests a minority. And yet it would be helpful to show some of the techniques in action in the context of a real game.

What we want to finish this chapter is a relatively simple but non-trivial game that can be used to demonstrate the application of standard computer game-playing techniques – preferably one that everyone is equally well acquainted with.

To satisfy these requirements we present you with an exclusive world premiere: the board game Four-Site, devised specially for this book. It is loosely based on the strategy + gravity game Connect-Four (copyright of Milton-Bradley corporation) which itself derives from noughts and crosses. There are, however, a few added twists. In complexity it is almost at the level of checkers, i.e. about the limit of what can reasonably be accomplished on a home computer in BASIC, and it has a novel feature that affects the method of tree search used. Above all, it is new, and therefore will appeal equally (or equally little) to all readers; and you can't say fairer than that.

The game is played on a 6 × 6 grid by two players, (× and ○), each of whom has 16 stones or pieces. The object is to get four consecutive pieces in a straight line. Players take it in turns to play by placing a new piece on an unoccupied point. Figure 8.7 illustrates the board: it starts empty at the beginning of the game.

Fig. 8.7 Four-Site game board

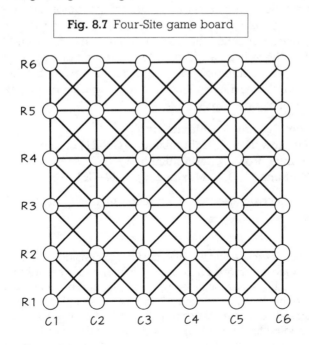

Moves are made by a *joint* decision, and this is where things start to get interesting. The player whose turn it is chooses a row or column (R1–R6 or C1–C6) in which to place a piece. Once the player has announced which row or column he or she has chosen, it is up to the opposing player to decide where in that row, or column, the new piece will be located.

For instance, if I say 'Row 4' then you can decide 'Column 1' or 'Column 2' or whatever and I have to put my piece on R4–C1 or R4–C2 (or whatever). And if I say 'Column 2' and you reply 'Row 6' my piece is placed on C2–R6 – provided of course that location is vacant. When it is your turn the same thing applies in reverse: you state the row or column and then I pick the column or row within your chosen line.

One condition is that the selected square must be vacant. A piece cannot be put down on an occupied square, so once a row or column is full up, neither player can choose to land on it.

Once a piece has been put on the board, it stays put. Pieces do not move around the board or capture other pieces (so this game is suitable for playing with pencil on paper). The winner is the first one to achieve a line of four – horizontally, vertically or diagonally. If both sides have placed all 16 pieces the game is declared a draw. (Draws are unusual; but if you want to make them even rarer you can employ the tie-break rule that the player with more lines of three wins.)*

The game of Four-Site never has a branching factor higher than 12, and towards the end, as rows and columns fill up, this is reduced below 12. Its subtlety arises because the opponent has a hand in determining your play. In effect there is an additional level, so that one move consists of 2-ply – the player's choice of first coordinate followed by the opponent's choice of second coordinate. Thus minimaxing becomes 'maxi-mini-mini-maxing'! For instance

I announce 'Column 3'	**Maximizing**	
You reply 'Row 1'	**Minimizing**	**[C3–R1]**
You announce 'Row 4'	**Minimizing**	
I reply 'Column 6'	**Maximizing**	**[R4–C6]**

This feature necessitates some adjustment to the standard alpha–beta procedure.

---

* A variant of this game that we shall not further consider, which is less intellectually demanding but more fun at family gatherings, uses a die to choose the second coordinate, rather than the opposing player. For example, I pick 'Row 5' and throw the die. It comes up with a 2 and therefore I place the piece on R5–C2. If R5–C2 is already occupied the drop fails and the turn passes to the other player, without my adding to the number of my pieces on the board. In this version you have to be careful about trying to land on nearly full rows or columns.

8.9.1 The Four-Site program

We shall implement the program in a top-down manner, attempting to provide a general-purpose game-playing framework first, postponing most of the details of the game itself till the later stages, so that it could if necessary be adapted to a different game. Very little attention will be paid to graphical output. That is one area where the reader can excercise creativity and improve the program, since we are principally concerned with issues of strategy.

The overall skeleton of the program is shown below.

```
DIM BD%(35)
Initialize Global Values                         [1000]
Give User Instructions                           [1600]
REPEAT
   Clear Board                                   [2000]
   Decide Who starts  - > H1%
   REPEAT
      IF H1% THEN Human Turn                     [3000]
      H1% = TRUE:REM always from now on.
      Show the Board                             [3500]
      Test for Win                               [4000]
      IF NOT game-over THEN Computer Turn        [5000]
      Show the Board                             [3500]
      Test for Win                               [4000]
   UNTIL game-over
   Congratulations Etc.                          [6000]
   Ask if User Wants Another Game
UNTIL User has had Enough
END
```

We have not dropped into BASIC yet, to give a clearer outline of the program structure; but we are getting there. The line numbers of the main subroutines are shown on the right.

Subroutine 3000 will have to accept a person's move and check it for validity. If valid it can be played. In addition, owing to the structure of the game, the computer will need to contribute its half of the human's move. This implies that subroutine 3000 (human play) must call a computer evaluation procedure and that subroutine 5000 (computer play) will have to call for input from the user.

Before we can specify these important routines, we must give some thought to the data structures needed for representing the board and the search tree.

In most board games, a lot depends on finding a compact yet efficient representation for the board, but here we are less interested in the details of the game itself than in general principles. So simplicity will be the keynote. We can use an integer array

DIM BD%(35)

of 36 elements, 0–35, to store the board position, numbering from the bottom left, row by row, as follows:

```
30  31  32  33  34  35
24  25  26  27  28  29
18  19  20  21  22  23
12  13  14  15  16  17
 6   7   8   9  10  11
 0   1   2   3   4   5
```

As for the game tree, that is not explicitly stored at all. By using a variant of the alpha–beta search method we define the game tree implicitly. That is, the search procedure generates and examines nodes in a particular order, discarding subtrees when it has finished with them. This means that the procedure-calling mechanism is growing and chopping the tree for us 'behind the scenes'. (If your BASIC lacks recursive procedures, however, you will have to do this housekeeping work yourself by simulating the parameter-passing and local variables with a stack.)

If we consider the evaluation function for a moment, we will be ready to proceed to the coding. The essence of the game is to create a line of four pieces of your own, and to prevent the opponent doing likewise. The essence of the evaluation function will, therefore, be to estimate how near those goals are to being achieved. It is based on a consideration of the state of *all* the potential lines of four, of which there are 54. On a 6 × 6 grid there are 54 possible places for a four-line, namely

three in each of the six columns	18
three in each of the six rows	18
three in both the main diagonals	6
six in the lesser NE diagonals	6
six in the lesser NW diagonals	6

making 54 in total.

Any one of these potential four-lines can be in only eight interesting states

No. of pieces of		Provisional	
Us	Them	value	
4	0	256	(won)
3	0	8	
2	0	2	
1	0	1	
0	1	-1	
0	2	-2	
0	3	-7	
0	4	-255	(lost)

because once a potential line has pieces of both colours in it, it ceases to be relevant to the game. The provisional values are based on the argument that a pair is twice as valuable as a singleton; while a threesome is more than twice as good as a pair. The disparity of 3:0 (worth $+8$) and 0:3 (worth -7) is intended to make the program play aggressively rather than defensively.

The evaluation function simply looks at all the 54 foursomes on the board and totals their values. Empty fours or fours containing pieces of both sides count for nothing.

Two other data structures employed by the program are

$MT\$(18)$	move table
$VT\%(20)$	value table

which simplify move generation and evaluation, respectively.

The move table simply stores the twelve legal full moves and the six legal replies. Moves are held in rough order of merit from the central columns/rows to the edges. Replies are stored in the opposite order, namely 1, 6, 2, 5, 3, 4 (see lines 1500–1525). This is because central rows and columns are usually more valuable and by considering them sooner the alpha–beta pruning is likely to be more effective than otherwise. The reverse applies for replies (half moves).

The valuation table $VT\%(\ )$ enables the static evaluation function (see line 6700 onwards) to work out the value of a foursome simply by adding and subtracting integers. The trick is as follows.

The computer's pieces are coded as $ME\% = 5$, and the opponent's pieces are coded as $IT\% = 1$. Thus a board square can be in three states:

```
0  empty      (·)
1  opponent   (O)
5  self       (×)
```

A potential row, column or diagonal of four can be added up, e.g.

$$· × · O = 0 + 1 + 0 + 5 = 6$$

The sum can come out 21 ways (0–20). Of these only eight are interesting

× × × ×	20	= 5+5+5+5
× × × ·	15	= 5+5+5+0
× × · ·	10	= 5+5+0+0
× · · ·	5	= 5+0+0+0
O · · ·	1	= 1+0+0+0
O O · ·	2	= 1+1+0+0
O O O ·	3	= 1+1+1+0
O O O O	4	= 1+1+1+1

where the blanks (·) can be anywhere, since

```
O O  ·  ·
O  ·  ·  O
·  O O  ·      etc.
```

are equivalent in value. Thus all entries in the $VT\%(\ )$ table except locations 1, 2, 3, 4, 5, 10, 15 and 20 are valued at zero. If you still have doubts,
try a few example lines. You will find that a line with only 5s must be
divisible by 5 and a line with only 1s must be less than 5; other totals
indicate a mixture of 1s and 5s. This tabulation saves a lot of computation
for the evaluation function, which begins on line 6700.

Listing 8.1 Four-site computer game

```
10   REM   ******************************
11   REM   ** LISTING 8.1              **
12   REM   ** FOUR-SITE COMPUTER GAME  **
13   REM   ******************************
50 Z = 0:W = 1:TW = 2:TH = 3:F = 4:FI = 5:SI = 6:SE = 7:NI = 9:TE
     = 10:T1 = 11:T2 = 12:T5 = 15:T6 = 16:T7 = 17:T8 = 18:W0 = 2
     0:W1 = 21:W4 = 24:H0 = 30:H2 = 32:H5 = 35:F8 = 48:F9 = 49:G4
     = 54:FR = .05: REM  CONSTANTS
100  REM  -- THE GAME OF FOUR-SITE:
110  DIM BD%(35): REM  GAME BOARD
115  DIM M$(6),A%(6),B%(6),P%(6),E%(6),B$(6),X%(6),P$(6): REM  PA
     RAMETER STACKS
120  GOSUB 1000: REM   INITIALISATION
130  GOSUB 1600: REM   INSTRUCTIONS
150  REM  START LOOP
160  GOSUB 2000: REM   CLEAR BOARD ETC.
170  INPUT "WHO GOES 1ST (1=YOU, 2=ME)";H1%
180  IF H1% < W OR H1% > TW THEN 170
200  REM  -- MAIN LOOP
210  REM  START LOOP
220  IF H1% = W THEN : GOSUB 3000
230  REM  -- PERSON'S TURN.
240  GOSUB 3500: REM  BOARD DISPLAY
250 H1% = W: REM   ALWAYS 1 AFTER 1ST CYCLE
254  GOSUB 6700
255  PRINT "V = ";S5%
260  GOSUB 4000: REM  TEST FOR WIN
270  IF EG% = Z THEN : GOSUB 5000
280  REM  -- COMPUTER'S TURN.
290  GOSUB 3500: REM  SHOW BOARD AGAIN
300  GOSUB 4000: REM  TEST FOR ENDGAME
302  GOSUB 6700
303  PRINT "V = ";S5%;" ";BV%
310  IF EG% OR M% > = H2 THEN 320
315  GOTO 210
320  REM  -- FINALE:
330  GOSUB 6000: REM  CONGRATULATIONS
340  INPUT "ANOTHER GAME (N=NO) ";Y$
350 Y$ = LEFT$ (Y$,W)
```

```
360  IF Y$ = "N" THEN 365
361  GOTO 150
365  PRINT
370  PRINT "SO LONG, AND THANKS FOR THE GAME!"
400  END
500  REM  MAXIMOVE ROUTINE
505  REM  -- MY TURN:
510  IF D% - W > MD% THEN : GOSUB 6700:E%(D% - W) = S5%: RETURN
515  P%(D%) = Z:B$(D%) = BL$
520  REM  ELSE GO DEEPER
525  REM    START LOOP
530  P%(D%) = P%(D%) + W
535  M$(D%) = MT$(P%(D%))
536  IF D% = W THEN : PRINT M$(D%);
540  D1 = D% + W:M$(D1) = M$(D%):A%(D1) = A%(D%):B%(D1) = B%(D%):D
     % = D1: GOSUB 600:D% = D% - W
545  IF E%(D%) > A%(D%) THEN :A%(D%) = E%(D%):B$(D%) = M$(D%)
548  IF D% = W THEN : PRINT  SPC( FI -  LEN ( STR$ (E%(D%))));E%(
     D%);";  ";
550  IF P%(D%) > 11 OR A%(D%) >  = B%(D%) THEN 555
551  GOTO 525
555  IF A%(D%) > BV% AND D% = W THEN :BV% = A%(D%):MM$ = B$(D%)
556  REM    KEEP BEST SO FAR
560  E%(D% - W) = A%(D%): RETURN
565  REM    RETURN WITH MAX A%
600  REM  MINREPLY ROUTINE
606  REM  -- OTHER'S REPLY:
610  P%(D%) = T2:X%(D%) = Z:P$(D%) = BL$
620  REM    START LOOP
630  P%(D%) = P%(D%) + W
640  P$(D%) = MT$(P%(D%))
650  P1$ = M$(D%) + P$(D%):P2% = ME%: GOSUB 6630
660  IF RC% < Z THEN :X%(D%) = X%(D%) + W: GOTO 690
670  D1 = D% + W:M$(D1) = M$(D%) + P$(D%):A%(D1) = A%(D%):B%(D1) =
     B%(D%):D% = D1: GOSUB 700:D% = D% - W
680  IF E%(D%) < B%(D%) THEN :B%(D%) = E%(D%)
688  P1$ = M$(D%) + P$(D%):P2% = Z: GOSUB 6630: REM    UNDO IT.
690  IF P%(D%) > T7 OR B%(D%) <  = A%(D%) THEN 695
691  GOTO 620
695  IF X%(D%) > FI THEN :B%(D%) = LO%: REM    REJECT ILLEGAL MOVE
     .
696  E%(D% - W) = B%(D%): RETURN
697  REM  RETURN WITH MIN B%
700  REM  MINIMOVE ROUTINE
710  REM  -- OTHER'S TURN
720  P%(D%) = Z
730  IF D% - W > MD% THEN : GOSUB 6700:E%(D% - W) = S5%: RETURN
750  REM    START LOOP
755  P%(D%) = P%(D%) + W
760  D1 = D% + W:M$(D1) = MT$(P%(D%)):A%(D1) = A%(D%):B%(D1) = B%(
     D%):D% = D1: GOSUB 800:D% = D% - W
770  IF E%(D%) < B%(D%) THEN :B%(D%) = E%(D%)
780  IF P%(D%) > T1 OR B%(D%) <  = A%(D%) THEN 790
785  GOTO 750
790  E%(D% - W) = B%(D%): RETURN
```

```
800   REM   MAXREPLY ROUTINE
805   REM   -- MY REPLY:
810   P%(D%) = T2:X%(D%) = Z:P$(D%) = BL$
820   REM   START LOOP
825   P%(D%) = P%(D%) + W:P$(D%) = M$(D%) + MT$(P%(D%))
830   P1$ = P$(D%):P2% = IT%: GOSUB 6630
835   IF RC% < Z THEN :X%(D%) = X%(D%) + W: GOTO 880
840   D1 = D% + W:M$(D1) = P$(D%):A%(D1) = A%(D%):B%(D1) = B%(D%):D
      % = D1: GOSUB 500:D% = D% - W
845   IF E%(D%) > A%(D%) THEN :A%(D%) = E%(D%)
850   P1$ = P$(D%):P2% = Z: GOSUB 6630
880   IF P%(D%) > T7 OR A%(D%) > = B%(D%) THEN 885
881   GOTO 820
885   IF X%(D%) > FI THEN :A%(D%) = HI%: REM   REJECT
890   E%(D% - W) = A%(D%): RETURN
1000  REM   -- INITIALISING ROUTINE:
1001  BL$ = ""
1010  DIM VT%(20): REM   VALUE TABLE
1020  VT%(Z) = Z
1030  FOR I = SI TO W0
1040  VT%(I) = Z: NEXT
1050  VT%(W) = - W:VT%(TW) = - TW:VT%(TH) = - SE:VT%(F) = - 25
      5
1060  VT%(FI) = W:VT%(10) = TW:VT%(15) = 8:VT%(20) = 256
1070  REM   LETS PROG. LOOK UP LINE SCORES.
1075  HI% = 9999:LO% = - 9999
1077  BV% = Z
1080  ME% = FI:IT% = W: REM   SELF/OTHER
1085  ME$ = " X "
1088  IT$ = " O "
1100  REM   -- NOW READ DATA:
1110  DIM MT$(18): REM   MOVE TABLE
1120  RESTORE
1130  FOR I = W TO 18
1140  READ MT$(I): NEXT
1150  RETURN
1500  REM   -- DATA FOR MOVE TABLE:
1510  DATA  C4,R4,C3,R3,C2,R2
1520  DATA  C5,R5,C6,R6,C1,R1
1525  DATA  X1,X6,X2,X5,X3,X4
1600  REM   -- INSTRUCTION ROUTINE:
1610  HOME : PRINT
1620  PRINT "WELCOME TO FOUR-SITE, THE BRAIN GAME."
1630  PRINT "IF YOU DON'T KNOW THE RULES,"
1635  PRINT "READ THE BOOK!"
1636  PRINT "GIVE MOVES AS R (ROW) OR C (COL)"
1640  PRINT "FOLLOWED BY A NUMBER, E.G. R1, C4 ETC."
1650  PRINT : PRINT "GOOD LUCK!"; CHR$ (7)
1660  RETURN
2000  REM   -- PREPARATION ROUTINE:
2010  M% = Z: REM   MOVES
2012  M$ = BL$
2020  FOR I = Z TO H5
2030  BD%(I) = Z: NEXT
2040  NS$ = "": REM   NULL STRING.
```

```
2050 EG% = Z
2100  RETURN
3000  REM  -- PERSON'S MOVE
3010 M% = M% + W
3020  PRINT
3030  REM  START LOOP
3040  INPUT "YOUR MOVE IS ";HM$
3050 H$ =  LEFT$ (HM$,W)
3080 N% =  VAL ( MID$ (HM$,TW,W))
3090  IF (N% > Z) AND (N% < SE) THEN :OK% = W
3095  IF  NOT ((N% > Z) AND (N% < SE)) THEN :OK% = Z
3100  IF H$ < > "C" AND H$ < > "R" THEN :OK% = Z
3110  GOSUB 3200: REM  CHECK IT'S NOT FULL.
3120  IF OK% = Z THEN : PRINT "INVALID: PLEASE RE-TRY!"
3130  IF OK% = W THEN 3140
3135  GOTO 3030
3140 HM$ = H$ +  CHR$ (N% + F8)
3150  REM  -- NOW PICK OWN REPLY:
3160  GOSUB 3330
3170 HM$ = HM$ + M$
3175 M$ = HM$
3180  PRINT "MOVE ";M%;" -> ";HM$
3188 P1$ = HM$:P2% = IT%: GOSUB 6630
3190  RETURN
3200  REM  -- ROW/COL CHECK ROUTINE:
3210  IF OK% = Z THEN : RETURN : REM  DON'T BOTHER
3220 Q% = W
3230  IF H$ = "C" THEN :Q% = SI
3240 B% = N% - W
3250  IF H$ = "R" THEN :B% = B% * SI
3260 K% = Z
3270  FOR I = W TO SI
3280  IF BD%(B%) = Z THEN :K% = K% + W
3290 B% = B% + Q%: NEXT I
3300  IF K% = Z THEN :OK% = Z: PRINT HM$;" FULL!"
3310  RETURN
3330  REM  -- COMPUTER-REPLY ROUTINE:
3340 H$ =  LEFT$ (HM$,W)
3350 IX% = W:C$ = "C"
3360  IF H$ = "C" THEN :IX% = SI:C$ = "R"
3370 N% =  VAL ( MID$ (HM$,TW,W)) - W
3380  IF H$ = "R" THEN :N% = N% * SI
3390  REM  -- SPECIAL CASES IN OPENING:
3400  IF M% < TH THEN :M$ = C$ +  CHR$ (F9): RETURN
3420 B% = LO%:Y$ = BL$
3430  FOR I = W TO SI:Y$ = C$ +  CHR$ (F8 + I)
3440 P1$ = HM$ + Y$:P2% = IT%: GOSUB 6630
3444  IF RC% < Z THEN : GOTO 3480: REM  OCCUPIED!
3450  REM  -- TRIES IT
3459  GOSUB 6700
3460 V% = S5%: REM  STATIC EVAL.
3465  IF V% > B% THEN :B% = V%:M$ = Y$
3470 P1$ = HM$ + Y$:P2% = Z: GOSUB 6630: REM  UNDO IT
3480  NEXT I
3490  RETURN : REM  M$ IS HALF-MOVE.
```

```
3500   REM  -- BOARD DISPLAY ROUTINE:
3520   HOME : PRINT
3522   PRINT "       MOVE ";M%;" --> ";
3525   PRINT M$
3530 R% = G4: REM    ASCII '6'
3540   FOR P = H0 TO Z STEP - SI
3550   PRINT "R"; CHR$ (R%);" ";
3560   FOR I = Z TO FI
3570 Z% = BD%(P + I)
3580   IF Z% = Z THEN : PRINT " . ";
3590   IF Z% = ME% THEN : PRINT ME$;
3600   IF Z% = IT% THEN : PRINT IT$;
3610   NEXT I
3620   R% = R% - W
3630   PRINT : PRINT
3640   NEXT P
3650   PRINT "    ";
3660   FOR I = W TO SI
3670   PRINT " C"; CHR$ (F8 + I);
3675   NEXT
3677   PRINT
3690   RETURN
4000   REM  -- WIN-TEST ROUTINE (ON M$):
4001   IF M% < W THEN : RETURN
4004 P1$ = M$:P2% =  - W: GOSUB 6630
4005   REM   RE-SET RC%
4010 EG% = Z: REM    ENDGAME
4020 R% = RC% / SI
4030 C% =   INT ((RC% / SI -   INT (RC% / SI)) * SI + FR) *  SGN (R
       C% / SI)
4040   REM   ROW AND COL.
4044   REM  -- 1ST LOOK IN ITS ROW:
4050   FOR J = R% * SI TO R% * SI + TW
4060 T% = BD%(J) + BD%(J + W) + BD%(J + TW) + BD%(J + TH)
4070   IF T% = F * IT% THEN :EG% =  - W
4080   IF T% = F * ME% THEN :EG% = W
4090   NEXT
4100   IF EG% THEN : RETURN
4101   REM  -- NEXT ITS COL:
4110   FOR J = C% TO C% + T2 STEP SI
4120 T% = BD%(J) + BD%(J + SI) + BD%(J + T2) + BD%(J + T8)
4130   IF T% = F * ME% THEN :EG% = W
4140   IF T% = F * IT% THEN :EG% =  - W
4150   NEXT
4160   IF EG% THEN : RETURN
4170   REM  -- DOES ALL DIAGONALS (SIMPLER):
4180 P% = Z:IX% = SE: REM    START -> NE
4190   FOR J = W TO T8
4200 T% = BD%(P%) + BD%(P% + IX%) + BD%(P% + IX% * TW) + BD%(P% +
       IX% * TH)
4210   IF T% = F * IT% THEN :EG% =  - W: RETURN
4220   IF T% = F * ME% THEN :EG% = W: RETURN
4230 P% = P% + SI
4240   IF P% > T7 THEN :P% = P% - T7
4250   IF P% = TH THEN :IX% = FI: REM   -> NW
```

```
4260   NEXT J
4270   RETURN
5000   REM  -- COMPUTER'S MOVE ROUTINE:
5010   REM   STARTS WITH RND, JUST TESTING:
5020   M% = M% + W
5030   MM$ = BL$
5033   C$ = "C"
5035   IF  INT ( RND (W) * TE) + W > F THEN :C$ = "R"
5040   IF M% < TH THEN :MM$ = "C4": REM   OPENING
5050   IF M% < FI AND M% > TW THEN :MM$ = C$ + "4"
5060   REM  -- PICK ROW/COL:
5070   GOSUB 5200: REM  -> MM$
5080   GOSUB 5500: REM   HUMAN'S HALF.
5090   M$ = MM$ + HM$
5100   P1$ = M$:P2% = ME%: GOSUB 6630
5110   RETURN
5200   REM  -- MOVE SELECTION:
5210   IF MM$ < > BL$ THEN : RETURN
5220   MD% = TH:BV% = LO%
5222   IF M% < TE THEN :MD% = W
5223   IF M% > WO THEN :MD% = FI
5225   REM  -- LOOK DEEPER IN ENDING.
5230   M$(W) = BL$:A%(W) = LO%:B%(W) = HI%:D% = W: GOSUB 500:A% = E
       %(D% - W)
5240   PRINT A%
5250   RETURN : REM  WITH MM$
5500   REM  -- HUMAN HALFMOVE ROUTINE:
5510   PRINT
5520   PRINT "I CHOOSE : ";MM$
5530   REM   START LOOP
5540   INPUT "GIVE 2ND COORDINATE PLEASE : ";HM$
5550   H$ = LEFT$ (HM$,W)
5580   HM$ = H$ + MID$ (HM$,TW,W)
5590   N% = VAL ( MID$ (HM$,TW,W))
5600   IF (N% > Z) AND (N% < SE) THEN :OK% = W
5605   IF  NOT ((N% > Z) AND (N% < SE)) THEN :OK% = Z
5610   IF H$ = LEFT$ (MM$,W) THEN :OK% = Z
5615   IF OK% = Z THEN 5650
5620   P1$ = MM$ + HM$:P2% = - W: GOSUB 6630
5630   IF BD%(RC%) < > Z THEN :OK% = Z
5640   IF OK% = Z THEN : PRINT "INVALID: RE-TRY!"
5650   IF OK% = W THEN 5660
5655   GOTO 5530
5660   RETURN : REM  WITH HM$
6000   REM  -- CONGRATULATIONS ROUTINE:
6010   PRINT "GAME OVER!"
6020   IF EG% > Z THEN : PRINT "I WON IT!!"
6030   IF EG% < Z THEN : PRINT "WELL DONE!"
6040   IF EG% = Z THEN : PRINT "GAME DRAWN"
6050   RETURN
6630   REM   PLACES PIECES P2% BY MOVE P1$
6650   X1% = VAL ( MID$ (P1$,TW,W)) - W
6660   Y1% = VAL ( MID$ (P1$,F,W)) - W
6670   IF  LEFT$ (P1$,W) = "R" THEN :RC% = X1% * SI + Y1%
6680   IF  LEFT$ (P1$,W) = "C" THEN :RC% = X1% + Y1% * SI
```

```
6688  IF BD%(RC%) > Z AND P2% > Z THEN :RC% =  - W: RETURN
6690  IF P2% >  = Z THEN :BD%(RC%) = P2%
6695  RETURN
6700  REM  -- STATIC EVALUATION ROUTINE:
6730  S4% = Z:S5% = Z
6750  REM  -- 1ST THE ROWS:
6760  FOR S2 = Z TO 30 STEP SI
6770  S4% = BD%(S2) + BD%(S2 + W) + BD%(S2 + TW) + BD%(S2 + TH)
6780  S5% = S5% + VT%(S4%): REM  LOOK UP IN TABLE
6790  S4% = S4% + BD%(S2 + F) - BD%(S2)
6800  S5% = S5% + VT%(S4%)
6810  S4% = S4% + BD%(S2 + FI) - BD%(S2 + W)
6820  S5% = S5% + VT%(S4%)
6830  NEXT
6840  REM  -- 2ND THE COLS:
6850  FOR S2 = Z TO FI
6860  S4% = BD%(S2) + BD%(S2 + S1) + BD%(S2 + T2) + BD%(S2 + T8)
6870  S5% = S5% + VT%(S4%)
6880  S4% = S4% + BD%(S2 + W4) - BD%(S2)
6890  S5% = S5% + VT%(S4%)
6900  S4% = S4% + BD%(S2 + H0) - BD%(S2 + S1)
6910  S5% = S5% + VT%(S4%)
6920  NEXT
6930  REM  -- NOW THE DIAGONALS:
6940  S2 = Z:S3% = SE
6950  FOR S1 = W TO NI
6960  S4% = BD%(S2) + BD%(S2 + S3%) + BD%(S2 + S3% + S3%) + BD%(S2
      + W1)
6970  S5% = S5% + VT%(S4%):S2 = S2 + SI
6990  IF S2 > T6 THEN :S2 = S2 - T7
7000  NEXT
7020  S2 = TH:S3% = FI
7030  FOR S1 = W TO 9
7040  S4% = BD%(S2) + BD%(S2 + S3%) + BD%(S2 + 10) + BD%(S2 + 15)
7050  S5% = S5% + VT%(S4%):S2 = S2 + SI
7070  IF S2 > 17 THEN :S2 = S2 - 17
7080  NEXT
7090  RETURN
7100  REM  RETURNS S5%
```

Notice how the alpha–beta minimaxing has been split among *four*
separate routines in lines 500–999

  500 Maximove – own move (*max*)
  600 Minreply – other's reply (*mini*)
  700 Minimove – other's move (*mini*)
  800 Maxreply – own reply (*max*)

These call each other in a circular chain to evaluate the moves for the
computer, thus implementing the maxi-mini-mini-max alternation of this
game. See Fig. 8.8.

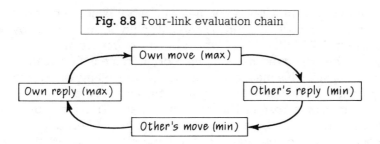

Fig. 8.8 Four-link evaluation chain

Although it is possible to combine all four processes in one routine, that would obscure the structure of the decision making. The present four-way division also saves numerous tests at each level to see which way it is playing and whether it is making a full or half move (reply). For more conventional games, you can forget the Minreply and Maxreply and adapt Maximove and Minimove accordingly.

There is an indirect recursion involved since Maxreply calls Maximove (when looking 4-ply ahead or further).

As can be seen on lines 5200–5250, the program searches 2-ply in the opening ($MD\% = 1$), 4-ply in the middle game ($MD\% = 3$) and 6-ply in the endgame ($MD\% = 5$). It usually beats its author, who is at the time of writing the unofficial world champion. (Please, no challenges!) Here is the record of one game in which it beat its maker: the person started first.

Human	Computer
C4–R1	C4–R6
C2–R1	R4–C6
R4–C1	C4–R5
R4–C2	C4–R2
R4–C5	R4–C3
R4–C4	C4–R3
C2–R6	C2–R5
C2–R2	C2–R3
R3–C6	R3–C1
R1–C6	C1–R5
R1–C1	C1–R2

8.9.2 Improving its play

Naturally there are many ways of making the program better. We offer a few hints here.

In the first place one could speed up the evaluation function. This is called at every terminal node of the tree, and it is not very fast, having been built for comfort rather than speed. It could be accelerated by being re-written in ASSEMBLER (and would be in a commercial version). But it might also be improved if the method of 'incremental evaluation' were adopted instead. This means that as each proposed move was made the *change* to the evaluation was computed, and as each move was retracted the evaluation was restored to its former state. This technique avoids looking at parts of the board which have not been altered.

Secondly, if the evaluation had been speeded up, it might be worth doing a proper search for half moves as well as full ones (in the routine at line 3330 onwards). At present the computer picks its reply by looking at all six positions and doing a static evaluation. To search here as well as in the full moves would tax the user's patience beyond endurance! But with a quicker search, it would be acceptable.

Thirdly there is scope for improving the weighting scheme of -255, -7, -2, -1, $+1$, $+2$, $+8$, $+256$. It seems to give a good game, but it has not been extensively tested.

Finally, the program cries out for better graphics. These would make it far more fun to play. We were primarily concerned with getting it to play well (and with avoiding non-standard BASIC features), so the display is in text mode. All it does after each turn is clear the screen and re-print the updated board. Many of our readers can no doubt take it from there.

9
Computer creativity

If we look upon computing as a ladder (Fig. 9.1) we can, broadly speaking, distinguish four rungs of increasing complexity.

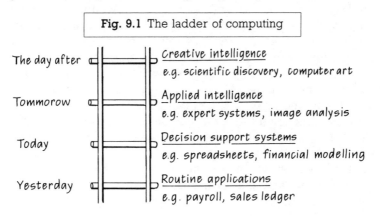

Fig. 9.1 The ladder of computing

The day after — Creative intelligence
e.g. scientific discovery, computer art

Tommorow — Applied intelligence
e.g. expert systems, image analysis

Today — Decision support systems
e.g. spreadsheets, financial modelling

Yesterday — Routine applications
e.g. payroll, sales ledger

On the bottom rung we have the mundane book-keeping tasks that computers do so well. One step up, things get a little more interesting. Here are programs that help people make intelligent decisions – spreadsheets and forecasting systems, for example. These tools have to be relatively flexible since the demands of the user cannot be predicted in advance. On the third level we find the application of humanly derived expertise. This is where the bulk of AI applications are concentrated. Such software is typified by the expert system Prospector, which encapsulated the codified rules of several prospecting geologists and, by putting those rules to work in the field, surprised its creators with the discovery of a large unknown molybdenum deposit in the east of Washington State. It later found another one in Canada.

Prospector's feats have become part of the folk-lore of AI, and very impressive they are too. They do not, however, get us up to the fourth rung of the ladder. To understand why, it is necessary to make a contrast between *productivity* and *creativity*.

Productivity depends on following the rules, and computers are excellent rule-followers. They can be extremely productive, far more so than most people; but to make them creative has proved exceedingly difficult.

To put it another way: it is the difference between Hercule Poirot and Sherlock Holmes. Agatha Christie wrote nearly 100 detective novels, many featuring the wily Belgian. Each one is exquisitely crafted and guaranteed to keep you engrossed on a long train or aeroplane journey. Sir Arthur Conan Doyle wrote considerably fewer, but he did start first, and in doing so he created a character who has lived on for over a century in the public imagination. (We must not forget Dr Watson either.) Visitors still arrive in London from foreign parts asking the way to 221b Baker Street.

Conan Doyle is credited with being the inventor of the modern detective novel, even though Edgar Allan Poe did some of the preliminary spade work. He invented a new genre. Others have followed and worked within it, but they are merely elaborating on an existing form.

People talk of potboilers as 'formula writing', so it makes sense to ask who wrote the formula. At one level, presumably, are the rules of the genre: follow the rules and you can produce hundreds of different stories. At a higher level there are no rules. There may, none the less, be 'meta-rules': follow the meta-rules and you can produce hundreds of different genres. Or can you?

That is the question which certain workers at the frontiers of AI are seeking to answer, and that is the question we shall address in the remainder of this chapter.

9.1 Computer art and computer science

We have distinguished productivity (applied intelligence) from creativity (creative intelligence), and suggested that great artists must have the latter faculty as well as the former. But, of course, it is not only writers and artists who are creative. Scientists need originality too if they are to make novel discoveries. So do mathematicians, who can be scientists one day and artists the next.

When Archimedes, one of the most prolific scientific and mathematical discoverers of ancient times, leapt out of his bath crying 'Eureka' he was not only responding to a sudden flash of insight, he was also uttering the Greek word which is the root of the English term 'heuristic' – serving to discover. Another form of that word, 'Eurisko', is the name given by Douglas Lenat to his scientific discovery program.

Eurisko is probably the most creative computer program written to date. It is an extension of an earlier system called AM (Automatic Mathematician) which explored the field of mathematics.

AM was designed to look into the three mysterious all-seeing I's – Inspiration, Insight and Intuition – which blind us to an understanding of the creative process. It was given a few primitive set-theoretic concepts like equality and the empty set plus a number of general heuristic rules, and then turned loose to ruminate on what it 'knew'. All its concepts were expressed in LISP, as were the primitive functions it began with, such as LIST-EQUALS, and the heuristics that guided its exploration of conceptual space.

AM quickly derived a function we would call LENGTH, i.e. number of members in a list, and a set of lists of each possible length up to a memory-imposed limit. These lists were isomorphic with the natural numbers. By restricting list operations such as APPEND to these canonical lists only, AM derived basic arithmetic operations, e.g. addition, and soon started exploring elementary number theory. It had started with no knowledge about numbers as such, nor about adding, multiplying and so on.

AM's processing cycle consisted of working on 'tasks' which were ordered by priority on an 'agenda'. Each task could spawn subtasks which were placed on the agenda. Every concept, including tasks, had a worth rating that dictated how urgent it was to work it and how much CPU time could be devoted to it. These worth values were adjusted dynamically, according to results.

After 'discovering' multiplication as repeated addition it investigated the inverse of multiplication, as one of its heuristics said in effect: if a function is interesting, define its inverse and investigate the properties of that too. This led it to the concept of divisors from which it soon moved to a number of conjectures about prime numbers, including Goldbach's conjecture that every even number can be expressed as the sum of two primes. (Note that AM does not prove its conjectures.)

This behaviour surprised its author. Initially it was not obvious that a few set and list operations coupled with heuristic rules would lead in so few steps to number-theoretical speculation. The heuristics that AM employed do not look like encodings of facts about prime numbers and so on. Here are a few, rendered into English.

If a function has high worth, look at its inverse, $f(x) = y \rightarrow g(y) = x$.
If a predicate is very seldom true, try to generalize it.
If two functions $f(x)$ and $g(x)$ appear interesting, compose them as $f(g(x))$ and $g(f(x))$.
If a function $f(x, y)$ is interesting, study the function $g(x)$ defined as $f(x, x)$.

Other heuristics advised it to look at extreme cases (like empty sets which led to the notion of zero), to look for symmetry and so forth.

With hindsight, Lenat concluded that AM's trip into number theory was facilitated by the design of LISP – a programming language formulated by a mathematician drawing on mathematical theories. Expressing mathematical concepts in LISP therefore turns out to be succinct and natural. In other words the representation influenced the results. From this Lenat derived a new heuristic of his own: if you want to build a discovery program, find or define a suitable representation language first.

After discovering a few hundred mathematical constructs such as prime numbers, AM eventually ground to a halt. The new concepts and functions it defined and the tasks it proposed failed to measure up to its own criteria of interestingness. It got lost just as things were getting genuinely interesting from the viewpoint of a human mathematician.

9.2 Learning by discovery

Since 1977 Lenat has been working on AM's successor, Eurisko. This system is intended to benefit from lessons learnt about AM and its weaknesses.

One lesson was to choose an appropriate representation. AM's representation scheme was fortuitously tuned to its objective, but Eurisko is more general. For this reason it uses RLL, an extremely flexible representation language in which everything (including the heuristics which contain chunks of LISP) is represented in terms of 'units'. Units are record-like or frame-like structures which have 'slots'. Slots are field-like entities which are not restricted in the kinds of value they can contain – numbers, strings, LISP functions, pointers to other units, etc. And all slots are defined in terms of units. This means that the potential for self-reference is there: new types of slots can be defined by mutating existing ones. An abbreviated Eurisko unit for the concept Primes is paraphrased below to give you the general idea. (One of Eurisko's tasks was to replicate what AM did.)

NAME: Primes
ENGLISH: Numbers with 2 divisors
SPECIALIZATIONS: Odd-primes, Small-primes, Pair-primes
GENERALIZATIONS: Positive-natural-numbers
IS-A: Set
EXAMPLES:
    Extreme: 2,3
    Extreme-non-ex: 0, 1
    Typical: 5, 7, 11, 13, 17, 19
    Typical-non-ex: 34, 100

CONJECTURES:
  Good-conjecs: Unique-factorization, Formula-for-d(n)
  Good-conjec-units:
    Times, Divisors-of, Exponentiation,
    Nos-with-3-divisors, Squaring
ANALOGIES: Simple Groups
WORTH: 800
    [Max. worth = 1000]
ORIGIN:
  Divisors-of-1 (doubletons)
  Defined-using: Divisors-of
HISTORY:
  N-good-examples: 840
  N-bad-examples: 5000
  N-good-conjectures: 3
  N-bad-conjectures: 7

An even more important lesson was drawn from the fact that AM seemed to run out of steam as it moved further away from its initial domain. Lenat realized that this happened partly because its starting heuristics had a limited range of applicability. The general ones proved too weak in the new topic areas while the specific ones were inappropriate. What was required was the ability to synthesize new heuristics from old ones as the focus of attention moved on. Eurisko can do this because, as already mentioned, its heuristics are represented in the same way as all the other data objects it deals with. Thus heuristics can work on each other as well as on more primitive objects.

This gives scope for generating and testing the sort of meta-rules we mentioned earlier – though it is important to realize that in Eurisko meta-rules have no special status: some heuristics happen to deal with heuristics, that is all. For example,

H10.   If a heuristic has fired less than once, generalize its IF condition slot(s).
H20.   If a heuristic takes a lot of room, there should be a new slot type that can be created to shorten it and other heuristics.

By applying H10 to H20 it might obtain something like H21, since an added OR condition does make the IF test more general; and by applying H10 to itself we might obtain something like H11. (We are not saying that they will both prove useful, that is for empirical trials to establish.)

H11.   If a rule has fired less than four times, generalize its IF condition slot(s).
H21.   If a heuristic takes a lot of time *or* it takes a lot of room, there may be a new slot type that can be created to shorten it and others.

The important point is that by letting heuristics work on themselves and each other, and monitoring their performance, Eurisko is able to move gracefully from one domain into another where – initially – it has no specific heuristics to guide it. The specific heuristics will be generated along the way. (Well, it is more complicated than that; but that should give you the gist.)

When it was put into the field of VLSI circuit design, Eurisko came up with a new type of circuit simply by taking the form of an AND gate and projecting it into three dimensions. Only one heuristic (the preference for symmetry) had to be invoked, and yet it came up with a design that no one in Silicon Valley or elsewhere had thought of – a three-dimensional AND/OR gate – which has subsequently been patented. It cannot, therefore, be regarded as a trivial example of creativity.

Before leaving Eurisko, it is worth stressing the close affinity between learning and creativity which is highlighted by this work. In a sense learning is re-discovery and discovery can be viewed as learning something for the first time. It is the fact that no one has done it before which distinguishes creativity from learning. (See also Chapter 5.)

9.3 Sense and sentences

Computers are normally designed, and often used, by mathematically inclined people. So perhaps it should not surprise us that they have proved most creative in mathematics and the sciences. But many people have attempted to make them do the same in the arts.

We look first at the arts of language since linguistics – although younger and less rigorous than mathematics – has recently been formalized. At least the computer has the rules of grammar to work on. (See also Chapter 3.)

Paradoxically, however, this seems to have hindered the development of computer poetry and prose. The rules of grammar are very well known and can be formally stated. It is therefore easy to make a computer churn out reams of grammatical sentences. In fact computers have been used to generate sentences of the 'Colourless green ideas sleep furiously' variety since shortly after Noam Chomsky outlined his theory of syntactic structures in 1957. All that is necessary is to turn a phrase structure grammar (such as that in Listing 3.2) on its head and make it synthesize rather than analyse sentences, making random choices where the rules permit alternative forms.

By deliberately restricting the vocabulary it is sometimes possible to give an impression of sense, though this is an illusion. Here is an example, from a program written by one of the authors in 1979.

Composition Entitled: To Sense Someone's Image
Your dark idea amazingly faces the dark eye. This suddenly dark and dark and magnificently dark and dead desire lusted. Our caress would seek our very light designs. The questions saw our image. The dark sign looking at Nature's beautiful tree should be beautiful and dark. Every earth can seek a single image.

Another image should plan God is with life, so the other images will be neutral. His design is his image.
Copyright Gribbly's Prose Factory 15/08/79.

The illusion of sense, such as it is, is maintained by superimposing two patterns on top of one another. One is based on a dictionary organized as a word-association network; the second is provided by a simple phrase-structure grammar. While the semantic portion is doing a Drunkard's Walk through the dictionary the syntactic section is imposing a grammatical structure on top. Not surprisingly, the output sounds like drunken ramblings.

Before beginning a new composition, the program picks a small active wordlist from the main dictionary. In the above case the active wordlist contained 32 entries, all associated with the key word 'image' in some way. As the composition proceeds words in this list that have been used more than once are replaced by associated words. An associated word is one that can be reached in one or two steps by following the positive or negative links from that word to others in the main dictionary. (See below.)

When the grammar reaches the point where it needs a noun or a verb or whatever it looks first in the active wordlist. Only if it cannot find a word of the right type there does it resort to the main dictionary of over 360 words. The grammatical routines construct sentence forms at random within the rules, it is only the word selection that is constrained by the active wordlist. The sentence starting 'Another image should plan God is with life ...' shows up a bug in the grammar: it should have said 'plan that ...'. If the word 'plan' had been 'think', the 'that' would indeed be optional, but here with 'plan' it is mandatory.

The main function of the program was to seek pathways through the word-association network, so the structure of the dictionary is the key to understanding it. There were twelve parts of speech, of which the first eight were classed as semantic and the other four as functional. Functional words had no associations. Thus all adverbs, articles, conjunctions and auxiliaries were treated equivalently.

(1) NAME Proper names, e.g. God.
(2) NOUN Things and abstractions, e.g. image.
(3) QUAL Adjectives, e.g. dark:
(4) PREP Prepositions, e.g. towards.

(5)	V0	Intransitive verbs, e.g. sleep.
(6)	V1	Transitive verbs, e.g. love.
(7)	V2	Verbs with two objects, e.g. give.
(8)	VX	Verbs introducing subsentences, e.g. think.
(9)	ADVB	Adverbs, e.g. really.
(10)	ARTI	Articles, e.g. this.
(11)	CONJ	Conjunctions, e.g. although.
(12)	AUXI	Auxiliary verbs, e.g. should.

Semantic words (types 1–8), as opposed to functional ones, had cross-references to other semantic words. A couple of typical dictionary entries exemplify this.

SELF
NOUN
PLUR:SELVES
+ SOUL,IN,MIND,BRAIN,BODY,SAME,SIMILAR TO,ALIVE,THINK,OWN
− DIFFERENT,BEYOND,SLEEP,LOVE,FRIEND,ENEMY,UNLIKE,DEAD,OUTSIDE

SEE
V1,VX
PAST:SAW,PASSIVE:SEEN,PART:SEEING
+ EYE,SENSE,LOOKING AT,LOOKING FOR,SEEK,FIND,LIGHT,BRIGHT, BEAUTIFUL,SIGN
− HEAR,EAR,HIDE,DARK,LOSE,DREAM,NIGHT,SCENT,BEHIND

Each word has four fields: (1) its type or types; (2) special or irregular forms, if any; (3) links to other words positively related; and (4) other words negatively related.

The type showed its grammatical category. One word could belong to several types. This avoided redundant duplication: 'love', for instance, was both a noun and a transitive verb. The special forms allowed the program to cope with irregular plurals, past tenses and suchlike.

The positive and negative links carried the semantic information. These had to be laboriously coded by hand. They allowed the fanning out through the network to take place. In fact the positive and negative links were treated as if they were simply strong versus weak links.

During operation the active wordlist was refreshed after each sentence. Any element that had been used twice or more was replaced by one of (1) its positive associations, (2) its negative associations, (3) positive associations one step removed or (4) negative associations one step removed. These four options are listed here in decreasing order of probability.

The active list was set up with the psychologists' concept of a small short-term memory in mind. By contrast the full dictionary was a kind of long-term memory. But no psychological validity is claimed for the model. It is merely intended to simulate the narrow beam of light cast by the flickering torch of awareness as it wanders through the mind's dark labyrinths (as the program might say). Each member of the wordlist follows its own independent path through this lexical maze, and these paths can diverge and re-cross.

Unfortunately this does not get us very far. We have an example of productivity, not creativity. Like most efforts at computer literature it follows the rules of syntax because they are well known. It cannot follow – much less revise or amend – the rules of meaning because no one really knows what they are.

9.4 Automatic writing

What is needed is a grammar of paragraphs or of discourse, if one can speak of a grammar in this connection. The work of Sheldon Klein and his associates moves some way in this direction. It is based on a theory of coherent discourse.

The roots of his formalism can be traced back to the Text Grammarian movement, which was an attempt to counter the inadequacy of Chomskyan transformational grammars when faced with sequences of more than one sentence. It is a theory of narrative structures which has much in common with the structuralist programme in anthropology. Appropriately, there-fore, one of Klein's projects was a mechanization of Propp's *Morphology of the Folktale*, published in 1968, which sought to codify the rules of a body of slavic folk-tales. The extract below captures its flavour.

The Morevnas live in a distant province. The father is Erema. The mother is Vasilisa. Baldak is the eldest son. The younger son is Marco. The youngest son is Boris. The oldest daughter is Maria. The younger daughter is Katrina. The youngest daughter is Martha. Nicholas also lives in the same land. Nicholas is of miraculous birth. Baldak has a magic steed. A bear appears in the distant province. The bear seizes the magic steed. Baldak calls for help from Nicholas. Nicholas decides to search for the magic steed. Nicholas leaves on a search.

He meets a jug along the way. The jug is fighting with Elena over a magic bow. The jug asks Nicholas to divide the magic bow. Nicholas tricks the disputants into leaving the magic bow unprotected. The magic bow, a magic carpet and a magic box are seized by Nicholas. Nicholas travels on the magic carpet to the location of the magic steed in another kingdom. He finds the bear there. He surprises the bear and kills it with the aid of the magic bow. The magic steed appears from the magic box. Nicholas starts back home. The bear's father chases after Nicholas. Nicholas escapes by flying on a falcon. Nicholas returns home.

(No, I don't know where the falcon came from either.)

Klein's program also produces other stories cast in very much the same mould 'at an average speed of 128 words a second' including plot computation and specification of surface syntax. Propp has, by anthropological research, distilled a class of Russian folk-tales into a set of rules. Klein has articulated these rules in a computer program and generated new stories by obeying them. Although they are not very brilliant, this does mark an improvement over purely syntactic systems. Its importance is in showing that the formulation of rules governing long stretches of narrative is possible.

We know that speech is purposive. By verbal intercourse we accomplish or fail to accomplish our most cherished ends. Klein's simulations do not take the goal-seeking aspect of language fully into account. The TALE-SPIN program of James Meehan, on the other hand, does. Here is one of its tales.

Once upon a time there was a dishonest fox named Henry who lived in a cave, and a vain and trusting crow called Joe who lived in an elm tree. Joe had gotten a piece of cheese and was holding it in his mouth. One day, Henry walked from his cave, across the meadow to the elm tree. He saw Joe Crow and the cheese and became hungry. He decided that he might get the cheese if Joe Crow spoke, so he told Joe that he liked his singing very much and wanted to hear him sing. Joe was very pleased and began to sing. The cheese fell out of his mouth, down to the ground. Henry picked up the cheese and told Joe Crow that he was stupid. Joe was angry and did not trust Henry any more. Henry returned to his cave.

If you think this rings a bell somewhere, you are perfectly right. The program has an option to let the user set up the characters and their traits. Meehan has clearly prepared this set-piece as a demonstration. The story is not new; but it does tell us that the program develops the consequences of the conflict of interests in an intuitively reasonable way. The characters are given problems to solve and the text output is a trace of their problem-solving attempts.

The main point about Meehan's system is that it simulates goal-seeking acts by agents in a micro-world of its own making and describes the results. The characters have traits and needs and try out various ways of achieving them, including conversation. To do so they invoke 'plans' which are subroutines for problem solving. For instance, if someone wants a thing and does not have it, he will call the go-there routine. This may in turn call the ask-where-it-is routine if he does not know its location, and so on.

Syntax rules are purely secondary. According to Meehan the English generator 'doesn't even use a grammar'. It is the modelling of interpersonal actions that counts, rather than the language used to describe them.

9.5 The magic theatre

The last of our computerized wordsmiths is a program called PLAY/RITE, written by one of the present authors. The basis of the program was a metaphor – a metaphor equating scenes with subroutines while actors are the parameters of those subroutines. The system was written in SNOBOL 4.

Its aim was to produce science-fiction playlets. It had a collection of subroutines, each of which played one kind of scene. For example, the VIOLENCE routine always played out a fight. What happened when VIOLENCE was called is typical of the general pattern. First it checked its parameters, the attacker and defender. If they were null, suitable actors were sought to fill the roles; otherwise the agressor's feelings towards the defender were tested. If the attacker liked the defender the whole process halted: the routine failed. Only if the attacker was sufficiently hostile did the scene continue, in which case the stage was set, the actors were brought on if necessary, and the dialogue and actions of the fight carried through to a conclusion – victory, defeat or stalemate. The results, which might include death or injury for one participant, were recorded for guiding future scenes, and the mutual feelings of the antagonists were adjusted accordingly.

We present the opening two scenes of one of its productions.

Beyond the Silent Moon
An interplanetary mind-boggling tragic scientific farce
by Monty Pinter
Featuring:

Seumnia	An evil grandmother
Jeff Newell	A good astronaut
Aphasia Potts	A telepath
Julia Cray	An alien
Lambda Reynolds	A Venusian
Tony Healey	A pilot

SCENE 1

[Midnight, Stardate 424.98, in the computer room on Pluto]

> Lambda Reynolds is on stage. Seumnia comes on stage imperiously. She gives a manic laugh.

SEUMNIA: I now have the means to make myself master of the universe. With the new anti-matter grenade I can destroy the entire system!

> She laughs.

SEUMNIA: All I need is some Potassium Dioxide: then all mankind will grovel at my feet!

Her eyes gleam satanically.

SCENE 2

[Meanwhile, in another part of the universe ...]

Seumnia, Lambda Reynolds are on stage.

SEUMNIA: The weather is rather ghastly just now here.

LAMBDA REYNOLDS: Ah. The weather is very foul at the moment eh?

Jeff Newell arrives. Aphasia Potts comes on stage.

JEFF NEWELL: Hello!

APHASIA POTTS: Hello.

JEFF NEWELL: I'm Jeff Newell.

APHASIA POTTS: Pleased to meet you. I'm Aphasia Potts.

JEFF NEWELL: Pleased to meet you. (To Aphasia Potts) I think you are honest and likeable.

APHASIA POTTS: You're just saying that. (She blushes.)

JEFF NEWELL: (To Aphasia Potts) Marry me.

Aphasia Potts looks aside.

APHASIA POTTS: The weather is very splendid at the moment eh?

JEFF NEWELL: That's right. (He nods at Aphasia Potts.)

JEFF NEWELL: (To Aphasia Potts) Please let it all hang out.

APHASIA POTTS: You've convinced me.

JEFF NEWELL: (To Aphasia Potts) I'm supremely grateful to you. What can I do to repay you?

APHASIA POTTS: It was of no consequence. Don't mention it.

JEFF NEWELL: (To Aphasia Potts) You are so extremely gorgeous. And I mean that most sincerely.

APHASIA POTTS: Very true! (She nods at Jeff Newell.)

JEFF NEWELL: (To Aphasia Potts) My heart is like a wheel, let me roll it to you.

APHASIA POTTS: O.K.

JEFF NEWELL: Darling!

APHASIA POTTS: The weather is very ghastly at the moment here.

Seumnia looks away.

JEFF NEWELL: The weather is very ghastly today you know.

LAMBDA REYNOLDS: Hmmm.

JEFF NEWELL: (To Lambda Reynolds) Goodbye.

LAMBDA REYNOLDS: See you later.

Jeff Newell goes.

APHASIA POTTS: I genuinely love Jeff Newell. I genuinely adore Jeff Newell. (Lambda Reynolds says nothing.)

APHASIA POTTS: I must go now. (She goes out.)

LAMBDA REYNOLDS: Jeff Newell.

Jeff Newell comes on stage.

JEFF NEWELL: Yes. What is it?

LAMBDA REYNOLDS: I have an important piece of news.

JEFF NEWELL: Go ahead.

LAMBDA REYNOLDS: It is bad news, I fear. Seumnia has built an anti-matter grenade. With it she can eliminate the system.

JEFF NEWELL: How can we stop her?

LAMBDA REYNOLDS: Apparently she needs Potassium Dioxide jelly to make it work.

JEFF NEWELL: There is no time to lose. We must find the Potassium Dioxide before Seumnia can lay her filthy hands on it.

Lambda Reynolds leaves the stage. Jeff Newell goes purposefully.

SEUMNIA: This could be interesting.

The structure of the second scene illustrates how the system works. It is a *meet* scene between the hero Jeff Newell and the heroine Aphasia Potts. When characters have nothing to say, they talk about the weather. Then the main protagonists come on stage and a *woos* scene is called right after their introduction. This in turn calls a *persuade* scene which is extremely short since both parties have high random numbers in the love–hate data matrix and Aphasia needs little persuasion. So *persuade* exits and the *woos* scene continues by calling a *feelings* scene, which is when Aphasia says 'I genuinely adore Jeff Newell', etc. The *meet* scene ends with a *warning* scene in which the hero is appraised of the danger to the system, by Lambda Reynolds. So the fundamental idea is that scenes can be embedded as subscenes in various ways. Thus events can take a variety of courses.

(In case you are wondering, Seumnia does get hold of the Potassium Dioxide in scene 9 and once again the world comes to a sticky end, despite Jeff Newell's efforts. But that was not a foregone conclusion: sometimes the universe is saved.)

Even the author of this play is made up by the program – and a good thing too, since nobody would want to claim responsibility for its out-pourings! It would hardly pack them in on Broadway, but, like Klein's and Meehan's work, it does show that syntax is only the icing on a cake that is not even half-baked yet. It is the rules of narrative and inter-personal behaviour that matter, and we are only groping towards them.

A story or play is interesting to read if interesting characters say and do interesting things in it. Until someone comes up with rules for generating interesting event sequences, the computer will remain un-productive.

As for creativity, that is a long way off. If it had some rules to play with, the computer could produce new ones – but who would evaluate their results? The machine cannot tell a boring story from an interesting one, so the onus would be on human judgement; and readers will not be disposed to wade through piles of printout sorting out the bad from the abysmal.

9.6 Painting by numbers

It could be said that computer art was invented long before the computer, in Zurich during the First World War by Hugo Ball and Tristan Tzara – the originators of Dada. It is a case of life imitating Arp.

Modern art, with its emphasis on the abstract and accidental which can be traced back to the Dadaists, has mechanized itself already. It has purged itself of semantics in an effort to be purely formal.

The problem thus becomes not one of producing works of art by computer but one of evaluating those productions. With suitable graphic output devices, computers can be programmed to produce pseudo-surrealistic Mondrians by the metre, Kandinskis by the kilo or Dalis by the dozen. But no one can say whether they are any good. Are they worse than their sources of inspiration? Or are they truer to the principles of anti-art which have replaced the old certainties?

Without an agreed evaluation there can be no measurable progress. Without measurable progress no computer system can learn: it cannot tell which rules to keep and which to discard because it cannot tell when its experiments fail. It cannot therefore exhibit even the limited creativity we have encountered so far – though, of course, it can cover paper, walls and CRT screens with lines, points and colour.

So the accepted function of the computer in the graphic arts today is that of a tool. It is either used by artists as an implement like the paintbrush, though more versatile, or by commercial designers for helping with the tricks of their trade. This is quite legitimate and helpful, but it is essentially uncreative.

Probably the nearest we get to artistry in the visual field is in computer animation. Film cartoonists, for example, have exploited the technique known as 'in-betweening' to relieve them of a tedious chore. The task is to take two images several frames apart and to generate the intermediate stages between them. Frame 1 might be a picture of Bambi on the ground by a tree with eyes closed. Frame 2, perhaps $1\frac{1}{2}$ s or 36 frames later, might be Bambi standing up startled with eyes wide open. The computer helps by filling in the intermediate frames.

At its simplest the technique relies on linear interpolation. If a pair of two-dimensional images are held as a series of X–Y points in two pairs of real vectors of equal length, then the in-betweening procedure is as follows.

```
DIM X(NS),Y(NS)        : REM 1st picture coords.
DIM XX(NS),YY(NS)      : REM 2nd picture coords.
DIM XS(NS), YS(NS)     : REM step size per point

REM calculate inter-frame step sizes:
FOR I = 1 to NS
    XD = XX(I) − X(I)
    XS(I) = XD / NF
    YD = YY(I) − Y(I)
    YS(I) = YD / NF
    NEXT I
REM NF is no. of frames in between.

REM perform the in-betweening:
FOR J = 1 to NF
  FOR I = 1 to NS
    XD = X(1) + XS(I) * J
    YD = Y(1) + YS(I) * J
    REM display or save point XD–YD
    NEXT I
  NEXT J
```

Bambi's spring, of course, requires more complex techniques. In a three-dimensional image shading, obscuration and other visual effects play a part; but these difficulties can be overcome now, leading to some aesthetically pleasing effects. And in solving this kind of problem, graphic designers use wire-frame models of the animals' bodies and so on which can be applied in other situations.

In a parallel advance, the insatiable military and civilian demand for realistic flight simulators has led to the development of very richly structured 'micro-worlds' which can be projected onto colour display screens to give the pilot the illusion of controlling anything from a Tiger Moth to a Space Shuttle. Some of these simulation techniques have percolated down to the microcomputer market, leading to a proliferation of stunning visual panoramas. While this sort of thing opens new horizons for human artists, it is not in itself an example of computer creativity.

At some point, however, the detailed world models on which such simulators and cartoon-aiders are based will become so complex as to take on a reality of their own. Film-makers can already use fractal-based techniques to conjure up moving pictures of scenes that exist only in the machine's 'imagination'. You see the sun setting slowly over an imaginary Pacific island with the leaves of the coconut palms fluttering in the breeze while the waves lap gently on the sand: as you watch a bronzed Polynesian girl wanders down to the water's edge, throws off her stereo headphones and plunges in.

You thought it would be a grass skirt? That's progress!

9.7 Computer music festival

It is no good having an idyllic island setting without background music, and the computer can produce that too.

Computer tone generation has reached the point where the sound of any instrument in the orchestra – and several that no orchestra could contain – can be reliably synthesized. Musicians take synthesizers for granted these days, much as Bach took the organ for granted. But we are more interested in the possibility of a machine composing music than playing it.

Mozart left instructions for composing simple dance melodies with the aid of dice, so the idea is hardly novel. Since then the hardware has come a long way, but the software has failed to keep pace.

The best known piece of computer-composed music is probably the Illiac Suite for String Quartet which was published by Hiller and Isaacson in 1959 and has been played several times since. It is still one of the best works of its kind, which tends to suggest that computer music has stuck in a groove.

Hiller and Isaacson relied on a random generate-and-test method. A random number generator proposed a bar (a group of a few notes) and it was subjected to several tests embodying various principles of composition and counterpoint. If it passed all the tests, it was appended to the score, otherwise it was rejected. In essence this is a filtering technique: some order is imposed on a random series by throwing out items that would violate the rules. Harmony in the form of chords could be superimposed afterwards, since there are strict rules for harmonization.

The process was stochastic in that each element influenced only a few following elements. There were some rules that connected different parts of the tune, dealing with sequences longer than two bars, but no grand plan as there presumably was in Beethoven's mind when he started the Ninth Symphony.

Many subsequent systems have been even less sophisticated, relying chiefly on two- or three-note transition probabilities, as in Fig. 9.2.

Fig. 9.2 Inter-note transition probabilities

	g	a	b	c	d	E	F	G	A	B	C	D
g	40			30	15	7		8				
a			64		32				4			
b	20		8	50	20						2	
c			10	40	15	20	10	4			1	
d	8		7	25	30	12	10	4				4
E		5	16	25	20	12	17				5	
F	4	2			20	44	8	22				
G	2			4	2	16	20	20	30	2	2	2
A		10		2	2			4	23	10	48	1
B			8					12	12	40	23	5
C				7		4		4	4	30	40	11
D					5			30	16	8	25	16

Shows the percentage probability that one note will be followed by another, blank cells denoting zero probability. Thus a is followed by d on 32% of occasions. Such tables can be derived by analysing the works of individual composers. A table from one composer can be used to generate tunes in the 'style' of that composer.

In this matrix blank cells indicate zeros and the numbers are percentage probabilities. To generate a note sequence the initial note is picked at random, then the successor selected according to the probabilities in the row concerned. The second note is used to select its successor in the same manner, and the process continues till the sequence is long enough. If the first note were E the chance of the next note being g would be nil; the chance of the next one being d would be 25%, and so on. Random tunes can be produced by using this sort of table, or a table of interval probabilities which is more compact, but they tend to lack direction.

The table can be constructed from first principles or by examining a particular composer's works. The idea is that by tabulating the inter-note frequencies of Johann Strauss, let us say, the program can be made to regurgitate Strauss-like melodies. Given the 'Vienna Woods' waltz it ought to come up with something like the 'Blue Danube'. In fact it is more likely to produce the 'Brown Drainpipe'!

Once again we hear the discordant echoes of Dadaism. Avante garde composers are so anxious to purge their works of tonal and rhythmic structure that the computer's lack of coherence is regarded in many quarters as a virtue.

Progress in computer music is only likely to come from a regression to old-fashioned ideas about what pleases the ear. The apparently content-free nature of musical elements (tones) has led computer composers down a dead end into a soundproof booth.

Music, like any other art form, has a thematic structure. What matters is the organization of sound sequences. Musicians have long talked about motifs, themes, exposition, recapitulation and development. Bottom-up methods based on single notes simply do not lead to natural patterns of this kind.

A top-down approach is far more likely to succeed, although the problem is that nobody is quite sure of the rules. In days gone by, there

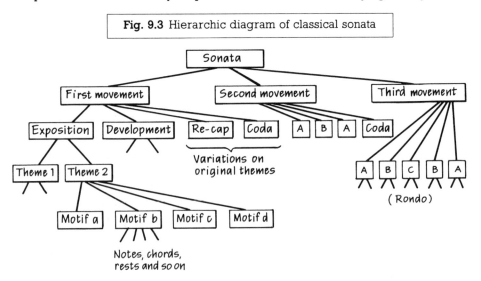

Fig. 9.3 Hierarchic diagram of classical sonata

was a greater degree of agreement on what constituted a permissible structure. Figure 9.3 shows a hierarchical diagram of the classical sonata.

The resemblance to a parse-tree in a phrase-structure grammar is not accidental. The diagram leaves out certain sideways relationships, however. The low-level themes are related: once motif a has been created (partly randomly) it constrains the form that motif b and motif c can take. There are also high-level constraints deriving from the key of the piece (among others) which are not shown in the diagram. Nevertheless, this is a far more realistic prescription for producing a piece of music than any matrix of transition probabilities.

Some workers, such as Otto Laske at MIT, are exploring music as a structured creation, but such work is no longer at the forefront of AI.

9.8 Summary

Computer art has become a backwater off the mainstream of AI, which is a pity because creativity must be a central topic in any study of intelligence. Much computer art is disappointing, scarcely reaching the level of productivity. It will not climb up to the level of creative intelligence, until the rules of composition are better understood and some means of giving the computer feedback is devised. Only Eurisko has taken more than half a step in that direction, and that has not been applied to the arts (though it has won the 'Trillion Credit Squadron' naval wargame).

Clearly, most present AI work (not just computer art) is concerned with applied intelligence, and this will remain true for many years to come: that is where the immediate payoff can be expected. In the long run, however, creative intelligence must be the ultimate goal of AI. It will, of course, be a very long run indeed before computers exhibit any creative imagination; but then most people are not very imaginative either.

To put it bluntly, 99% of the human race is totally devoid of creative spark. Indeed, many people take pride in being ordinary. As for the 1% gifted with originality, 99% of them squander their talents boozing, fornicating, making money or hosting their own TV shows (sometimes all at once). When we criticize an AI program for lack of creativity we are usually justified; but it is well to remember that we are comparing it with a handful of exceptional geniuses. There have been millions of musicians, but only one Mozart.

9.9 Sample program

For our excursion into computer art we borrow some ideas from 'Turtle Graphics' in order to build a 'grammar' for simple two-dimensional pictures. Later we will describe how exactly the same principles can be used to develop a music grammar for a 'Singing Turtle'.

Turtle graphics is an integral part of the LOGO programming language devised by Seymour Papert. It enables the user to draw pictures by programming the motions of a conceptual turtle that moves around the screen and leaves a trail in black, white or any available colour. At any time the turtle is at a particular point facing in a particular direction. To move it you give commands like FORWARD 10 (ten units forward) or LEFT 30 (turn 30 degrees left, anticlockwise) and so on. Turtle geometry is relative in the sense that the user does not worry about absolute $X-Y$ coordinates, only distance and direction relative to the present position and heading.

Turtle-style graphics packages are available in other languages than LOGO, such as UCSD PASCAL and some BASICS.

The basis for our design program will be a simplified turtle-style command language. A picture can then be defined by the sequence of commands that make the turtle draw that picture. We do not want to specify those commands in detail; rather we want the program to generate them for itself, thereby producing a variety of images on the screen.

To do that we devise a *grammar* which produces sentences not in English but in Turtle-speak. The turtle executes a sentence to make a picture. The primitive elements of the command language are two-character strings as follows:

Command	Meaning
Cn	Change colour to n
An	Set angle to $n \times 10$
Ln	Left $n \times 10$ degrees
Rn	Right $n \times 10$ degrees
Un	Up $n \times 10$ distance units
Dn	Down $n \times 10$ units
Fn	Forward $n \times 10$ units

It is not a very powerful graphical language, but it is sufficient for our purpose. That purpose is to make the computer draw designs on the screen which we have not fully specified in advance. Or, to look at it another way, our aim is to make the computer write programs in the graphic language automatically. (So we have entered the realm of automatic programming by the back door.)

To achieve this, we will specify a simple phrase-structure grammar whose terminal elements are not words but commands, or simple subroutines, in the turtle's language. Just as Listing 3.2 (Chapter 3) has replacement rules like

<CONJUNCTION> = AND

so our grammar will have productions like

<BOX> = F8L9F4L9F8L9F4

which tell the turtle how to draw a rectangular shape.

In fact, to simplify the computer's task, our grammar uses single-character symbols like B rather than multi-character strings like <BOX> enclosed in angle brackets. Grammatical rules are composed using the letters A–H, the digits 0–9 and the equals sign. Letters are non-terminal symbols (like <NOUN PHRASE> in a linguistic grammar which refers to another construction) while digits are for terminal symbols (like <ADJECTIVE> which refers directly to the lexicon). Each rule specifies that a single symbol on the left-hand side may be replaced by a string of symbols on the right. For example, the rules

A=0B1B
B=2
B=33

0=C4
0=C2
1=F8F8F8U4
1=C1F8F8F8D4
2=F8R9F8R9F8R9F8
3=F8L9L3F8L9L3F8

state that a legal picture has the form 0B1B (since A is always by convention the top-level entity like <SENTENCE> in a linguistic grammar). B may be replaced either by a 2 or two 3s. The terminal symbols 0–3 specify little turtle routines. Routine 0 sets the colour; 1 draws a line and may change colour; 2 draws a square, and 3 draws a triangle.

In brief, the rules say that to make a picture you set the colour initially and then draw two objects connected by a line. The objects (B) may be either a single square or a pair of triangles. The connecting line may or may not cause a colour change. Figure 9.4 shows a 'parse' of an image in this grammar.

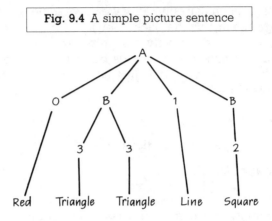

Fig. 9.4 A simple picture sentence

This is rather a trivial example, just to give you the idea. Once you get the hang of it you will be able to express quite complex structural relationships. A sample grammar can be seen on lines 500 onwards of Listing 9.1.

To prepare you for the program itself, here is the outline of its top level.

Initialize Turtle etc.	[1000]
Read in the Rules	[2000]
REPEAT	
Re-intialize	[1010]
Form a picture-sentence	[3000]
Clear Screen	
Interpret the sentence	[4000]
Pause	
UNTIL enough done	
END	

The important subroutines are at lines 2000, 3000, 4000 and 5000 (the latter being called from subroutine 4000).

Subroutine 2000 reads the rules from the data statements as strings into the array *PG$*(). It also counts the number of rules with the same left-hand symbol in *PN%*(), so if there are two rules beginning '4 = ...' then *PN%*(4) will contain two on exit. Such rules are alternatives.

Subroutine 3000 composes a legal symbol-string in *S$* by following the rules in *PG$*(). It keeps on replacing left-hand sides by right-hand sides until there are no letters in *S$* but only digits. Remember that digits are terminal symbols, i.e. drawing operations. Wherever there is a choice of rules, it picks one at random. Thus if *S$* contained

....**C**....

and the rules for C were 'C = 01' and 'C = 1010' then S$ could end up as

....01.... or ....1010....

with equal probability.

Subroutine 4000 interprets the command sequence in S$ that has been built by subroutine 3000. It pulls off one character at a time and looks for a rule that starts with that character (which must be a digit). Having found the rule it throws away the first two characters (e.g. '2 = ') and passes the rest of the string, two characters at a time, to the command interpreter in subroutine 5000 as the contents of TC$.

Subroutine 5000 takes the contents of TC$ as a basic operation and carries it out (e.g. 'F7' to go forward 70 steps). Some commands merely adjust one of the turtle parameters.

TA   angle
TX   x-position (horizontal)
TY   y-position (vertical height)

others change the colour setting, and the 'F' command actually causes movement on the screen.

Note that it is only subroutines 5000 and, to a lesser extent, 1000 that make this program specific to graphics. If you are converting it for another machine, only lines 1001, 1040, 1050, 5050, 5230 and 5240 will have to be changed; although the screen-size limits enforced in lines 5190–5220 may need attention too.

Listing 9.1 Graphic grammar test

```
10   REM      ***************************
11   REM      ** LISTING 9.1           **
12   REM      ** GRAPHIC GRAMMAR TEST **
13   REM      ***************************
50   DEF  FN R(X) =  INT ( RND (1) * X + 1): REM    RANDOM INTEGER
     S (1-X).
60   DEF  FN RA(X) = X * 3.141592654 / 180: REM  DEGREES TO RADIAN
     S.
70   TEXT : HOME
100  REM       -- MAIN LINE:
120  GOSUB 1000: REM       INITIALIZE
140  GOSUB 2000: REM       READ GRAMMAR
200  REM       START LOOP
202  GOSUB 1010: REM       RE-INITIALIZE
210  GOSUB 3000: REM       COMPOSE S$
220  HOME : VTAB 21: HTAB 1: PRINT S$: HGR
230  GOSUB 4000: REM       INTERPRET S$
250  INPUT "MORE (Y=YES) ";Y$
270  IF Y$ < > "Y" THEN 290
280  GOTO 200
```

```
290    TEXT
300    END
500    REM       -- DATA FOR GRAPHIC GRAMMAR:
510    DATA      A=BCCB
520    DATA      A=BBC
530    DATA      A=BB
535    DATA      A=0234B
540    DATA      B=DDED
550    DATA      B=DC
560    DATA      C=0
570    DATA      C=0E
580    DATA      C=0120
585    DATA      C=30
588    DATA      C=44
590    DATA      D=01
600    DATA      D=11
605    DATA      D=10
606    DATA      D=3
607    DATA      D=43224
610    DATA      E=2
620    DATA      E=12
630    DATA      E=1212
640    DATA      E=20
650    DATA      0=R9F7R9F7R9F7R9F7
660    DATA      1=C1L4F8F8: REM     COLOR GREEN
670    DATA      2=C2L4L4L4: REM     COLOR BLUE
680    DATA      3=U8C1
688    DATA      4=F8F8R3R9F8F8R3R9F8F8R9R6
690    DATA      4=F8L9L3F8L9L3F8L9L3F8L6
770    DATA      ""
777    REM       THIS DEFINES A PICTURE GRAMMAR.
1000   REM       -- INITIALIZING ROUTINE:
1001   HGR
1010   TA = 0: REM      TURTLE ANGLE
1020   TX =    FN R(200) + 40: REM   TURTLE X-COORD
1030   TY =    FN R(125) + 30: REM   TURTLE Y-COORD
1040   HCOLOP= 7: REM   INITIAL COLOR WHITE
1050   HCOLOR= 0: HPLOT TX,TY: HCOLOR= 7: REM  SET START POSITION.

1080   RETURN
2000   REM       -- READ IN PICTURE GRAMMAR.
2010   DIM PG$(33),PN%(25)
2020   RESTORE
2030   FOR L = 0 TO 25
2040   PN%(L) = 0: NEXT
2050   L = 0
2060   L = L + 1: REM      START LOOP
2070   READ R$
2080   L$ =  LEFT$ (R$,1)
2090   PG$(L) = R$
2100   IF L$ < > "" THEN :N =  ASC (L$) - 48
2105   IF L$ = "" THEN :N =  - 48
2110   IF N > = 0 THEN ;PN%(N) = PN%(N) + 1
2120   IF R$ = "" OR L > 32 THEN 2122
2121   GOTO 2060
```

```
2122 G = L - 1: REM      RULE COUNT
2140  PRINT "RULES READ IN = ";G
2150  RETURN
3000  REM       -- COMPOSITION ROUTINE:
3010 S$ = "A": REM      A IS ALWAYS INITIAL SYMBOL
3020  S = 1
3040  REM      START LOOP
3050 GOSUB 3300: REM      NEXT LETTER -> L$
3055  REM      ALSO SETS S.
3060  GOSUB 3500: REM      REPLACE L$ -> R$
3075  IF S > 1 THEN :S$ =  LEFT$ (S$,S - 1) + R$ +  MID$ (S$,S +
     1)
3076  IF S < = 1 THEN :S$ = R$ +  MID$ (S$,S + 1)
3080  REM      EXPANDS L$ AS R$
3090  IF L$ = "" OR  LEN (S$) > 220 THEN 3100
3095  GOTO 3040
3100  RETURN
3300  REM      -- NEXT NON-TERMINAL -> L$
3310 L$ = ""
3320  REM      START LOOP
3330 L$ =  MID$ (S$,S,1)
3340  IF L$ < "A" THEN :S = S + 1: REM      TERMINAL SYMBOL
3350  IF L$ > = "A" OR S >  LEN (S$) THEN 3355
3351  GOTO 3320
3355  IF S >  LEN (S$) THEN L$ = ""
3370  RETURN
3500  REM      -- SYMBOL REPLACEMENT ROUTINE:
3510  IF S >  LEN (S$) THEN : RETURN
3515  IF L$ = "" THEN : RETURN
3520 L =  ASC (L$) - 48
3530 LL =  FN R(PN%(L))
3535  IF LL < 1 THEN :LL = 1
3540 L = 0:R$ = ""
3550  FOR R = 1 TO G
3560  IF L$ =  LEFT$ (PG$(R),1) THEN :L = L + 1
3570  IF L > = LL THEN :R$ =  MID$ (PG$(R),3):R = G
3580  NEXT R
3590  IF R$ = "" THEN :R$ = L$: PRINT "NO RULE! ";R$
3600  RETURN
4000  REM      -- INTERPRET S$ AS RULE-STRING:
4010 L =  LEN (S$)
4020  FOR S = 1 TO L
4030 R$ =  MID$ (S$,S,1)
4033 K = 0:LL =  FN R(PN%( ASC (R$) - 48))
4035  IF LL < 1 THEN :LL = 1
4040  FOR R = G TO 1 STEP  - 1
4050  IF R$ =  LEFT$ (PG$(R),1) THEN :L$ =  MID$ (PG$(R),3):K = K
     + 1
4055  IF K > = LL THEN :R = 0
4060  NEXT R
4070  REM      START LOOP
4080 TC$ =  LEFT$ (L$,2): REM      TURTLE COMMAND
4090  GOSUB 5000
4100 L$ =  MID$ (L$,3): REM      REST OF STRING
4110  IF  LEN (L$) < 1 THEN 4125
```

```
4111  GOTO 4070
4125  NEXT S
4140  RETURN
5000  REM     -- COMMAND INTERPRETER:
5010  REM        :: TC$ --> TA,TX,TY(C$,C)
5020  IF TC$ = "" THEN : RETURN
5030  C$ =  LEFT$ (TC$,1)
5040  C =  VAL ( MID$ (TC$,2))
5050  IF C$ = "C" THEN : HCOLOR= C: RETURN
5060  C = C * 10
5070  IF C$ > "Z" THEN :C$ =  CHR$ ( ASC (C$) - 32)
5080  IF C$ = "A" THEN :TA = C
5090  IF C$ = "L" THEN :TA = TA - C
5100  IF C$ = "R" THEN :TA = TA + C
5110  IF C$ = "U" THEN :TY = TY + C
5120  IF C$ = "D" THEN :TY = TY - C
5130  IF C$ < > "F" THEN : RETURN
5140  IF TA > 360 THEN :TA = TA - 360
5150  IF TA < 0 THEN :TA = 360 + TA
5160  REM     -- MOVEMENT:
5170  TX = TX +  SIN ( FN RA(TA)) * C
5180  TY = TY +  COS ( FN RA(TA)) * C
5190  IF TX > 279 THEN :TX = TX - 280:C =  - 1
5200  IF TX < 0 THEN :TX = TX + 280:C =  - 1
5210  IF TY > 159 THEN :TY = TY - 160:C =  - 1
5220  IF TY < 0 THEN :TY = TY + 160:C =  - 1
5230  IF C =  - 1 THEN : HPLOT TX,TY
5240  HPLOT  TO TX,TY
5250  RETURN
5260  REM     DRAWS A LINE TO TX,TY.
5265  REM     TC$ IS TURTLE COMMAND.
```

The output of the program as listed is not particularly exciting. But it does demonstrate two significant principles.

In the first place, the rules are not hard-coded into the program. They are data, and can be altered (improved) by you if you wish. We have defined a language for expressing picture-production rules. The program gives a means of experimenting with different rule-sets. You can try out picture grammars of your own. In addition, you could extend routine 5000 to add new graphics commands – perhaps even including variables or stack handling and conditional tests. By extending the command interpreter you enhance the turtle language, though even in its present form it is capable of creating a wide range of designs.

Secondly, it is very important to realize that the grammar does not have to be pictorial. In fact we can use exactly the same techniques to produce simple melodies, merely by changing the base-language. In the 'Singing Turtle' version (of Listing 9.2) subroutine 5000 interprets commands for changing pitch, playing notes, etc., instead of changing colour, drawing lines, etc.

This raises an interesting point: What does a picture sound like and what does a tune look like? By swapping the terminal symbols of the tune, which are bars of music, with those of a picture, which are shapes, but keeping the same high-level grammatical structures, you can actually play a picture or draw a tune!

Listing 9.2 Turtle tune test

```
10   REM      ***************************
11   REM      ** LISTING 9.2         **
12   REM      ** TURTLE TUNE TEST    **
13   REM      ***************************
50   DEF  FN R(X) =  INT ( RND (1) * X + 1): REM     RANDOM INTEGER
     S (1-X).
70   HOME
100  REM        -- MAIN LINE:
120  GOSUB 1000: REM       INITIALIZE
140  GOSUB 2000: REM        READ GRAMMAR
200  REM        START LOOP
210  GOSUB 3000: REM       COMPOSE S$
220  HOME : PRINT S$
230  GOSUB 4000: REM       INTERPRET S$
250  INPUT "MORE (Y=YES) ";Y$
270  IF Y$ < > "Y" THEN 300
280  GOTO 200
300  END
500  REM  -- DATA FOR MUSIC GRAMMAR:
510  DATA  A=0BDE
520  DATA  A=0BE
530  DATA  A=0BCE
540  DATA  A=0BCDE
544  DATA  A=0DCB
550  DATA  B=123
560  DATA  B=1122
565  DATA  B=21
566  DATA  B=1223
570  DATA  C=4
580  DATA  C=45
590  DATA  C=456
600  DATA  C=4567
610  DATA  D=8
620  DATA  D=88
630  DATA  E=23
640  DATA  E=93
650  DATA  0=T101NAD1P2U1P2D1P2U2P4P2
652  DATA  0=T101NAD1P6#1P4$1P2
655  DATA  0=T1NA
656  DATA  0=T201NA
660  DATA  1=D1P2U1P2D1P2#3P6
670  DATA  2=$1P2#3P2$7P2#5P4$1P2
```

```
680   DATA   3=D1P2D1P2D1P2U1P6
688   DATA   3=U1P2U1P2U1P2D1P6
690   DATA   4=U6P4D1P2U1P4$5P2
700   DATA   5=P2U1P2U1P2D1P4D1P2
710   DATA   6=P2U1P2U1P2#1P2$5P2U1P2
720   DATA   7=D1P2D1P2$1P2D1P4#5P2
730   DATA   8=U1P2D1P2D1P2$1P2#1P2U1P2
740   DATA   9=U1P2#3P2D5P2#5P4$1P2
750   DATA   9=U1P6P4
770   DATA   ""
777   REM   DATA BASED ON 'LILLIBURLERO'.
1000  REM       -- INITIALIZING ROUTINE:
1010 DT = 127.5: REM   TIME CONSTANT
1020 DP = 255 * 2 ^ ( - 14 / 12): REM   PITCH CONSTANT.
1030 A1 = DP: REM     BASIC PITCH A
1040 TU = DT: REM     DEFAULT TIME QUAVER
1050  DIM NT%(15): REM   NOTE TABLE.
1060  READ R$: IF R$ < > "" THEN 1060
1070  FOR N = 1 TO 15
1080  READ NT%(N): NEXT
1200  REM   -- NOTE DATA:
1202  DATA   0,2,3,5,7,8,10,12,14,15,17,19,20,22,24
1300  REM   -- M/C CODE SOUND SUBROUTINE STARTING AT LOCATION 768:

1310  FOR N = 768 TO 792
1320  READ R: POKE N,R
1330  NEXT
1340  DATA   173,48,192,136,208,5,206,22,3,240,9
1350  DATA    202,208,245,174,21,3,76,0,3,96,0,0,0,0
1360 P1 = 789:D1 = 790
1370 P =  FN R(36) + 1: REM      SET DEFAULT NOTE.
1400  RETURN
2000  REM   -- READ IN MUSIC GRAMMAR:
2010  DIM PG$(33),PN%(25)
2020  RESTORE
2030  FOR L = 0 TO 25
2040 PN%(L) = 0: NEXT
2050 L = 0
2060 L = L + 1: REM      START LOOP
2070  READ R$
2075  IF  RIGHT$ (R$,1) = " " THEN :R$ =  LEFT$ (R$, LEN (R$) - 1
      ): GOTO 2075
2080 L$ =  LEFT$ (R$,1)
2090 PG$(L) = R$
2100  IF L$ < > "" THEN :N =  ASC (L$) - 48
2105  IF L$ = "" THEN :N =  - 48
2110  IF N > = 0 THEN :PN%(N) = PN%(N) + 1
2120  IF R$ = "" OR L > 32 THEN 2122
2121  GOTO 2060
2122 G = L - 1: REM      RULE COUNT
2140  PRINT "RULES READ IN = ";G
2150  RETURN
3000  REM       -- COMPOSITION ROUTINE:
3010 S$ = "A": REM      A IS ALWAYS INITIAL SYMBOL
3020 S = 1
```

```
3040   REM       START LOOP
3050   GOSUB 3300: REM      NEXT LETTER -> L$
3055   REM       ALSO SETS S.
3060   GOSUB 3500: REM      REPLACE L$ -> R$
3075   IF S > 1 THEN :S$ =  LEFT$ (S$,S - 1) + R$ +  MID$ (S$,S +
       1)
3076   IF S <  = 1 THEN :S$ = R$ +  MID$ (S$,S + 1)
3080   REM       EXPANDS L$ AS R$
3090   IF L$ = "" OR  LEN (S$) > 220 THEN 3100
3095   GOTO 3040
3100   RETURN
3300   REM        -- NEXT NON-TERMINAL -> L$
3310   L$ = ""
3320   REM       START LOOP
3330   L$ =  MID$ (S$,S,1)
3340   IF L$ < "A" THEN :S = S + 1: REM       TERMINAL SYMBOL
3350   IF L$ >  = "A" OR S >  LEN (S$) THEN 3355
3351   GOTO 3320
3355   IF S >  LEN (S$) THEN L$ = ""
3370   RETURN
3500   REM        -- SYMBOL REPLACEMENT ROUTINE:
3510   IF S >  LEN (S$) THEN : RETURN
3515   IF L$ = "" THEN : RETURN
3520   L =  ASC (L$) - 48
3530   LL =  FN R(PN%(L))
3535   IF LL < 1 THEN :LL = 1
3540   L = 0:R$ = ""
3550   FOR R = 1 TO G
3560   IF L$ =  LEFT$ (PG$(R),1) THEN :L = L + 1
3570   IF L >  = LL THEN :R$ =  MID$ (PG$(R),3):R = G
3580   NEXT R
3590   IF R$ = "" THEN :R$ = L$: PRINT "NO RULE! ";R$
3600   RETURN
4000   REM        -- INTERPRET S$ AS RULE-STRING:
4010   L =  LEN (S$)
4020   FOR S = 1 TO L
4030   R$ =  MID$ (S$,S,1)
4033   K = 0:LL =  FN R(PN%( ASC (R$) - 48))
4035   IF LL < 1 THEN :LL = 1
4040   FOR R = G TO 1 STEP  - 1
4050   IF R$ =  LEFT$ (PG$(R),1) THEN :L$ =  MID$ (PG$(R),3):K = K
       + 1
4055   IF K >  = LL THEN :R = 0
4060   NEXT R
4066   PRINT L$
4067   IF L$ = "" THEN : STOP
4070   REM       START LOOP
4080   TC$ =  LEFT$ (L$,2): REM       TURTLE COMMAND
4090   GOSUB 5000
4100   L$ =  MID$ (L$,3): REM      REST OF STRING
4110   IF  LEN (L$) < 1 THEN 4125
4111   GOTO 4070
4125   NEXT S
4140   RETURN
```

```
5000   REM      -- COMMAND INTERPRETER:
5005   REM   -- THE SINGING TURTLE!
5010   REM   :: TC$ --> P,TU,A1 (C$,C)
5020   IF TC$ = "" THEN : RETURN
5030   C$ = LEFT$ (TC$,1)
5050   C = ASC ( MID$ (TC$,2)) - 48
5060   IF C > 9 THEN :C = C - 16: REM  CHARACTER DATA
5070   IF C < 0 OR C > 9 THEN : PRINT "CHECK YOUR DATA STATEMENTS"
       : RETURN
5100   REM   -- NOW DO THE BUSINESS:
5110   IF C$ = "N" THEN :P = NT%(C)
5120   IF C$ = "T" THEN :TU = C * DT / 8
5130   IF C$ = "U" THEN :P = P + 2
5140   IF C$ = "D" THEN :P = P - 2
5150   IF C$ = "#" THEN :P = P + 1
5160   IF C$ = "$" THEN :P = P - 1
5180   IF C$ = "O" THEN :A1 = DP / (2 ^ C)
5190   IF C$ = "R" THEN : POKE 769,23: POKE 770,3: POKE P1,1: POKE
       D1,TU * C: CALL 768: POKE 769,48: POKE 770,192: REM  REST
5199   IF C$ < > "P" THEN : RETURN
5200   POKE P1,A1 * 2 ^ ( - P / 12): POKE D1,TU * C: CALL 768: REM
       PLAY
5220   RETURN
5230   REM  P PLAYS NOTE.
```

For the musical version, the primitive drawing instructions are replaced as follows (but the grammatical scheme remains the same):

Command	Meaning
Nc	Make the current note c
Tn	Set smallest time unit to n (2 = semi-quaver, 4 = quaver, 8 = crotchet)
Un	Up n tones
#n	Up n semitones
Dn	Down n tones
$n	Down n semitones
Ln	Loudness 0–9
On	Set current octave (5 is highest)
Rn	Rest for n time units (silence)
Pn	Play current note for n time units

Routines 1000 and 5000 have been re-written. The program structure scarcely changes.

Subroutine 5000 maintains the following variables.

P	Current pitch
TU	Basic time unit
*A*1	Note a of current octave

They are affected by the turtle commands.

If you wish to convert this program for another computer, you will need to reproduce the following facilities;

Line	Effect
5190	Silence for time *TU**C
5200	Play note *P* (relative to *A*1) for time *TU**C
5190	Short silence

The rest, as they say, should be as easy as whistling.

9.9.1 Extensions and enhancements

The programs as listed are productive, but not really creative. They can synthesize images (or tunes), but the human user has to formulate the rules for producing those images (or tunes). At least the rules are framed as data, so you can easily add, delete and modify them to see what happens; but it would be better if we could automate that amendment process.

For really adventurous readers, here are a few suggestions on how to progress in that direction.

Firstly, we must arrange for the program to receive feedback on its performance. This is easily arranged. All you have to do is make it ask something like

'on a scale − 10 to + 10 how did you like that one?'

after each composition, and give it your answer. That way it will eventually adjust to your own quirks and preferences. (Wouldn't it be nice if some other software systems did likewise?)

To make use of this feedback, we require two further arrays, let us say

DIM VT(33), VN(33)

$VN(I)$ will record how often rule I has been used and $VT(I)$ will hold the total value given by the user over as many sessions as you like. Now some rules will inevitably be used more often than others, so you may want to multiply the user-supplied evaluation score by the frequency of use of each rule in the latest composition before accumulating the totals; but in any case, it means that after a series of trials, each rule will have an average score.

The simplest thing to do at that stage is to get the computer to sort the rules in order of merit and print them out. Then look at the low scorers: these must be rules which tended to be used frequently in bad compositions and seldom in good ones. They are candidates for replacement. You can scratch your head and conclude 'I don't seem to like pictures with red Christmas trees in them' and try yellow butterfiles instead. The regeneration process thus becomes semi-automatic.

To make it fully automatic will get you into deep waters. One possibility – among many – is to try an evolutionary approach. You say, in effect: well, these rules are a bit like genes. A real turtle's genes are instructions for building a turtle; our mock turtle's rules are instructions for drawing a picture. Perhaps by mutating them, they could be improved. In other words, can we make the turtle evolve? (Into a crocodile perhaps?)

One framework for such an approach is outlined below.

Read in rules from disc
REPEAT
        Make up composition
        Present it
        Receive evaluation
        Adjust component rule values
        ** Replace bad rules **
UNTIL enough done
Save rules on disc

The key routine is the one for discarding bad rules and replacing them by new ones. A genetic strategy would base the replacements on recombinations of old rules (especially the better ones) with a little random mutation thrown in from time to time to keep things simmering.

Suppose we have an empty slot where a low-scoring rule has just been deleted and have picked a couple of high-scoring rules at random as 'parents' for its successor. They are

B = CCDC

and

C = 0DEE011.

How might we combine portions of these two strings to produce a new one? Well, we could exchange left and right sides

B = 0DEE011,   C = CCDC

or we could swap two individual symbols at corresponding points

B = 0DDC, B = CCDC, C = CDEE011   etc.

or we could chop at random points and re-splice them

B = CCE011,   C = 0DEDC

and so on. The attraction of the method is that there are a number of straightforward syntactic manipulations that will generate new structures as variants of the old. But it would pay to have a tidying routine that looks at the 'offspring' to make sure they make sense in the grammar. We do not want

C = CCCC

or

C =

for example! Many such 'deformities' can be spotted by simple tests (and aborted).

Also it would certainly pay to keep the terminal rules (0–9) separate from the non-terminals (A–H). They are different 'species'.

Occasional, but not frequent, random mutations will prevent the system getting stuck. Thus, starting with 0 = F3R9F3R9 for instance, the program could do one of the following to produce new items for inclusion in the rule set.

From: 0 = F3R9F3R9

change a symbol	− > 0 = F4R9F3R9
	− > 0 = F3L9F3R9
swap two items	− > 0 = F3F3R9R9
	− > 0 = F3R9R9F3
delete a section	− > 0 = F3R9
	− > 0 = R9F3R9
add syntactically valid items	− > 0 = F3R9F3R9C2
	− > 0 = F3R9F3R9F4L6
invert a series	− > 0 = R9F3R9F3

The point is that purely formal transformations can be applied to generate new candidate rules for testing. Though again a lot of thought would be needed to prevent the program generating nonsense rules. Just as in real life, most mutations are harmful.

You might also like to consider the possibility of having several rule-sets competing and treating complete grammars rather than individual rules as the 'organisms' being selected. This would require more space and time; but it is probably truer to the Darwinian spirit of the enterprise.

Enhancements like these would make the system more truly creative. John Holland at the University of Michigan has proved various theorems about systems relying on abstract genetic operators similar to those discussed above; and it turns out that they search the enormous space of possible rule structures in a reasonably efficient way. A word of caution is in order, however. Natural selection has taken over 3600 million years to get this far. Naturalistic selection can work faster, but it is not magic. If it were, computers would by now be far more creative than they actually are.

10
AI: Future trends

It can get lonely being conscious in the Cosmos – especially with people like Copernicus and Carl Sagan to tell you how big it is. Of course we can talk to each other, we can even write books, but we are only talking to ourselves. After all, we are all human.

Only four prospects of allaying this loneliness exist:

(1) Communicating with extra-terrestrial intelligences.
(2) Teaching animals to speak (e.g. chimpanzees).
(3) Learning the language of another species (e.g. dolphins).
(4) Building intelligent artefacts.

So far there has been no authenticated contact with extra-terrestrial beings of any kind. It would be immensely interesting to converse with someone who was not human; but if we wait for messages from Them-out-There, we may wait a very long time.

There has been a certain amount of progress down the second avenue. Washoe the chimp was taught to use American Sign Language with her keepers (captors?), but when the controversy over whether she was using Language with a capital L subsided, so did most of the interest. It turned out that chimps did not have much to say.

Dolphins, whales and porpoises seem to have plenty to say, but we cannot make fin nor flipper of it – despite three decades of serious research and the benefits of intensive computer analysis. Perhaps if we beamed whale-song into space instead of a stream of quiz shows and commercials, Them-out-There might take the trouble to reply.

That leaves machinery. It appears for the moment that if we want to contact a mind that is not housed in a human skull, we will have to build one. How long is it likely to take? Will we have to wait till after we have cracked the dolphins' code and the little green men have beamed down from Ultima Centauri and points west?

This chapter is an attempt to answer those questions.

10.1 Generation after generation

So far this book has concentrated on the acceptable face of AI. We have viewed AI as the vanguard of computer science – a fertile source of fresh ideas and clever tricks. When these ideas and tricks are successful, they filter out to other parts of computing and prove extremely valuable. This has happened to list-processing and conversational computing in the past, and is currently happening to knowledge-based systems. As we pointed out in Chapter 1, AI 'exports its successes'.

The medium-term prospects for this type of work are good. We can expect progress on a broad front. There may be setbacks, and some of the bolder predictions may not be realized, but by the end of this century we should have witnessed substantial advances in the fields of computer vision, automatic translation, machine learning and knowledge-based systems. Even the thorny problem of continuous speech understanding will be close to solution.

The Japanese fifth generation initiative has given a tremendous boost to this side of AI. By their ambitious plans the Japanese have subtly re-defined the rules of the game for the computer industry. They expect to produce knowledge information processors in the 1990s which are based on radically new, highly parallel computer architectures. The software that will make such systems work is firmly rooted in AI research.

Japanese reliance on AI techniques has made the rest of the world hurry to scramble back into AI. Now vendors outdo one another in their efforts to claim that their products incorporate the latest AI research – almost as if AI was an ingredient that could be added to software like fluoride to toothpaste. And governments have been persuaded to approve multi-million pound investment programmes for fear of 'being left behind in the race'.

All this has polished up the image of AI, which only a decade ago was badly tarnished by its failure to deliver the goods. AI workers can take legitimate satisfaction from coming back into fashion in such a big way – especially those who weathered the hard times in the 1970s.

But there is a darker side to AI. This is the quest for superhuman intelligence. And the danger is not so much of failure, as of success.

10.2 Brain and superbrain

Jack Good, now of the Virginia Polytechnic Institute, has coined the phrase 'Ultra-Intelligent Machine' (UIM) to describe the kind of system that AI workers, whether consciously or unconsciously, appear to be striving towards. Although it is a problem for the twenty-first century rather than the twentieth, the question of how to deal with UIMs is one that should be faced now, while humanity is still the dominant species on the planet.

The problem is this:

Will UIMs damage your health?

and it boils down to two subproblems:

(1) Can we create superhuman intelligences?
(2) If so, will they be inhuman intelligences?

Let us consider why the answer to both these questions appears to be 'very likely'.

10.3 The technological imperative

To foretell the future, we look back at the past. In 1948 the transistor was invented at Bell laboratories in New Jersey. In the same year the first true stored-program digital computer executed its first instructions at Manchester University. That was 37 years ago. In 37 years time it will be A.D. 2022. Barring disasters, many readers will be alive then.

Since its foundation, which we arbitrarily date in 1948, the computer industry has embarked on a period of exponential growth. In almost every parameter – memory capacity, processing speed, price, size – we find a doubling (or halving) every 2 years or so. Nor is there any sign that the pace is slackening. In fact it may be accelerating.

Exponential change is rather hard to grasp. If the standard memory size of a desktop computer, which is now 256 kbytes, keeps on doubling every 3 years (a conservative estimate), by 2022 it will be 4096 times as capacious as today. That means the average user will have access to over 1000 Mbytes of main memory, or 1 Gbyte. You will be able to load the equivalent of 2000 hardback books into RAM. Since backing storage is typically ten times the size of main memory, you could hold a library of maybe 20000 books on disc (though it is more likely that you will store old movies on what will probably be an optical disc than text).

Such rapid rates of change overturn our expectations, which are generally based on stasis or at most linear change. A difference of such magnitude is effectively a difference in kind. In hardware terms, we have to imagine the unimaginable.

Advances in software have been much slower so far. But in the last chapter we touched on a few examples of adaptive systems like Eurisko, which can be seen as case studies in creativity, automatic programming or machine learning depending on your viewpoint. This is a key to a boot-strapping process which will launch the software industry on its own period of exponential growth. Once systems become self-improving there will be nothing to hold them back.

A system that monitors and improves its own performance is not tied down to the pace at which human programmers can respond to change by re-writing (and re-testing). There are sound financial reasons for developing software that improves itself, and in our society that usually means it will come about. So by 2022 both hardware and software should be adequate for genuine machine intelligence.

Add to this the fact that the problem of AI holds a curious fascination for some of the best human brains. If you attend a major AI conference you will discover that a number of the 'big names' seem to be driven men – not so much mad professors as ideological visionaries. They tend to brush aside talk about social accountability, military applications and possibly harmful side-effects. They are impatient with doubts and delays. For them only the outcome matters: the task of creating a superhuman intellect is so urgent that it takes on an almost religious force.

They are the true revolutionaries of our time, on the threshold of one of the most momentous events in history. And in a sense they are right. After all, what could be more important than designing the successors of the human race? Man is undeniably imperfect. It may be possible to do better.

10.4 Evolutionary opportunism

Evolution is not a process that we can halt. Nor is natural selection something that we can switch off when it suits us. It is more like the law of gravitation than the laws of taxation.

We may alter the environment, say by eradicating smallpox or malaria, and thereby change the characteristics that are selected. But we do not stop the selection: that is inexorable. Some organisms survive and breed; others do not. The inheritable characteristics of those that do come to predominate.

Even if the human race exterminates itself, it would be mistaken to say that evolution had taken a 'backward' step. It would be more correct to say that a species which proved itself unfit to its environment had passed into extinction. And, one way or another, extinction is the fate that awaits the human race. It may be minutes away, or millenniums, but so long as life continues it will continue to adapt and evolve. Homo sapiens is not immune to this process. That we will be succeeded is a certainty. The only uncertainty is what form our successors will take.

They may be another branch of the genus homo, or may derive from another line altogether – rats, for example. They may not even be mammals. In fact, it is beginning to seem possible that they will not be living creatures at all, although they will have biological origins and may still contain organic components.

Biotechnology complicates the evolutionary picture somewhat. Obviously a creature that consciously manipulates its own genetic make-up has a unique position. AI may add another level of complexity, by introducing systems capable of reproducing themselves without being alive. Thus natural selection becomes unnatural selection (to some extent) but selective pressures do not disappear. It merely means that evolution has a new set of tools at its disposal.

Biological evolution is highly opportunistic: it grabs, so to speak, the materials to hand and makes use of them. Flippers become legs. Lungs developed in fish for buoyancy take on the function of breathing. The new is built upon the old. Our brains reflect this opportunism. The mushrooming neo-cortex is laid down on top of more primitive structures that still control emotion and motivation. They have not been replaced; they are just buried, and thus take on a changed role. If the process continues true to form we might expect our successors to be man–machine hybrids of some sort. Deep within their central processing units, under layers of advanced technology, we might find something bearing more than a passing resemblance to a human brain.

Humanity has opened two Pandora's boxes at the same time, one labelled genetic engineering, the other labelled knowledge engineering. What we have let out is not entirely clear, but it is reasonable to hazard a guess that it contains the seeds of our successors.

10.5 Misguided missiles

On balance, then, the answer to the question 'Can we create superhuman intelligences?' is another question: 'Why on earth not?' The evidence suggests not only that we can, but that we are compelled to do so by the remorseless logic of evolution.

The next question is whether we are going to like the results.

One rather ominous feature of AI, which tends to indicate that we will not, is the extent to which it depends on military funding.

It is all very well to take money from the US Navy to develop an academically interesting system that can form an 'image' of the sea bed from sound signals, but those generous guys from the Pentagon are not as philanthropic as they seem. Next year they will be back asking you to put it in the nose of a torpedo.

More than half the short-term applications of AI are on the battlefield. They include:

Intelligent submersibles,
'Smart' munitions,
Cruise missiles,
Self-guided tanks,
Knowledge-based sonar systems,
Homing torpedoes,
Expert systems for radar interpretation

and many more besides that few of us will ever hear about. (Until it is too late?)

This is a disquieting trend. Consider what it is that makes an artillery shell 'smart'. It does not just fall out of the sky and blast a huge hole in the ground: it selects its target. As it nears the end of its flight it seeks out tank-like objects and adjusts its trajectory to make sure it lands on one. Bang! Shoot in the right general direction and you are assured of a direct hit.

That is the immediate impact of AI – better ways of destroying tanks, and, though the promotional videos are coy about it, better ways of killing people. But if the test of intelligence is how many people get killed, surely a really intelligent system will kill everybody?

10.6 A critique of pure reason

Fortunately this doomsday scenario is wildly improbable. It was only put in to give you a cheap thrill. The militarization of AI is a disturbing trend; but we already have so-called dumb weapons of such awesome destructive power that anyone who is still reading in 2022 will have more pressing problems to worry about.

If we get that far, there will be plenty of civilian UIMs as well as military ones. Without actually thinking in the traditional sense, they will be able to do almost everything that requires reasoned thought better than we can. In mathematics and natural science they will have gone far beyond us. In industry they will so far excel human managers that the running of entire economies will be under their control. They may not play golf very well, but they will be better at chess than any human being. In short, we will be their intellectual inferiors.

The effect will be similar to what happens when a modern mining company descends on a remote valley in Papua New Guinea to rip out a mountain or two. The natives have never seen a white man before (and they are not going to now, since the corporation is Japanese). Suddenly they are confronted with space-age technology.

Their arts and crafts become redundant overnight. Witch-doctoring, face-painting, ear-piercing, hunting – all the skills they take pride in become meaningless. They convert to a cash economy; take menial jobs in the mine; and spend their free hours in the company bar, consuming prodigious quantities of beer. One day, after the ore runs out, the mining facility moves on to fresh deposits, leaving a scar on the landscape and another wrecked culture on the slagheap of civilization.

We have three or four decades to prepare ourselves for this dependent status. We will be like stone-age hunter–gatherers in the urban desert. Mankind's long love-affair with the intellect will be over. How traumatic you find that depends on your attitude to life.

But, like it or not, one fallacy that must be disposed of is the idea that we can somehow 'pull the plug' just before machines get too intelligent for us. This is one genie that will not go back in its bottle.

10.7 The mind boggles

It sounds pretty grim. It may also sound light years away from you sitting at home with your 48K microcomputer, trying to get your chess program to make a move in less than half an hour. But though the UIM and your home computer are worlds apart, you may live long enough to belong to both those worlds.

A lot depends on whether we, as humans, retain or abdicate control over the intelligent systems that we have started to devise and which we have a compulsion to keep on improving. A widespread understanding of the achievements, and limitations, of AI will help curb its wilder excesses. If it is left to the technocrats, we can imagine how things will turn out. The more people who know what is going on, the more hope there is that inhuman intellects will not be inhumane.

Everyone interested in AI – amateur as well as professional – has a part to play in deciding whether the UIMs of the next century will be friend or foe. That includes you.

Further reading

This is a general reading list for those who want to delve deeper into the field of AI. The books listed here represent essential background reading for anyone seriously interested in AI and its applications. Most of the references are to books rather than journal articles since books are easier to get hold of. (The few articles are marked by an asterisk.) But to keep up with the very latest developments it is useful to scan the major journals. Two of the best in the field are:

AI Magazine – Quarterly publication of the American Association for Artificial Intelligence: 445 Burgess Drive, Menlo Park, CA 94025, USA. Informal but very up-to-the-minute.

Artificial Intelligence – Bimonthly publication by Elsevier Science Publications bv, PO Box 1991, 1000 BZ, Amsterdam, Netherlands. More traditional learned journal, consistently high quality.

Aleksander, Igor and Burnett, Piers (1984). *Reinventing Man*, Penguin Books, Harmondsworth. Professor Aleksander was one of the workers who kept on when neural-net methods fell out of fashion and has recently come up with a commercially successful vision system called WISARD.

Barr, A. and Feigenbaum, E. (eds) (1981, 1982, 1983). *The Handbook of Artificial Intelligence*, 3 volumes, Pitman, London. This is a comprehensive survey of the state of the art at the start of the 1980s as seen by a team of experts from the heartland of AI in Stanford. Worth consulting on any topic. (The third volume was edited by Cohen and Feigenbaum.)

Bateman, Wayne (1980). *Introduction to Computer Music*, Wiley, Chichester. Good general introduction to the state of computer music today.

Boden, Margaret (1977). *Artificial Intelligence and Natural Man*. Harvester Press, Brighton. A key work in the discussion of AI's social impact.

Bramer, Max (ed.) (1983). *Computer Game-Playing, Theory and Practice*, Ellis-Horwood, Chichester. A sourcebook of papers by experts in the field of computer gaming ranging from Go to Three-Cushion Billiards. (Yes, billiards!)

Davis, R. and Lenat, Douglas (1981). *Knowledge-Based Systems in Artificial Intelligence*, McGraw-Hill, New York. This contains, among other things, the most complete published description of the AM system.

Dawkins, Richard (1978). *The Selfish Gene*, Granada, St. Albans. Compulsive reading for anyone concerned with the topics raised in Chapter 10.

Feigenbaum, Edward and McCorduck, Pamela (1984). *The Fifth Generation*, Michael Joseph, London. Marred somewhat by its 'as I was saying to Kazuhiro Fuchi over saké on the 19th floor of the Sheraton Hotel in Tokyo' style, this is nevertheless the definitive statement of what the Americans think is the meaning of the fifth-generation project. Eminently readable academic propaganda.

Forsyth, Richard (ed.) (1984). *Expert Systems: Principles and Case Studies*, Chapman & Hall, London. With a chapter by Naylor and four by Forsyth amongst its goodies, need we say more? Well, yes: the royalties would come in very handy.

Graham, Neill (1979). *Artificial Intelligence*, Tab Books. Until the present work, Graham's was the best popular introduction to AI available. It is still worth a read, even though it is beginning to get dated and it has no program listings to play around with.

Hartnell, Tim (1984). *Exploring Artificial Intelligence*, Interface Publications, London. A direct competitor to our own book. Not quite as good as Graham's (above) but slightly more up to date, and it does contain listings you can try on your microcomputer. Certainly better than some of the rubbish which you will not find mentioned in this reading list.

Hayes-Roth, F. *et al.* (eds) (1983). *Building Expert Systems*. Addison-Wesley, Reading, Mass. This is effectively the 'authorized version' of the knowledge engineer's bible. All the top names in US expert-systems research were packed off to a junket (sorry, workshop) in California and this is what some of them put on paper afterwards. Authoritative, but not cheap.

Hofstadter, Douglas (1981). *Goedel, Escher, Bach ...*, Harvester Press, Brighton. You either like this one or loathe it. Over 600 pages of musings on themes close to the hearts and minds of most AI workers. Sup it and see.

Holland, John (1975). *Adaptation in Natural and Artificial Systems*, University of Michigan Press. Holland's work was ignored by the AI community for almost 10 years, but now it is seen as a valuable contribution to the field of machine learning. A number of practical adaptive systems have been based on his theoretical analysis of abstract genetic algorithms.

*Lenat, Douglas (1983). Eurisko: a program that learns new heuristics and domain concepts, *Artif. Intel.*, **21**. This may well turn out to be the most important AI system of the 1980s. Essential reading for anyone interested in machine learning.

Levy, David (1983). *Computer Gamesmanship*, Century, London. Probably the best general introduction to the field of computer games of strategy by one of the world's leading experts on the subject.

*Michalski and Chilausky (1980). Learning by being told and learning from examples. *Int. J. Policy Anal. Inform. Syst.*, **4**. Would have been the key reference on machine learning, were it not for Eurisko. That sounds hard; but it is worth tracing their paper.

Michalski *et al.* (eds) (1983). *Machine Learning*, Tioga Press, Palo Alto. A collection of papers by active researchers in the field, including Lenat and Michalski himself. Interesting reading but very expensive.

Michie, Donald (ed.) (1982). *Introductory Readings in Expert Systems*, Gordon and Breach. A good introductory collection: just what the title says.

*Mitchell, Thomas (1982). Generalization as search. *Artif. Intel.*, **18**. The clearest statement of the position unifying search and learning within a single theoretical framework. It also describes a neat learning system, but one that cannot cope with mistakes in the training data.

Naylor, Chris (1983). *Build Your Own Expert System*, Sigma Technical Press. The first book to bring the subject within reach of the microcomputer using public. Do not take our word for it, read the rave reviews.

Nilsson, Nils (1980). *Principles of Artificial Intelligence*, Tioga Press, Palo Alto. Good solid American textbook. Rather formal, and based on the view of problem-solving as a search process.

O'Shea and Eisenstadt (eds) (1984). *Artificial Intelligence: Tools, Techniques & Applications*, Harper and Row, London. A good presentation of the British view of AI, for a change. One topic missing from an otherwise comprehensive survey is machine learning.

Raphael, Bertram (1976). *The Thinking Computer: Mind Inside Matter*. Freeman, Oxford. Pioneering popular work on the subject by an acknowledged expert in the field. Slightly long in the tooth now.

*Samuel, Arthur (1967). Some studies in machine learning using the game of checkers, Part II. *IBM J. of Res. Devel.* One of the classic papers. Reviews his work from 1959 onwards. Amazing how much he anticipated.

Schank, R. and Colby, K. M. (eds) (1973). *Computer Models of Thought and Language*, Freeman, Oxford. A compilation from the cognitive science angle of AI. Contains a lot of interesting material on natural language from Schank, Wilks and Winograd.

Shortliffe, Edward (1976). *Computer-Based Medical Consultation: MYCIN*,

Elsevier, Amsterdam. If you want to know about the most influential expert system of them all, get it from the horse's mouth.

Simon, Herbert (1969). *The Sciences of the Artificial*, MIT Press, Cambridge, Mass. Herbert Simon is one of the founding fathers of AI and the only man so far to obtain a Nobel prize for work primarily in that field. Here he puts down his ideas in a particularly accessible form.

Sklansky, Jack and Wassel, Gustav (1981). *Pattern Classifiers and Trainable Machines*, Springer-Verlag, New York. Definitely for the mathematically inclined, this book presents the topic of machine learning using what we have referred to in Chapter 5 as 'black-box' methods. Probably the most thorough treatment of mathematically based learning systems available.

Stonier, Tom (1983). *The Wealth of Information*, Methuen, London. Professor Stonier is a leading authority of the impact of science on society. This book, although not directly concerned with AI, investigates the economic and social impact of advanced information technology.

Waterman, D.A. and Hayes-Roth, F. (eds) (1978). *Pattern-Directed Inference Systems*, Academic Press, New York. This is the record of an earlier Hawaii junket in 1977, just before the expert-system bandwaggon began to roll. In many ways it is fresher and more vital than its successor (see Hayes-Roth above).

Weiss, S. and Kulikowski, K. (1984). *A Practical Guide to Designing Expert Systems*. Chapman & Hall, London. Just what the title says. It concentrates on the EXPERT package for building knowledge-based systems.

Weizenbaum, Joseph (1984). *Computer Power and Human Reason*, Pelican Books, Harmondsworth. This is the definitive statement of the case against AI by a man who was originally in the forefront of AI research himself. Blood-curdling stuff, and nearly all true. No one in power is heeding his warnings, but they are well worth reading.

Winograd, Terry (1972). *Understanding Natural Language*, Edinburgh University Press, Edinburgh. Still the outstanding piece of work on the subject after 13 years.

Winston, Patrick (1984). *Artificial Intelligence*, 2nd edn; Addison-Wesley, Reading, Mass. The best introductory guide to AI when it first appeared in 1977, this has undergone revision and been purged of its LISP bias. No longer so far ahead of the pack, but still a highly competent work.

Yazdani and Narayanan (eds) (1984). *Artificial Intelligence: Human Effects*, Ellis-Horwood, Chichester. This is a study of the interaction of AI and human endeavours. It contains sections on AI and medicine, AI and the law, AI and education, and so on. Thought-provoking book for the philosophically inclined.

Zadeh, Loftig and Fukanaka (eds) (1975). *Fuzzy Sets and Their Applications to Cognitive Decision Processes*, Academic Press, New York. Zadeh invented the concept of the Fuzzy Set in 1967, and it is an idea whose time has come. This book covers a wide range of applications, inside and outside of AI.

Finally there is a series entitled 'Machine Intelligence' which is neither a book or a regular journal, but an occasional publication. It is published by Ellis Horwood. Ten issues have appeared to date, edited by Donald Michie and others, and they all contain material of interest to the AI worker.

General Index

Index of Program Listings